The Insider's Complete Guide to

AP Art History

VOL 3 | Beyond the European Tradition with Global Contemporary

by LARRY KRIEGER

The Insider's Complete Guide to

AP Art History

Volume 3

Beyond the European Tradition with
Global Contemporary

LARRY KRIEGER

ISBN: 978-0-9852912-4-2

An INSIDER TEST PREP publication of Larry Prep LLC

Art Direction & Design by Station16 (Station16 LLC)

For more Insider resources visit
www.InsiderTestPrep.com

LETTER FROM THE AUTHOR

The AP Art History Framework challenges students to study 250 required works, representing ten very different content areas. Students across America report that their AP Art History classes often have to rush through the latter content areas on works beyond the Western tradition. This problem inspired me to create this book series, giving equal attention to Western and non-Western works.

My research also identified a dearth of materials on non-Western works. The existing prep books limit their coverage to a short series of bullet points, while the textbooks offer short paragraphs on the topics.

I hope that my book will rectify these problems. This volume contains 84 essays on the works in Content Areas 6-10. These artworks are numbered Images 167-250; I have opted to use the same image numbering system used by the AP College Board.

Each narrative discusses the context, content, form, and function of these works. In addition, each discussion ends with a special Making Connections feature, linking the focused work with another one of the required images. For example, the Making Connections feature for *Travelers among Mountains and Streams* compares Fan Kuan's use of shifting perspective with Bruegel's use of linear perspective in *Hunters in the Snow*.

Many students and teachers have justifiably noted the lack of multiple-choice practice questions in other test prep books. I have studied all the released questions for both the old and new APAH Frameworks. Based upon this analysis, I have written 80 multiple-choice questions designed to provide coverage of the works covered in this volume.

Finally, Volume 3 concludes with a distinctive Glossary. It provides clear and concise definitions for each all-caps term found in the individual essays. In addition, our Glossary links these definitions to relevant examples from the required list of works.

I hope you will find this book a valuable and informative aid that will help you prepare for the APAH exam!

Larry Krieger

TABLE OF CONTENTS

ABOUT THE AUTHOR

Larry Krieger earned his B.A. and M.A.T. from the University of North Carolina at Chapel Hill and his M.A. from Wake Forest University. In a career spanning more than 40 years, Mr. Krieger taught in urban, rural, and suburban public high schools in North Carolina and New Jersey. He taught a variety of AP subjects including Art History, U. S. History, European History, and American Government. Mr. Krieger has published popular books in all of these subjects.

Mr. Krieger's AP Art History courses were renowned for their energetic presentations, commitment to scholarship, and dedication to helping students achieve high AP exam scores. Almost half of Mr. Krieger's students scored fives, with 40 percent scoring fours and about 10 percent scoring threes. Mr. Krieger has never had an AP student score a one or two. In 2004 and 2005, the College Board recognized Mr. Krieger as one of the nation's foremost AP Art History teachers.

ACKNOWLEDGEMENTS

Books do not write or publish themselves. They require the work of a number of dedicated and creative people.

The plan for this book necessitated obtaining permissions for a large number of photographs. I quickly realized that the permissions process would be very difficult. I was extremely fortunate to obtain the professional services of Sheri Gilbert, a Freelance Permissions Editor located in Rochester, New York. Sheri did a remarkable job negotiating with artists, museums, and photo agencies. Thanks to her indefatigable effort, we successfully obtained permissions from all around the world.

Photographs and text must be assembled into a well-designed book. I began the project by challenging Station16 in Atlanta to create a book of which we would all be proud. I believe that they more than met this challenge. As always, Brenton created distinctive designs, Jesh shaped the manuscript into flowing layouts, and Margo supervised the entire project and advised me on a number of pedagogical decisions.

I would like to thank my wife Susan for her support. Every page of this book benefited from her "close reads." Susan spotted misplaced modifiers, passive voice, and unconnected thoughts. She gave each essay a grade and encouraged me to always be "clear, concise, and interesting!"

And finally, I would like to thank my mother for her encouragement. Mom's love for art and sense of humor in the face of a long illness helped to inspire me. Unfortunately, mother passed away just before we completed the book. I would like to dedicate this book to her memory.

Content Area 6
AFRICA

AFRICA

Content Area 6 includes 14 works created between 1000 C.E. and 1914 C.E. The African artists and architects who produced these works come from a wide variety of ethnic and geographic backgrounds. They are a product of not one, but many "Africas."

Our unit presents the 14 African works in the chronological order provided in the College Board's AP Art History Framework. This organization will enable you to quickly find a specific work of art. It is important to stress that African works cannot be neatly packaged into a few mutually exclusive categories. Indeed, many of the works can be placed in multiple groupings.

The College Board encourages teachers and students to arrange the works in a wide variety of meaningful topical categories. Cultural themes and geographic locations are two of the most commonly used ways of organizing the study of African art.

CULTURAL THEMES

ROYAL POWER AND AUTHORITY

Image 167: Conical Tower and circular wall of Great Zimbabwe
Image 169: Wall plaque, from Oba's palace
Image 170: *Sika dwa kofi* (Golden Stool)
Image 171: *Ndop* (portrait figure)
Image 177: *Lukasa* (memory board)
Image 178: Aka elephant mask
Image 180: Veranda post of enthroned king and senior wife

MASKS/MASQUERADES

Image 173: *Female (Pwo) mask*
Image 174: Portrait mask (*Mblo*)
Image 175: *Bundu* mask
Image 178: Aka elephant mask

CONTINUITY WITH LINEAGES, ANCESTORS, AND SPIRITS

Image 171: *Ndop* (portrait figure)
Image 172: Power figure (*Nkisi n'kondi*)
Image 176: *Ikenga* (shrine figure)
Image 177: *Lukasa* (memory board)
Image 179: Reliquary figure (*byeri*)

INITIATION ASSOCIATIONS

Image 173: *Female (Pwo) mask*
Image 175: *Bundu* mask

ARCHITECTURAL STYLES

Image 167: Conical Tower and circular wall of Great Zimbabwe
Image 168: Great Mosque of Djenné

GEOGRAPHIC REGIONS

WEST AFRICA

Image 168: Great Mosque of Djenné
Image 169: Wall plaque, from Oba's palace
Image 170: *Sika dwa kofi* (Golden Stool)
Image 174: Portrait mask (*Mblo*)
Image 175: *Bundu* mask
Image 176: *Ikenga* (shrine figure)
Image 178: Aka elephant mask

CENTRAL AFRICA

Image 171: *Ndop* (portrait figure)
Image 172: Power figure (*Nkisi n'kondi*)
Image 173: *Female (Pwo) mask*
Image 177: *Lukasa* (memory board)
Image 179: Reliquary figure (*byeri*)
Image 180: Veranda post of enthroned king and senior wife

EAST AND SOUTH AFRICA

Image 167: Conical Tower and circular wall of Great Zimbabwe

Werner Forman Archive / Bridgeman Images

IMAGE 167

Conical Tower and circular wall of Great Zimbabwe

Southeastern Zimbabwe

Shona peoples

c. 1000–1400 C.E.

Coursed granite blocks

The word "Zimbabwe" derives from a Shona term meaning "houses of stone" or "venerated houses." Both meanings provide insights into Great Zimbabwe, the largest and most important collection of stone ruins in sub-Saharan Africa. Built between 1000 and 1400 C.E., Great Zimbabwe served as a royal center where kings governed from "venerated houses." The Great Enclosure and the Conical Tower are symbols of Great Zimbabwe's rich past and sources of national pride for the people of modern Zimbabwe.

A SPECTACULAR STONE ENCLOSURE

At its peak during the 14th century, Great Zimbabwe may have supported a population of 18,000 inhabitants. The overwhelming majority of these people lived in crowded earthen and mud-brick structures that have not survived. In contrast, an elite group of rulers and their families enjoyed a luxurious lifestyle within the confines of a walled structure known as the Great Enclosure.

A 820-foot-long elliptical-shaped outer wall defines the boundaries of the Great Enclosure. The towering structure rises 32 feet above the surrounding savanna. A second inner wall runs along part of the outer wall and forms a narrow parallel passageway leading to the Conical Tower. The tower is 18 feet in diameter and rises to a height of 30 feet.

The two walls and Conical Tower contain over one million granite blocks quarried from nearby hills. An astonished 16th-century Portuguese historian reported that despite their "marvelous size," the granite stones had "no mortar joining them." Requiring over 30 years to build, the Great Enclosure was a stunning architectural feat that displayed great precision and craft.

There is no evidence that the Great Enclosure functioned as a defensive fortress. Instead, its formidable walls separated the royal family from their subjects. The walls thus symbolized the ruler's power. Shaped like a granary, the Conical Tower may have underscored the ruler's role as a custodian of bountiful harvests.

A LUCRATIVE TRADING NETWORK

Great Zimbabwe's granite walls were more than just symbols of royal authority; they were also a testament to the city's great wealth. Between approximately 1000 and 1450 C.E., mines in the Zimbabwe Plateau and Limpopo

Valley produced about two-fifths of the world's total mined gold. The rulers of Great Zimbabwe controlled and taxed the flow of gold from these inland mines to Kilwa and other port cities along East Africa's famed Swahili Coast. Great Zimbabwe was thus an integral part of a lucrative trading network connecting Africa to Arabia, India, and China. During the peak of their power, Great Zimbabwe's rulers collected glass from Arabia, pottery from Persia, and even prized porcelain from China.

FORGOTTEN BUT NOT LOST

A combination of factors caused Great Zimbabwe to decline. During the 15th century, gold reserves gradually dwindled, causing trade routes to shift northward. At the same time extensive cattle overgrazing and a prolonged drought exhausted the soil. Faced with the loss of their economic foundation, residents abandoned Great Zimbabwe, and the city fell into obscurity.

European explorers "discovered" Great Zimbabwe during the late 1800s. At first, they could not believe that the ancestors of local Shona people had the ability to construct such sophisticated ruins. They theorized that the Biblical Queen of Sheba had commissioned the city as a replica of the palaces where she stayed in Jerusalem. However, radiocarbon dating has enabled modern archaeologists to conclusively debunk this fanciful theory.

Great Zimbabwe now stands as an important source of national pride and unity. In 1980 national leaders celebrated their newly independent state by proudly naming it Zimbabwe.

MAKING CONNECTIONS

THE GREAT ENCLOSURE AND THE WALLS AT SAQSA WAMAN

The walls of the Great Enclosure and the walls of Saqsa Waman in Cuzco (Image 159) share a number of common characteristics. Both structures used heavy stones that required decades to quarry and transport. Skilled Shona and Inka masons carefully cut the stones and fit them together without the use of mortar. Known as ASHLAR MASONRY, this painstaking process produced stone walls that endured for centuries.

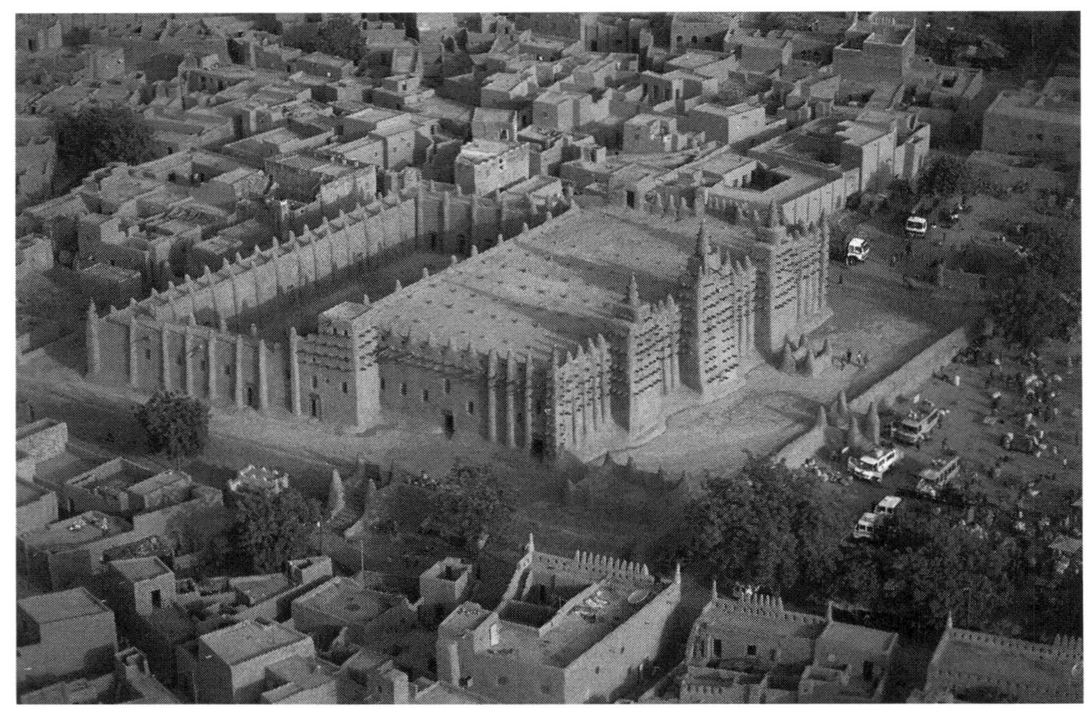

George Steinmetz / National Geographic Creative

IMAGE 168

Great Mosque of Djenné

Mali

Founded c. 1200 C.E.; rebuilt 1906–1907
Adobe

Djenné is the oldest known city in sub-Saharan Africa. The Great Mosque of Djenné is located in present-day Mali on the flood plain of the Bani River. It is the largest mud brick building in the world and one of the most famous landmarks in Africa. The Great Mosque is widely recognized as a symbol of the city of Djenné and a source of pride for the nation of Mali.

ISLAM AND DJENNÉ

During the 8th century C.E., Arab traders ventured across Northern Africa into the savannah region south of the Sahara Desert. These Muslim merchants enjoyed great commercial success by trading gold, ivory, and salt. At the same time, they introduced their Islamic faith to the people and rulers they encountered.

Local African chiefs frequently adopted Islam. According to tradition, sometime during the 13th century Djenné's 26th chief, Koi Konboro, converted to Islam. He then erected a mosque in Djenné as a sign of his religious devotion. Mali's emergence as a powerful sub-Saharan empire enabled Djenné to become a prosperous commercial and religious center.

Very little is known about the appearance of Koi Konboro's mosque. As Mali's fortunes declined, his mosque slowly deteriorated. During the 1830s a second less impressive mosque replaced it. After the the French gained control over Mali, they funded a new mosque between 1906 and 1907 on the same site where the original once stood. This building still stands and is universally known as the Great Mosque of Djenné.

"WE DO IT ALL BY HAND"

Djenné's Great Mosque is composed of cylindrical mud bricks about the size of a soft-drink can. The entire community contributes to the process of creating this surprisingly durable construction material. "We do it all by hand," one mason proudly boasted. "Every man leaves a part of himself in each brick."

The Great Mosque's imposing presence further underscores its importance. Aware of the threat posed by damaging floods, skilled masons built the Great Mosque on a platform raised about 10 feet above ground level. As a result, the Great Mosque dwarfs the surrounding buildings and the adjacent marketplace. Six sets of stairs provide access to the mosque. They symbolize the transition from the everyday life found in the marketplace to a sacred space.

THE QIBLA WALL

Image 168 features the Great Mosque's famous eastern wall. Known as the QIBLA or prayer wall, it ensures that worshippers inside the Great Mosque face toward the Kaaba (Image 183) in Mecca. Although the outside temperature often rises above 100 degrees, the two-foot thick walls provide insulation from the hot African sun.

Three large symmetrically arranged towers dominate the qibla wall. Reaching a height of over 50 feet, the towers serve as minarets. The pinnacles at the top of each minaret are crowned with ostrich eggs, symbolizing purity and fertility. A muezzin climbs a spiral staircase inside the tower five times a day. He then uses a loudspeaker to amplify his voice as he recites a call for prayer.

The wall facade also contains distinctive projecting beams. Known as TORONS, the bundles of palm sticks provide a decorative ornament. They also help reduce cracking caused by frequent changes in humidity and temperature.

REPLASTERING THE GREAT MOSQUE

The Great Mosque's mud brick walls are stronger than those made with conventional rectangular bricks. However, mud bricks are vulnerable to erosion from rain. As a result, the Great Mosque requires frequent maintenance.

The entire Djenné community takes an active role in maintaining the Great Mosque. During an annual spring festival known as *Crepissage*, thousands of devoted citizens replaster the mosque's rain-soaked walls. This festive occasion includes music, food, and a race to recognize the fastest runners delivering plaster to the mosque.

Experienced members of Djenné's mason's guild direct the work. The TORONS provide ready-made scaffolding, enabling volunteers to reach all parts of the walls. This new coat of mud plaster protects the walls and gives them a smooth, sculpted look.

MAKING CONNECTIONS

THE GREAT MOSQUE OF DJENNÉ AND THE MOSQUE OF SELIM II

Minarets are essential parts of a mosque's architectural plan. However, their number and style vary. The Great Mosque of Djenné includes an innovative design in which its three symmetrical minarets are part of the QIBLA wall. In contrast, the renowned Ottoman architect Sinan positioned four identical minarets at each corner of the Mosque of Selim II (Image 84). Shaped like rockets, the slender minarets enabled Sinan to enhance the mosque's soaring vertical thrust.

The Michael C. Rockefeller Memorial Collection, The Metropolitan Museum of Art. Gift of Nelson A. Rockefeller, 1965

IMAGE 169

Wall plaque, from Oba's palace

Edo peoples

Benin (Nigeria)

16th century C.E.

Cast brass

This small but revealing brass plaque sheds light on many aspects of West African history. Originally created to express royal power, it also illustrates 16th-century commercial relations between Portugal and the West African Kingdom of Benin. The plaque's layered meanings do not stop in the 16th century. It provides a vivid and painful connection to the consequences of British imperialism during the late 19th century Scramble for Africa.

THE POWER OF THE OBA

The figure of the Oba, or ruler, of Benin dominates the plaque. Although we do not know his name, we do know that the people of Edo believed he was descended from the gods. As a divine ruler, the Oba exercised absolute power over every aspect of life in his kingdom.

The royal sculptors emphasized the Oba's undisputed power by placing him in the center of the plaque. They skillfully used HIERARCHICAL SCALE to underscore the Oba's relative importance compared to that of the surrounding figures. Two smaller palace attendants hold shields to protect their ruler's head from the hot tropical sun. Two smaller swordbearers support the Oba's outstretched hands. In addition, miniature figures can be seen hovering in the corners, and a tiny figure supports the Oba's royal feet.

The royal sculptors used a distinctive canon of proportion designed to emphasize the Oba's head. Recall that the ancient Greek sculptor Polykleitos created a canon of human proportion prescribing that the human head be 1/6 of the body's size (see Image 34). In contrast, Benin's royal sculptors portrayed the Oba with an enlarged head that was about one-third of their ruler's total height. This canon is consistent with Benin's understanding of the Oba as the kingdom's "Great Head." As the center of wisdom and thought, the head controls the body. Similarly, as the center of leadership and power, the Oba controls the Kingdom of Benin.

THE IMPORTANCE OF TRADE

The first Portuguese caravels reached Benin in about 1485. Their unexpected arrival soon led to mutually profitable trade. The Portuguese coveted Benin's rich supply of pepper, ivory, gold, and slaves. The Oba coveted the Portuguese rich supply of coral beads, horses, and brass bracelets known as *manillas*. For example, in 1548 one German merchant house supplied Portugal with 432 tons of brass for the West African trade.

Image 169 provides visual evidence of the trade between Benin and Portugal. The royal sculptors melted the *manillas* and then used the LOST WAX PROCESS to create the brass plaques. Since brass never rusts or corrodes, the metal implied that an Oba would reign over Benin forever.

European horses and Mediterranean coral were also prized as symbols of the Oba's power and wealth. The sight of the Oba seated sidesaddle on a large horse must have awed the people of Benin. The rings of red coral beads covering their ruler's neck provided a dazzling display of his wealth. Taken together, the brass plaques provided an unparalleled visual record of Benin's elaborate court rituals and long history.

THE DESTRUCTION OF BENIN

When Portuguese influence gradually faded, the British emerged as the dominant European power in West Africa. In 1897 a small British delegation demanded a meeting with the Oba to negotiate more favorable trade agreements. Since he was conducting state ceremonies, the Oba requested that the meeting be delayed. However, the British arrogantly rejected this request. A group of insulted local chiefs then ambushed the British party and killed most of its members.

News of the "Benin Massacre" shocked and enraged the British. Within five weeks London retaliated by dispatching a powerful force of 1,200 well-armed soldiers on a Punitive Expedition to punish the Oba. The British force raided Benin City, exiled the Oba, and seized over 2,500 works of art including 900 brass plaques, one of which became Image 169. The British shipped the looted artistic treasures back to London, where they were sold to museums and private collectors.

Benin is now part of Nigeria. Many Nigerians argue that the Punitive Expedition robbed their nation of its rightful artistic heritage. Their complaints are part of a wider debate over whether artistic treasures such as the Benin plaques and the Elgin Marbles (Image 35) should be returned to their homelands.

MAKING CONNECTIONS

HIERARCHICAL SCALE

Benin sculptors relied upon HIERARCHICAL SCALE to visually indicate the relative importance of the Oba and his various subordinates. Artists in Ancient Egypt and Sumeria also used this convention. For example, Narmer towers above his sandal-bearer and defeated foes in the beautifully carved Palette of King Narmer (Image 13). In the Standard of Ur (Image 16), the *lugal* or literally "big man" dominates figures in both the "War" and "Peace" panels.

© Marc Deville / Gamma-Rapho via Getty Images

IMAGE 170

Sika dwa kofi (Golden Stool)

Ashanti peoples (south central Ghana)

c. 1700 C.E.

Gold over wood and cast-gold attachments

The Ashanti are the largest ethnic group in the modern West African state of Ghana. Their memorable history stretches back to the late 17th century, when King Osei Tutu unified a number of previously independent chiefs. The unification and subsequent rise of the Ashanti Kingdom is closely tied to a remarkable object known as the Golden Stool.

OSEI TUTU AND THE *GOLDEN STOOL*

In the late 1690s Osei Tutu, a warrior-chief of Kumasi, attempted to unify a loose confederation of Ashanti states. According to Ashanti tradition, Osei Tutu's chief priest Okomfo Anokye assembled the various chiefs and then dramatically extended his arms towards the heavens. A Golden Stool miraculously descended from a cloud and landed on Osei Tutu's lap. Awed by this divine symbol, the proud chiefs swore allegiance to Osei Tutu.

THE SOUL OF THE ASHANTI PEOPLE

The Ashanti believe that the Golden Stool contains the *sunsum,* or soul, of their people. Just as individuals cannot live without a soul, so the Ashanti people would disappear from history if they lost their Golden Stool.

The Golden Stool is covered with pure gold. It is 18 inches high, 24 inches long, and 12 inches wide. It is never placed on the ground and is so sacred that no one has ever sat on it. New kings are lowered and raised over the Golden Stool without touching it.

"GIVE IT TO ME TO SIT ON"

Legitimized by the Golden Stool, the Ashanti Kingdom flourished. The royal treasury in Kumasi contained over 20,000 pounds of gold dust. But this great wealth did not protect the Ashanti from British imperialism. In 1874, British soldiers burned Kumasi. Determined to suppress all resistance, the British royal governor Sir Frederick Hodgson imperiously demanded that the Ashanti surrender the Golden Stool and "give it to me to sit upon."

Hodgson's arrogant insult touched off a rebellion known as the War of the Golden Stool. Although the British suppressed the revolt, the Ashanti claimed victory because they prevented Hodgson from seizing the Golden Stool and sending it to the British Museum in London. Today, the Golden Stool is housed in the Ashanti royal palace in Kumasi, Ghana.

MAKING CONNECTIONS

THE GOLDEN STOOL AND JOWO RINPOCHE

The Golden Stool and the Jowo Rinpoche (Image 184) are both revered cultural icons believed to have celestial origins. Housed in the Jokhang Temple in Lhasa, the Jowo Rinpoche is a larger than life-size image of the historical Buddha. According to tradition, the celestial architect Viswakarma carved the image during Buddha's lifetime. This belief in celestial origins gives great sacred power to both the Golden Stool and the Jowo Rinpoche.

© Brooklyn Museum of Art, New York, USA / Bridgeman Images

IMAGE 171

Ndop (portrait figure) of King Mishe miShyaang maMbul

Kuba peoples (Democratic Republic of the Congo)

c. 1760–1780 C. E.
Wood

The Kuba Kingdom flourished between the 17th and 19th centuries in the southwestern region of what is today the Democratic Republic of the Congo. Known as a major center of artistic creativity, the kingdom's sculptural tradition featured a series of carved *ndops* or "portrait statues" of Kuba rulers. Rubbed with oil to protect it from insects, Image 171 is the oldest *ndop* and one of Africa's earliest surviving wood sculptures.

AN IDEALIZED DEPICTION OF KINGSHIP

A highly skilled royal sculptor created the figure shown in Image 171 for King Mishe miShyaang maMbul. The nearly two-foot-high *ndop* is an idealized depiction of a *nyim* or Kuba ruler. Like all existing *ndop* statues, the *nyim* is seated cross-legged on a platform. This elevation underscores the *nyim*'s royal status as a leader raised above his people.

The sculptor portrayed King Mishe miShyaang maMbul with an enlarged head about one-third of the ruler's total height. This traditional canon of proportion emphasized the head's role as the seat of intelligence, knowledge, and power. The *nyim*'s expressionless face imparts a sense of dignity while reinforcing a feeling of royal distance.

Although the *ndop* is relatively small, it contains a number of symbols intended to convey the *nyim*'s wealth and royal lineage. The bracelets, armbands, and closed eyes shaped like cowrie shells all project an impressive display of regal opulence. Known as a *shody*, the distinctive hoe-shaped head ornament provides a visual link to a headdress worn by one of the founders of the Kuba Kingdom.

Although the *ndop* does not contain any distinguishing physical characteristics, it does include a prominent relief located on the front of the base. Known as an *ibol*, the image of a drum with a severed hand is a customized visual signifier chosen by King Mishe miShyaang maMbul.

"THEY WILL BE ABLE TO REMEMBER ME"

The *ndop* was more than a visual reminder of the *nyim*'s wealth and power; it also served as a carefully preserved surrogate that absorbed the king's spiritual essence. This prepared the *ndop* for its essential function as a source of future instruction and inspiration. At the beginning of the 20th century, a Kuba ruler quoted an early *nyim* who explained the *ndop*'s vital role for his people: "When they look at this statue they will be able to remember me and think I am looking at them consoling them when they are sad, giving them inspiration and new courage."

MAKING CONNECTIONS

THE *NDOP* AND THE BENIN WALL PLAQUE

The *ndop* and the Benin wall plaque (Image 169) both present idealized depictions of royal power. Unlike representations of Roman emperors and European monarchs, West African sculptors did not strive to create realistic images. Instead, the *ndop* and Benin wall plaque present rulers with unusually calm expressions and enlarged heads emphasizing their great wisdom.

IMAGE 172

Power figure *(Nkisi n'kondi)*

Kongo peoples (Democratic Republic of the Congo)

c. late 19th century C. E.
Wood and metal

A *nkisi n'kondi*'s body punctured with nails is one of the most easily recognized figures in the AP Art History curriculum. However, a *nkisi n'kondi* should not be dismissed as an amusing curiosity. The figure served as an important public object that played an integral role in the administration of justice for Kongo communities.

A CARVER AND A RITUAL SPECIALIST

Like all other *minkisi* (plural of *nkisi*), Image 172 was the collaborative work of an expert wood carver and a ritual specialist known as a *nganga*. The carver skillfully shaped a single block of wood into an imposing figure who leans forward as he stands upon raised blocks. Image 172's wide-open eyes, bent knees, and hands on hips create a distinctive pose that conveys a heightened sense of alertness. This *nikisi* is clearly ready to spring into action!

Although the carved image presents a formidable presence, it remained an empty vessel until the *nganga* completed his role by combining herbs, bits of animal bones, special minerals, and ancestor relics into a spiritually charged matter called *bilango*. The *nganga* then placed this material into a hollow cavity typically located in the figure's belly, believing this location was the *nkisi*'s spiritual center. The *nganga* then sealed the cavity with a piece of glass. Packed in resin, this potent medicine attracted a spiritual force, thus giving the *nkisi* its power.

DIVERSE FUNCTIONS

A *nkisi n'kondi* served its community in a number ways. It could be used positively to provide protection from misfortune, cure physical ailments and resolve disputes. Or it could be used negatively to hunt down evildoers and violators of agreements. Supervised by the *nganga*, members of the community accessed a *nkisi*'s power by driving a nail or other pointed object into the figure. These sharp objects captured the *nkisi n'kondi*'s attention thus activating the spiritual power residing in the figure. The word *n'kondi* or "hunter" underscores a *nkisi*'s ability to swiftly track down thieves and other wrongdoers.

A *nkisi n'kondi* could also be used to finalize a binding agreement between neighboring communities. In one documented example, representatives of two warring villages inserted a nail into a *nkisi n'kondi* and then solemnly vowed, "Between your village and my village we have an accord. You may not seize hostages from us and we will not seize hostages from you. If one of our people does something to the other group, we will meet to talk and not fight." The parties understood that the *nkisi n'kondi* would severely punish anyone who violated this agreement. The *nkisi*'s range of punishments included unleashing deadly afflictions and destructive natural forces such as thunderstorms and fire. Aware that the *nkisi n'kondi* would show no mercy to violators of the agreement, the parties could pay the *nganga* a substantial fee to remove the nail, thus annulling the accord.

The metal pieces embedded in each *nkisi n'kondi* provide a historic record of the agreements, disputes, and medical ailments experienced by a Kongo community. The number of nails indicates a *nkisi*'s power and efficacy. For example, Image 172 contains 380 sharp objects. This *nkisi n'kondi* must have been a truly formidable guardian who effectively served his community

MAKING CONNECTIONS

MAINTAINING SOCIAL ORDER

Although separated in time by over 2,500 years, Kongo chiefs and the Babylonian king Hammurabi both used public objects to help maintain social order. A *nkisi n'kondi* invoked spiritual powers to deter antisocial behavior and enforce agreements. Hammurabi used a written code of laws displayed on an eight-foot tall stele (Image 19) to create a uniform code of justice for the diverse groups within his kingdom. Like the Kongo chiefs, Hammurabi also used spiritual powers to inspire awe among his people. The top portion of his great stele displays a prominent relief showing the sun god Shamash presenting Hammurabi with the code of laws.

Photograph by Franko Khoury / National Museum of African Art / Smithsonian Institution

IMAGE 173

Female (Pwo) mask

Chokwe peoples (Democratic Republic of the Congo)

Late 19th century C.E.
Wood and metal

The Chokwe people are an ethnic group who reside in northeastern Angola and the southwestern part of the Democratic Republic of the Congo. The Chokwe won renown as successful traders and gifted artists. Image 173 is an outstanding example of *Pwo*, a traditional Chokwe mask used during important ceremonial rituals to honor a founding female ancestor.

AN IDEAL WOMAN

A professional woodcarver crafted Image 173 to honor an ideal Chokwe woman who had successfully given birth. The carver skillfully combined the features of a particular woman with traditional Chokwe stylistic traits. The completed *Pwo* mask includes real earrings and a meticulously woven wig.

Although it is just over 15 inches high, the *Pwo* mask conveys a great deal of information. For example, the mask contains a number of pounded dots representing SCARIFICATION patterns. The *cingelyengelye* or cruciform design on her forehead may have derived from the Cross of the Order of Christ introduced by 17th-century Portuguese monks. The tears under the *Pwo*'s eyes mark her pride as a mother and sorrow at the inevitable dissolution of the close ties with her son.

The *Pwo*'s half-closed almond-shaped eyes dominate the mask. The Chokwe craftsman used kaolin, a fine, white clay crushed into a powder, to create the whiteness around the *Pwo*'s eyes. The figure's eyes draw attention to her inner wisdom and suggest a connection to the spiritual realm.

MASKS AND MASQUERADES

The *Pwo* mask was more than an impressive work of art; it was also a vital part of a MASQUERADE. Like other West African communities, the Chokwe performed masquerades that combined performers, dancers, music, masks, and costumes. The *Pwo* mask played an especially important role in initiation ceremonies for adolescent boys by dramatizing Chokwe cultural traditions. The masks are thus part of a total experience that cannot be fully conveyed in a static museum exhibit.

The Chokwe are a MATRILINEAL society, in which descent is traced through the female line. The *Pwo* mask underscores the prominence of women among the Chokwe. A male dancer dressed like a woman wore the *Pwo* mask. The dancer used graceful steps to honor the special importance of Chokwe mothers.

MAKING CONNECTIONS

PWO AND *MBLO* MASKS

Neither the *Pwo* mask nor the *Mblo* portrait mask (Image 174) are realistic representations of a person's physical features. Rather, both Chokwe and Baule sculptors sought to create idealized faces to honor women. Accomplished male dancers wore the masks as part of elaborate public masquerades.

Jerry L. Thompson / Art Resource, NY

IMAGE 174

Portrait mask *(Mblo)*

Baule peoples (Cote d'Ivoire)

Early 20th century C.E.
Wood and pigment

The Baule include about 400,000 people who live in compact villages in the Cote d'Ivoire. The Baule are noted for their fine wood sculptures and carved ceremonial masks. Image 174 is an outstanding example of a *Mblo* portrait mask carved in about 1913 for a masquerade performed in the village of Kami.

A RARE MASK

The *Mblo* mask shown above is exceptionally rare. Unlike most African masks, the names of both the carver and his subject are known. Carved by Owie Kimou, the mask is just over 14 inches high. The small but impressive work is an idealized portrait of Moya Yanso, a woman renowned in Kami for her great beauty and extraordinary dancing skills.

STYLISTIC ATTRIBUTES

Owie Kimou used traditional stylistic attributes to convey Moya Yanso's physical beauty and wisdom. The mask's gracefully shaped, wrinkle-free face portrays a woman in the prime of her life. At the same time, the mask's high forehead and small almost closed mouth convey intelligence and composure, qualities of reserve highly esteemed by the Baule.

Owie Kimou used two additional attributes to enhance the mask's artistic quality. The figure's left eye is a little higher than its right eye. This subtle asymmetry gives the mask a feeling of complexity. Kimou also placed six projecting tubular pieces above Yanso's head. Included for beauty, they have no iconographic significance.

THE CLIMAX OF A GBAGBA MASQUERADE

Moya Yanso's *Mblo* mask appeared at a climactic moment of a *gbagba*, an elaborate Baule masquerade that included drummers, singers, and dancers. As the *gbagba* unfolded, highly skilled male dancers performed a series of increasingly complex dances. In order to heighten the drama, selected villagers carefully concealed the *Mblo* mask. Then at a climatic moment, Moya Yanso's husband appeared wearing her *Mblo* mask. Yanso also played a vital role in the performance as she danced alongside of her husband. Audience members participate by dancing, clapping, and drumming.

MAKING CONNECTIONS

THE BAULE *MBLO* MASK AND THE KUBA *NDOP*

The Baule *Mblo* portrait mask and the Kuba *ndop* (Image 171) are both idealized portraits that embody admired traits of wisdom and reserve. However, skilled carvers created the works to serve very different functions. The *Mblo* mask honors a respected woman during a public masquerade. In contrast, the *ndop* served as a visual display of royal power and a source of future instruction and inspiration.

Schomburg Center, NYPL / Art Resource, NY

IMAGE 175

Bundu mask

Sande Society

Mende peoples (West African forests of Sierra Leone)

19th to 20th century C. E.

Wood, cloth, and fiber

The Mende primarily live in small villages in the southern third of Sierra Leone. Most Mende art is associated with elaborate initiation ceremonies. The helmet illustrated by Image 175 has the distinction of being one the few ritual masks worn by African women.

THE SANDE SOCIETY

The Sande Society, a fellowship of Mende women, prepares young girls for their roles as wives, mothers, and community members. Their existence is well known to the entire village. Nonetheless, the Sande Society is often described as "secret" because it hides some of its rituals from the eyes of uninitiated children and Mende men.

The Sande initiation process includes taking young girls to a secluded spot in the forest where they are taught the spiritual knowledge, medicinal skills, and rich traditions necessary for adulthood in Mende society. The rituals include performing a clitoridectomy, a form of female genital mutilation. The Sande Society believes this procedure is important because it prepares young girls for the pain of childbearing.

THE MASK

A public masquerade celebrates the girl's transformation into adulthood. A talented Sande dancer appears in full costume as *Sowo*, the water spirit of the Sande Society. She wears a black gown of raffia fibers that conceal her identity. A two-to-four-pound conical helmet rests over her head on her shoulders. A coat of palm oil gives the mask a black, lustrous shine, representing healthy and beautiful skin.

The ideal mask has clearly defined features that embody Mende ideals of physical and moral beauty. The highly stylized neck rings signify fertility, good health, and high status. The high forehead conveys character and wisdom, while the small mouth and ears represent a person who will neither speak nor listen to gossip. The intricately styled coiffure indicates elegance, wealth, and femininity.

MAKING CONNECTIONS

THE *BUNDU* MASK AND THE YAXCHILAN LINTELS

The *Bundu* Mask and the Yaxchilan lintels (Image 155) are examples of how art can be used to support rituals we deem cruel. For example, the Yaxchilan lintels depict Lady Xook pulling a thorn cord through her tongue. Mayan nobles performed this painful act to feed their gods and help maintain order in their cosmos. The *Bundu* mask and the Yaxchilan lintels illustrate that artistic works cannot be separated from the belief systems that created them.

Werner Forman / Art Resource, NY

IMAGE 176

Ikenga (shrine figure)

Igbo peoples (Nigeria)

c. 19th to 20th century C. E.
Wood

The Igbo constitute the largest ethnic group in what is today southeastern Nigeria. Their arts are both varied and complex. The *ikenga* is a masculine sculptural genre celebrating the Igbo's belief in the importance of individual achievement.

EARNED STATUS

The Igbo lived in a remote inland location that enabled them to enjoy an extended period of independence. As a result, they did not develop a centralized government. The absence of a rigid class of powerful chiefs created a relatively open society celebrating individual achievement and success.

The *ikenga* reflects the importance of earned status in Igbo culture. *Ikenga* figures honor the power and skills of a man's right hand. As an indispensable center of action, the right hand often wields weapons that enable Igbo men to earn recognition as intrepid warriors.

HORNS AND KOLA NUTS

Ikenga figures vary in size and sculptural style. However, all figures include a set of ram horns. The distinctive horns in Image 176 symbolize calculated aggressiveness and ambition. According to Igbo tradition, a ram fights first with his head. The head therefore initiates all action.

Modern museums display their *ikenga* as isolated figures in a plexiglass case. In contrast, an Igbo awarded his *ikenga* a place of honor in a personal shrine. He regularly offered his *ikenga* sacrifices of palm wine, pounded yams dipped in soup, and prized kola nuts. During the early 1900s, George T. Basden worked as a missionary among the Igbo. He concluded that, "Without the *ikenga*, no household would rest in peace, its absence would be considered fatal."

MAKING CONNECTIONS

THE *IKENGA* AND *BAHRAM GUR FIGHTS THE KARG*

Both the wooden figure of an *ikenga* and the watercolor *Bahram Gur Fights the Karg* (Image 189) reflect the great value the Igbo and the Persians placed on individual achievement. Most *ikenga* depicted a warrior holding a weapon in his "strong right arm." Similarly, Bahram Gur is shown holding a fearsome weapon he has just used to slay a monstrous horned wolf known as a Karg. This feat contributed to Bahram Gur's legend of personal bravery and success.

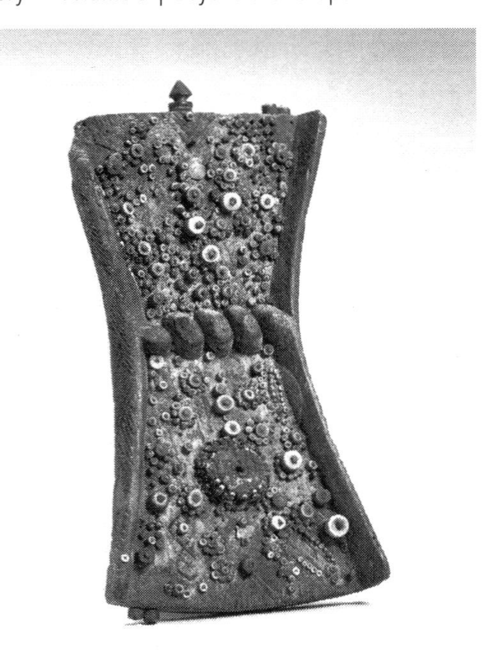

Private Collection, Photo © Heini Schneebeli / Bridgeman Images

IMAGE 177

Lukasa (memory board)

Mbudye Society

Luba peoples (Democratic Republic of the Congo)

c. 19th to 20th century C.E.

Wood, beads, and metal

The Luba kingdom was located in what is now the southeastern corner of the Democratic Republic of the Congo. Its origins and expansion began in the 1500s. Within a century, the Luba emerged as a powerful political and economic presence in central Africa. Luba artists left a distinctive legacy that included beautiful carved representations of women and unique *lukasa* memory boards.

THE MBUDYE SOCIETY

The Luba state's rapid expansion rested upon the twin principles of sacred kingship and rule by a council. This model of government provided the Luba with a durable and flexible political system.

Like other cultures, the Luba developed a way to record and remember their history. The Mbudye Society evolved during the 1700s as a special council charged with preserving the Luba's legendary past and major political achievements. The Mbudye Society included trusted "men of memory" trained to remember and interpret vast stores of information.

A COMPLEX ARCHIVE OF INFORMATION

The Mbudye Society developed a remarkable mnemonic device to help them recall details of their kingdom's long history. Known as a *lukasa*, the small objects appeared to be nothing more than a flat piece of wood studded with brightly colored beads and bits of shell and metal. However, each *lukasa* actually contained a wealth of symbolic information. A senior member of the Mbudye Society would "read" the *lukasa* by holding the board in his left hand and then tracing its design with his right forefinger. This tactile contact facilitated his ability to recall past legends and events.

Each *lukasa* functioned as a complex archive of information. "Reading" its conceptual map enabled elite members of the Mbudye Society to recall vital information about court ceremonies, cultural heroes, clan migrations, geographic landmarks, and a ruler's genealogical records. The Mbudye Society reader did more than just recall the past; he also used the symbols to interpret contemporary events. As the keepers of knowledge, the "men of memory" thus played a key role in sustaining the rituals and authority of the Luba state.

MAKING CONNECTIONS

THE *LUKASA* AND THE BENIN PLAQUES

The Luba *lukasa* and the Benin wall plaques (Image 169) both functioned as historic documents. The Benin plaques provided detailed images of the Oba and his warrior chiefs, court officials, and lesser attendants. Although these plaques suggest a decorative purpose, art historians believe they served as an archive enabling Benin officials to recall information about court rituals, costumes, and even hairstyles.

Image copyright © The Metropolitan Museum of Art. Image Source: Art Resource, NY

IMAGE 178

Aka elephant mask

Bamileke (Cameroon, western grasslands region)

c. 19th to 20th century C.E.
Wood

The Bamileke live in the lush grasslands of central and eastern Cameroon. Their ornate Aka elephant masks are among the best known and must striking works of art from sub-Saharan Africa. The intricate beadwork featured in this mask is one of the trademarks of their artistic legacy.

AN ELABORATE ELEPHANT COSTUME

The Bamileke people have traditionally recognized the elephant as a potent symbol of royal authority. The Aka mask successfully evokes the features of an elephant. The two large circles suggest the elephant's ears while the long front panel alludes to its trunk.

The mask features a lavish display of colorful beads. Imported from Venice and the Middle East, the coveted glass beads imply great wealth. Their colors also convey symbolic messages. For example, black denotes the relationship between the living and the dead, white refers to ancestors and medicines, and red symbolizes life and women. In addition, the beads form repeating triangular patterns that allude to leopard spots, an important symbol of royal power.

A long tunic and distinctive headdress completed the costume. Wearing a headdress was an important privilege reserved for special ceremonies. Composed of bright red feathers from the African gray parrot, the headdress added a flamboyant and memorable feature that impressed awed spectators.

THE KUOSI SOCIETY MASQUERADE

An elite masking society known as the Kuosi owned and wore the Aka elephant masks. The Kuosi included members of the royal family, wealthy title holders, and ranking warriors. Kuosi members displayed their elephant costumes during an impressive MASQUERADE. As spectators cheered, a single column of Kuosi masqueraders dramatically emerged from a large house in the palace compound. Many embellished their costumes by wearing expensive ivory bracelets and rare leopard pelts. Accompanied by an orchestra of drums and iron gongs, the masquerade symbolically underscored the power of the elephant and thus the Bamileke king.

MAKING CONNECTIONS

TRADING NETWORKS

Long-distance trading networks played an important role in the creation of both the Aka elephant mask and the Screen with the *Siege of Belgrade* (Image 94). The Bamileke acquired highly prized beads from trading networks extending across Africa to Venice and the Middle East. The Spanish authorities in Mexico City learned about folding screens (or *biombos*) and lacquerware from Manila galleons carrying Japanese goods to New Spain.

Brooklyn Museum, Frank L. Babbott Fund, 51.3

IMAGE 179

Reliquary figure *(byeri)*

Fang peoples (southern Cameroon)

c. 19th to 20th century C.E.

Wood

The Fang lived in the dense rainforests of equatorial Africa. During a period of over three centuries, they slowly migrated into present-day southern Cameroon and northern Gabon. Their gradual village-by-village movement created a migratory culture that valued portable objects such as the reliquary figure illustrated in Image 179.

THE IMPORTANCE OF RELIQUARIES

The Fang believed that their ancestors could continue to wield power from the afterlife. It thus became imperative to preserve the remains of great men who founded lineages and great women who gave birth to numerous healthy children. The Fang prepared cylindrical bark containers or RELIQUARIES to conserve skulls and other prized ancestral relics. They could then consult the relics on significant matters such as where to locate a village, how to prevent an illness and when to fight a battle.

THE IMPORTANCE OF GUARDIAN FIGURES

Because of their great spiritual power, the relics required additional protection. This led the Fang to attach wooden guardian figures known as *byeri* to the top of each reliquary. From this secure position, a *byeri* could protect the sacred relics from evil spirits and from the forbidden gaze of women and uninitiated boys. The guardian sculptures also played an important role in ritual ceremonies. During these occasions, clan leaders used the *byeri* as puppets to help instruct boys about the history of their people.

THE IMPORTANCE OF HARMONY BETWEEN OPPOSITES

Fang sculptors did not create a *byeri* as a portrait of a specific ancestor. Instead, it embodied a complex but harmonious combination of contrasting traits. For example, the *byeri* in Image 179 juxtaposed the large head of an infant with the bulging muscles of an adult. This union of juvenile and adult characteristics underscored the continuity between infants, adults, and ancestors. Newborn traits such as a prominent belly button and a high domed forehead emphasize an ongoing life cycle in which infants form a crucial link between the living and the dead.

The *byeri*'s expression also contributed to the harmony between opposing qualities. The figure's calm, expressionless face presented a sense of tranquility much admired by the Fang. Yet at the same time, the *byeri*'s clasped hands, large eyes, and tense muscles project a coiled energy ready to strike out at any threat to the irreplaceable relics stored inside the reliquary.

A NEW FUNCTION

During the late 1800s, French colonial officials banned *byeri* as unacceptable idols contradicting the Biblical injunction against graven images. Forced to comply with this demand, the Fang destroyed many *byeri* and sold others to Western collectors. Today, the surviving *byeri* have a new function in museums, where visitors and students can admire the Fang sculptors' abstract interpretation of the human form.

MAKING CONNECTIONS

THE *FANG BYERI* AND THE QIN TERRA COTTA WARRIORS

The Fang *byeri* and the Qin terra cotta warriors (Image 193) both originally functioned as guardians. The *byeri* guarded a reliquary containing sacred bones, providing a link between the living and their ancestors. The army of terra cotta warriors guarded the tomb of Qin Shi Huangdi, the First Emperor of China. They thus performed the vital function of protecting the emperor in his afterlife. Interestingly, both the Fang *byeri* and the Qin terra cotta warriors have a new contemporary function as major museum exhibits.

The Art Institute of Chicago / Art Resource, NY

IMAGE 180

Veranda post of enthroned king and senior wife

Olowe of Ise

Yoruba peoples

c. 1910–1914 C.E.

Wood and pigment

The Yoruba live in southwestern Nigeria and southern Benin. They are a diverse people with a rich cultural and artistic heritage. Yoruba artists produced a wide range of works designed to glorify their king and his court. Olowe of Ise (c. 1873–c. 1938) is the most important and admired Yoruba sculptor of the 20th century.

"THE MASTER CARVER"

An *oriki* is a Yoruba praise song extolling a specific person. A song dedicated to Olowe of Ise reveals the extent of his fame. Sung by one of his wives, the *oriki* lavishes praise on Olowe as "a great man" who was an "excellent husband," "a great dancer," and most of all a "master carver." Possessed of unrivalled skills, Olowe inspired awe and wonder as a sculptor "who carves the hardwood of the iroko tree as though it were as soft as a calabash."

Olowe's artistic reputation began when he carved a program of sculptures for the royal court in Ise. As his fame spread, other Yoruba kings commissioned Olowe to carve decorative containers, elaborate doors, and striking veranda posts. Image 180 was one of four figurative posts created for the king of Ikere's palace courtyard. Carved from a single piece of wood, the veranda post is a masterpiece that uses high relief figures to successfully portray key ideals of leadership in Yoruba society.

THE SENIOR WIFE

Olowe's innovative composition deliberately features a tall female figure who towers above a seated king. Known as the senior wife, the figure's size visually emphasizes the importance of Yoruba women as the source of human life and the embodiment of formidable spiritual powers. The senior wife's strong, solid body provides an architectural support for the veranda while also functioning as a visual reminder that Yoruba men cannot rule without the support of Yoruba women.

Olowe uses physical traits as ornaments to provide additional information about the senior wife. Her large eyes suggest alertness and the ability to detect potential enemies. The senior wife's intricate hairstyle, the gap between her front teeth, and the SCARIFICATION pattern on her face all signify great beauty and high social status. The bracelets around her neck, wrist, and waist all proclaim her lofty royal position.

THE KING

Olowe carved the king as a smaller figure than his senior wife. The king nonetheless occupies a central position in the overall composition. Seated on a prominent throne, the ruler wears beaded jewelry almost identical to the ornaments worn by his wife. The two figures convey a carefully presented balance between the king's overt political authority and his wife's understated but real spiritual authority.

THE ROYAL CROWN

Visitors entering the palace courtyard would focus their attention on the large beaded conical crown worn by the king. The crown was a Yoruba king's most important symbol of royal power and authority. According to Yoruba tradition, the beaded crown is a link in a continuous line of rulers dating back to the original Yoruba kingdoms. Olowe underscored this connection by using the crown to depict the all-seeing faces of previous rulers.

Olowe completed the royal couple by placing a bird perched on the peak of the king's crown. The bird symbolizes the presence of older women, female ancestors, and female deities. Known collectively as "our mothers," these groups command great respect for possessing supernatural powers that enable a king to rule. This explains why during the royal coronation the senior wife performed the critical role of placing the crown on the king's head.

MAKING CONNECTIONS

OLOWE OF ISE AND OWIE KIMOU

Most of the early collectors of African art identified the works by the name of the ethnic group that produced them. As a result, they saw no reason to ask for the names of the artists whose works are now displayed in museums around the world. Although the artists were known and recognized by their patrons, they are now anonymous. Olowe of Ise and Owie Kimou (Image 174) are exceptional African artists with known identities. Their work clearly illustrates that African artists had distinctive individual styles within their regional artistic traditions.

Content Area 7

WEST AND CENTRAL ASIA

WEST AND CENTRAL ASIA

Content Area 7 includes 11 works created between 400 B.C.E. and 1540 C.E. The artists, architects, sculptors, and weavers in these regions produced a wide variety of exceptional works.

Our unit presents the 11 works in this content area in the chronological order provided in the College Board's AP Art History Framework. This organization will enable you to quickly find a specific work of art.

The College Board encourages teachers and students to arrange the works in a wide variety of meaningful topical categories. Here are several possible arrangements:

HELLENISTIC ART

Image 181: Petra, Jordan: Treasury and Great Temple

BUDDHIST ART

Image 182: Bamiyan Buddha
Image 184: Jowo Rinpoche

ISLAMIC ART

Image 183: The Kaaba
Image 185: Dome of the Rock
Image 186: Great Mosque, Isfahan
Image 187: Folio for a Qur'an
Image 188: Basin (*Baptistère de St. Louis*)
Image 189: *Bahram Gur Fights the Karg*
Image 190: *The Court of Gayumars*
Image 191: The Ardabil Carpet

SACRED ARCHITECTURE

Image 183: The Kaaba
Image 185: Dome of the Rock
Image 186: Great Mosque, Isfahan

LUXURY OBJECTS

Image 188: Basin (*Baptistère de St. Louis*)
Image 191: The Ardabil Carpet

ILLUMINATED MANUSCRIPTS

Image 187: Folio for a Qur'an
Image 189: *Bahram Gur Fights the Karg*
Image 190: *The Court of Gayumars*

Graham Racher

De Agostini Picture Library / C. Sappa / Bridgeman Images

IMAGE 181

Petra, Jordan: Treasury and Great Temple

Nabataean, Ptolemaic, and Roman

c. 400 B.C.E.–100 C.E.

Cut rock

The ruins of Petra are located in a seemingly inhospitable desert in southwestern Jordan. And yet, at its peak in the first century C.E., Petra boasted a population of about 30,000 people who lived in one of the wealthiest and most remarkable cities in the ancient world. Petra's dramatic location and stunning rock-cut architecture now attract over 600,000 annual visitors who marvel at a site that ranks as one of the New Seven Wonders of the World.

THE NABATAEANS

A nomadic Bedouin tribe known as the Nabataeans transformed Petra from one of the driest places on Earth into a thriving urban oasis. They accomplished this feat by first taking advantage of Petra's strategic location at the intersection of lucrative trade routes. Caravans traveling north from southern Arabia carried boxes of frankincense and myrrh that Romans prized for use in religious rites. At the same time, caravans traveling west from Persia carried sacks of equally coveted spices from India.

The Nabataeans were more than masters of trade; they were also masters of water. Although Petra itself is dry, underground springs exist in the surrounding area. In addition, sudden downpours can produce flashfloods. The Nabataeans built a system of dams, cisterns, and conduits to store and move water to and around their city.

The Nabataeans' command of trade and water enabled them to become what the Roman writer Pliny called "the richest race on Earth." During the 300-year period between the first century B.C.E. and the second century C.E., the Nabataeans used their great wealth and engineering skill to create a spectacular city. At its peak, Petra covered an area as large as Manhattan Island, New York.

THE TREASURY WAS NOT A TREASURY

For the past 2,000 years, visitors to Petra have reached the Treasury by traveling through a narrow 1,000-yard-long natural gorge known as the Siq or "Shaft." The first glimpse of the Treasury inspires awe and amazement. Carved from a rose-colored cliff, the façade is 80 feet wide and 127 feet high.

The Treasury's immense façade includes an exceptional array of architectural orders and figurative details. Six towering Corinthian columns flank the entrance. On either side, statues of the mythological brothers Castor and Pollux welcome visitors. The Treasury's upper level features a broken or interrupted pediment. Nabataean sculptors added an eclectic display of griffins, eagles, winged victories, and six axe-wielding mythological women known as Amazons.

The Treasury's ornate façade fueled speculation that the structure must have housed fabulous riches. Indeed, in the climatic scene in the Hollywood film *Indiana Jones and the Last Crusade*, Indy enters the Treasury to search for the Holy Grail, the fabled drinking vessel Jesus Christ used at the Last Supper. Modern archaeologists, however, do not believe that the Treasury contained either riches or the Holy Grail. Instead, evidence indicates that three small interior chambers may have held the royal sarcophagi of Aretas IV, a powerful Nabataean ruler who reigned from 9 B.C.E. to 40 C.E.

THE GREAT TEMPLE MAY HAVE BEEN MORE THAN A TEMPLE

The Treasury was one of many impressive structures in Petra. At its peak, the city boasted a bustling, colonnaded street. Residents and visitors shopped in markets filled with luxury goods, enjoyed entertainment in an 8,000-seat stone amphitheater, and lived in lavish villas.

During the early 1990s, archaeologists from Brown University began excavating previously hidden ruins at a site now known as the Great Temple. Constructed during the last quarter of the first century B.C.E. and then enlarged in the following century, the Great Temple featured a monumental stairway leading to a large stone platform surrounded by over 100 columns. These features led scholars to hypothesize that the building served as a temple to Dushara, Petra's principle deity.

Recent discoveries have suggested that the Great Temple may have had additional functions. The Brown archaeologists discovered a series of stone seats that may have been part of an important meeting space. They have also uncovered the remains of an elaborate garden-pool complex located next to the Great Temple. These findings open the possibility that the Great Temple functioned as a center of both religious and political activities.

DECLINE, NEGLECT, AND REDISCOVERY

Petra's golden age ended when the Roman Empire absorbed the city in 106 C.E. Within a short time, Petra began to lose its wealth and power as Rome shifted trade to land routes and more accessible seaports. Then on May 19, 363 C.E., a massive earthquake shook the city. As the quake rumbled through Petra, it destroyed vital dams and unleashed a catastrophic flood. Petra never recovered from this natural disaster. Abandoned by its residents, the once-proud city deteriorated into sand-swept ruins known only to local Bedouin tribes. After centuries of neglect, the Swiss explorer Johann Ludwig Burckhardt rediscovered Petra in 1812. Today, Petra is a source of great pride and tourist revenue for modern Jordan.

MAKING CONNECTIONS

PETRA AND GREAT ZIMBABWE

Petra and Great Zimbabwe (Image 167) share a number of common characteristics. Both rose to economic prominence as integral parts of luxury trading networks. Rulers in both cities used their wealth to fund the construction of monumental works featured in Images 167 and 181. As their vital trade routes shifted, both cities lost revenue and began to decline. Natural disasters that included a devastating earthquake in Petra and a prolonged drought in Great Zimbabwe caused irreversible decline. Both cities slipped into obscurity, only to be rediscovered by 19th-century European explorers.

Borromeo / Art Resource, NY

IMAGE 182

Bamiyan Buddha
Bamiyan, Afghanistan

Gandharan

c. 400–800 C.E. (destroyed in 2001)
Cut rock with plaster and polychrome paint

Just over 1,400 years ago, anonymous sculptors carved two colossal statues of the Buddha into a sandstone cliff overlooking the Bamiyan Valley in what is today Afghanistan. Standing 180 and 125 feet tall, the elaborately decorated images ranked as the largest standing Buddhas ever created. In 2001, the Taliban rulers of Afghanistan deliberately destroyed the two statues and reduced the celebrated images to piles of rubble. Today only empty cavities remain where the towering Buddhas once stood.

THE BAMIYAN VALLEY AND BUDDHISM

The Bamiyan Valley is located in the heart of Afghanistan's rugged Hindu Kush mountain range. Although the valley is just 120 miles northwest of Kabul, modern travelers find its remote location difficult to reach. However, that was not the case 1,500 years ago. At that time, the Bamiyan Valley occupied an important strategic position along the famous Silk Road.

The Silk Road comprised an overland network of trade routes linking China and Central Asia with India and ultimately the Mediterranean Sea. The Bamiyan Valley's fertile fields attracted merchants and Buddhist missionaries. Thus between 500 and 750 C.E., the region served as both a commercial hub and an important Buddhist spiritual center.

Xuanzang, a renowned Chinese Buddhist monk, visited the Bamiyan Valley in 643 C.E. He reported seeing a flourishing Buddhist community that included "several tens" of monasteries housing "several thousand monks." The sight of yellow-robed monks chanting prayers to mark the passage of their monastic day fascinated Xuanzang. But he was even more intrigued by the unexpected sight of two colossal statues of the Buddha.

THE BAMIYAN BUDDHAS

The two massive Buddhas faced the widest part of the Bamiyan Valley. Although impressed by their size, Xuanzang was even more astonished by their color and ornamentation. The large Buddha dazzled with its "golden color" and "brilliant gems." About half a mile to the east, the second Buddha "was cast in separate pieces [of copper] and then welded together into shape." Each Buddha stood in a niche, with its robes attached to the back wall. This enabled pious worshippers to circumambulate, or walk around, the statue's free-standing feet and legs.

The two Buddhas' bright red and yellow colors gradually faded, and their gems disappeared. However, both statues contained distinctive flowing robes that provided striking evidence of what is known as the GANDHARAN style. Gandhara is the name given to a region in modern Pakistan and Afghanistan, conquered by Alexander the Great in 330 B.C.E. Alexander introduced classical art and culture to Gandhara. His successors adopted a Gandharan style that combined realistic Hellenistic elements, such as flowing robes, with Buddhist subject matter.

The Bamiyan Buddhas served as centerpieces of a flourishing Buddhist community. Both statues manifested the power and piety of their royal benefactors. Visible for miles, they provided pilgrims and merchants with a dramatic reminder to follow Buddhist practices. The two timeless images also marked a momentous development in Buddhist art. The gigantic Bamiyan statues represented Buddha as more than a gifted teacher; he was now presented as a guiding, enduring, and universal spiritual presence.

"ALL FAKE IDOLS MUST BE DESTROYED"

During the 9th and 10th centuries, Islam gradually replaced Buddhism in the Bamiyan Valley. The colossal Buddhas remained under Muslim rule for the next thousand years. Although they suffered from neglect and occasional vandalism, the statues nonetheless remained largely intact.

The safety of the Bamiyan Buddhas became endangered when the Taliban gained control over Afghanistan in 1996. They enforced a strict interpretation of Islamic law that included severe restrictions imposed on Afghan women and ultimately a prohibition against all figurative religious images.

On February 26, 2001, Mullah Mohammad Omar issued a decree declaring, "All fake idols must be destroyed." Mullah Omar ignored international protests by forcefully insisting, "I am a smasher of idols, not a seller of them." During the next month, the Taliban used artillery, anti-aircraft guns, and finally dynamite to completely demolish the Bamiyan Buddhas.

MAKING CONNECTIONS

ICONOCLASM—ART UNDER ATTACK

The demolition of the Bamiyan Buddhas provides a contemporary example of ICONOCLASM, the deliberate destruction of images for religious or political purposes. Iconoclasm has been a recurring practice since ancient times. The Egyptian pharaoh Akhenaton (Image 22) launched a campaign to destroy temples and monuments dedicated to traditional gods. In 730 C.E., the Byzantine emperor Leo III issued an edict against graven images such as *Virgin (Theotokos) and Child between Saints Theodore and George* (Image 54). Eight centuries later, Spanish conquistadores destroyed Aztec (Image 157) and Inka (Image 159) temples. During the 20th century, Hitler and his lieutenants ridiculed and defaced paintings by "degenerate" Expressionist artists such as Ernst Ludwig Kirchner (Image 133).

Flickr: Mosquée Masjid el Haram á la Mecque

IMAGE 183

The Kaaba

Mecca, Saudi Arabia

Pre-Islamic monument; rededicated by Muhammad in 631-632 C.E.
Granite masonry, covered with silk curtain and calligraphy in gold and silver-wrapped thread

All religious faiths have a spiritual center. In Islam, the Kaaba is the unquestioned spiritual magnet for followers of the world's second largest monotheistic faith. Kaaba is an Arabic word meaning "cube." The Kaaba is located near the center of the Great Mosque in Mecca. Although Muslims pray toward the Kaaba five times a day, they do not worship the shrine. Instead, they worship what they believe the Kaaba represents–Allah, the one God.

THE PRE-ISLAMIC KAABA

According to Islamic tradition, God ordained Abraham and his son Ishmael to build the Kaaba as a holy shrine for worship. While Abraham was building the Kaaba an angel brought the Black Stone, which he then placed in the structure's eastern corner. Following Ishmael's death, the Kaaba became a holy site for Bedouin tribes. As time passed, the Bedouins gradually turned to polytheism and idolatry. Thus, although the Meccans worshipped Allah as their chief deity, He shared His power with over 300 other gods and goddesses whose statues filled the Kaaba. The idols attracted throngs of people who came on pilgrimages to worship these deities.

THE KAABA AND MUHAMMAD

Muhammad was born in 570 C.E. into a minor branch of a powerful Meccan clan. He took great interest in religion and often spent time alone in prayer and meditation. At the age of 40, Muhammad experienced a vision that sent him on a path that would alter the course of history. According to tradition, while Muhammad meditated in a cave outside Mecca, the angel Gabriel appeared and declared, "O Muhammad! Thou art the messenger of Allah, and I am Gabriel."

During the next years, Muhammad received more revelations and openly announced himself as the Prophet of Allah who was divinely commissioned to lead the Arab people to a new monotheistic faith. However, many influential Meccans refused to accept his revolutionary ideas and warned that he posed a threat to the city's profitable pilgrimage trade.

Faced with this hostility, Muhammad fled to the city of Medina. Within a short time he attracted many followers to a new religion known as Islam, meaning "surrender to God." In 630 C.E., the Prophet and 10,000 of his followers made a triumphant return to Mecca. Muhammad boldly entered the Kaaba and exultantly proclaimed, "Truth has come and falsehood has vanished!" He then destroyed all the idols in the Kaaba and allowed only the Black Stone to remain.

THE KAABA AND ISLAMIC DUTIES

Prior to his death in 632 C.E., Muhammad established religious duties that all observant Muslims must follow. Known as the Five Pillars of Islam, these guiding tenets of faith include two duties—prayer and pilgrimage—that are closely tied to the Kaaba.

Daily prayer is one of the hallmarks of Islam. Muhammad fixed the Kaaba as the QIBLA or direction for all five prayers. Most mosques contain a semicircular niche known as a MIHRAB that identifies the qibla wall. The act of praying to the same point symbolizes the unity of all Muslims.

Pilgrimage to Mecca is a second Pillar of Islam that is closely linked to the Kaaba. Known as the *Hajj*, the pilgrimage to Mecca is a duty that must be carried out at least once in the lifetime by all adult Muslims who are physically and financially capable of undertaking the journey. The *Hajj* occurs from the 8th to the 12th (and in some cases the 13th) days of the last month of the Islamic calendar.

For most pilgrims, seeing the Kaaba for the first time is an unforgettable experience. "I've been praying in this direction for years," explained a pilgrim. "It's a dream come true. I can't believe I am actually here." Like two million other pilgrims, this worshipper began her spiritual journey by walking around the Kaaba seven times.

MAKING CONNECTIONS

CIRCUMAMBULATION

CIRCUMAMBULATION is the act of moving around a sacred object. It is an integral part of Islam and Buddhist devotional practices. Islamic pilgrims circumambulate the Kaaba seven times in a counterclockwise direction. For Muslims, this direction emphasizes that their action is not connected to the directional movement of the sun or planets. They believe that Allah is independent of all time and place. In contrast, Buddhists circumambulate venerated sites such as the Great Stupa at Sanchi (Image 192) in a clockwise direction. This direction suggests the journey of the Earth around the Sun, thus bringing devout pilgrims into harmony with the cosmos. The clockwise direction is also a gesture of great respect that always keeps the Buddha to the pilgrim's right. It symbolically underscores a pilgrim's goal of following a right and therefore a true path to enlightenment.

Erich Lessing / Art Resource, NY

IMAGE 184

Jowo Rinpoche

Enshrined in the Jokhang Temple
Lhasa, Tibet

Believed to have been brought to Tibet in 641 C.E.
Gilt metals with semiprecious stones, pearls, and paint

Lhasa has been the center of the Tibetan Buddhist world for over a thousand years. The city's many historic sites include the Jokhang Temple, Tibet's most important and sacred place of worship. The Jowo Rinpoche is enshrined inside the Jokhang Temple. The revered statue depicts the historic Buddha, also known as Buddha Shakyamuni.

BUDDHA SHAKYAMUNI

Prince Siddhartha Gautama was born around 563 B.C.E. near the foothills of the Himalayas in what is now Nepal. Deliberately protected from human suffering, he was brought up in luxury and splendor. Anxious to know the truth about life, Siddhartha ventured outside the palace walls. He promptly encountered human suffering in the forms of disease, old age, and death. These disturbing sights forced Siddhartha to question life's endless cycle of pain.

At the age of 29, Siddhartha renounced his life of ease and family pleasure. He took a last look at his sleeping wife and infant son and left his palace to become a wandering monk. During the next six years, Siddhartha attempted to solve the riddle of life by extreme fasting. At one point, he could press his stomach and feel his backbone. But fasting did not provide an answer–Siddhartha had neither escaped from the world of suffering nor gained wisdom.

In 537 B.C.E., Siddhartha began to meditate under a sacred Bodhi tree. After 49 days, he finally attained enlightenment. Siddhartha now understood that suffering is caused by desire and that the way to end pain is to end all desires. The historic Buddha Shakyamuni devoted the next 40 years to teaching the truths he had discovered.

THE JOWO RINPOCHE— ORIGINS AND MEANING

Legend has it that Vishvaharma, the celestial king of craftsmen, created the larger-than-life-size image of the historical Buddha Shakyamuni now housed in the Jokhang Temple in Lhasa. Unable to confirm this legendary account, modern scholars now believe that the Jowo Rinpoche, or "precious one," was probably made in India sometime during the early seventh century C.E.

The Jowo Rinpoche was created to act as the Buddha's proxy following his *parinirvana*, or departure from the world. The sculpture portrays Buddha seated under the Bodhi tree at the moment just before the historical Buddha Shakyamuni achieved enlightenment. Buddha's legs are crossed in the lotus position, or *padmasana*. The sculpture uses MUDRAS, or symbolic hand gestures, to convey the dramatic moment. Buddha sits in a gesture of meditation with his left hand, palm upright, in his lap. At the same time, his right hand touches the ground in a gesture calling the earth to witness his spiritual authority. The earth then roared, "I bear you witness!"

THE JOWO RINPOCHE IN TIBET

According to ancient accounts, the Indian king Dharmapala gave the Jowo Rinpoche to the Emperor of China. In 641 C.E., the Chinese princess Wencheng, the daughter of the Tang emperor Taizong, included the sacred image in her dowry. She then brought the Jowo Rinpoche to the Tibetan king Songtsen Gampo when she became his second wife. The Jowo Rinpoche's arrival marks the beginning of the foundation of Buddhism in Tibet.

Songtsen Gampo constructed the Jokhang Temple to house the Jowo Rinpoche. Although regularly expanded over the centuries, the temple's original core remains largely intact. The Jokhang Temple is now the spiritual heart of Tibet. Buddhist pilgrims who pray before the richly gilded and jeweled statue shown in Image 184 believe that viewing the image will facilitate their path to enlightenment.

THE JOWO RINPOCHE IN AMERICA

Pious pilgrims no longer have to journey to Tibet to see the Jowo Rinpoche. On May 30, 2008, the Drikung Meditation Center in Arlington, Massachusetts, installed a full-size replica of the revered statue. Pilgrims believe that their devotion transforms the statue from an ordinary object into a real Buddha. Seeing the Jowo Rinpoche will thus create a positive energy for each viewer.

MAKING CONNECTIONS

THE JOWO RINPOCHE AND THE ORIGINAL *VIRGIN OF GUADALUPE*

The Jowo Rinpoche and the original *Virgin of Guadalupe* (see Image 95) share many common characteristics. Devotees believe that both images emerged from a miraculous creation. The Jowo Rinpoche is permanently installed in the Jokhang Temple in Lhasa, while the *Virgin of Guadalupe* is permanently installed in the Basilica of Our Lady of Guadalupe in Mexico City. Viewers to these sites believe that each image provides a source of profound blessing. And finally, the Jowo Rinpoche and the original *Virgin of Guadalupe* have served as important unifying symbols for both Tibet and Mexico.

SEF / Art Resource, NY

Erich Lessing / Art Resource, NY

IMAGE 185

Dome of the Rock

Jerusalem

Islamic, Umayyad

691–692 C.E. with multiple renovations
Stone masonry and wooden roof decorated with glazed ceramic tile, mosaics, and gilt aluminum and bronze dome

The Dome of the Rock's golden dome dominates the skyline of Jerusalem's Old City. It is the oldest extant Islamic monument and is only surpassed by Mecca and Medina as an Islamic holy site. The Dome of the Rock is neither a mosque nor a mausoleum. It is instead a shrine for pilgrims who come to the Temple Mount to see a rock, known as the Foundation Stone, that is sacred to both Jews and Muslims.

SACRED SIGNIFICANCE

The Foundation Stone has deep roots in Jewish history. According to Jewish tradition, it is the "navel of the Earth," the place where God gathered the dust to create Adam. The Old Testament relates that Abraham came to the Foundation Stone to sacrifice his son Isaac as a demonstration of faith. The stone is also revered as the location of the Holy of Holies, an inner sanctum within Solomon's Temple that contained the Ark of the Covenant.

For Muslims, the Foundation Stone marks a sacred part of the Prophet Muhammad's Night Journey to Jerusalem. According to Islamic tradition, the archangel Gabriel guided Muhammad and a fabulous winged steed from Mecca to the sacred Foundation Stone in Jerusalem. Muhammad then led Abraham, Moses, Solomon, Jesus, and other prophets in prayer. Following the prayers, Gabriel escorted Muhammad to the pinnacle of the rock, where a ladder of golden light materialized. They then ascended through the heavens to Allah's presence, where the Prophet received additional instructions for his followers. Muhammad and Gabriel then descended to the Foundation Stone, remounted the steed, and returned to Mecca.

A BOLD STATEMENT

The titanic struggle between Christianity and Islam began in 637 C.E. In that year a powerful Muslim army of 60,000 men burst out of Arabia and stunned the Byzantine Christian empire by capturing Jerusalem. Within a decade Muslim forces conquered Byzantine Egypt, Palestine, and Syria and even toppled the Sassanid rulers of Persia.

In 661 an influential Meccan family known as the Umayyads gained power and brought stability to the vast and still-expanding Islamic empire. Despite their ties to Mecca, the Umayyads established their capital at Damascus, a thriving and centrally located city in Syria.

The leaders who followed Muhammad are called caliphs, meaning "successors to the Prophet." In 687, Caliph Abd al-Malik launched an ambitious project to construct a magnificent domed building over the sacred Foundation Stone. The caliph's decision combined piety and shrewdness. The new Islamic shrine would instill a sense of pride among devout Muslims. At the same time, it would use architecture to provide a bold statement emphasizing the power and wealth of the Umayyad dynasty.

ARCHITECTURAL PROGRAM

Byzantine architecture strongly influenced the builders of the Dome of the Rock. Like San Vitale in Ravenna (Image 51), the Dome of the Rock was built on an octagonal plan. A dome supported by a circular drum topped both structures. The Dome of the Rock's drum stands above a circuit of twelve columns and four piers. The interior space is filled with light, which enters through 16 windows in the drum and 40 windows in the eight-sided lower panels.

Skilled craftsmen created the distinctive golden dome by melting down 100,000 gold coins. This shimmering sight far surpassed the drab dome atop the nearby Christian Church of the Holy Sepulchre. Over time, the golden crown disappeared and was replaced with copper and gold-colored aluminum plates. During the early 1990s, King Hussein of Jordan provided funds to gild the dome with 5,000 glittering new gold plates. The restored dome thus remains a symbol of Jerusalem and one of the glories of Islamic art.

DECORATIVE PROGRAM

Beautiful tiles cover the Dome of the Rock's exterior façade. These tiles date back to the mid-16th century when the Ottoman Sultan Suleyman the Magnificent ordered the replacement of the weathered original glass mosaics with over 40,000 blue and gold glazed ceramic tiles. In Islamic art, blue is the color of the sky and suggests infinity, while gold represents knowledge of Allah.

The dazzling exterior façade provides a foretaste of the decorative wonders inside the Dome of the Rock. Forbidden by Muslim beliefs to depict Allah, Muhammad, or any figural form, mosaicists instead portrayed crowns, jewels, chalices, and other royal motifs. These objects may have been intended to provide visual references to the triumph of Islamic forces over the Byzantine and Persian empires.

A Qur'anic inscription, more than 785 feet in length, surrounds the interior walls. It underscores Islam's central message, that "There is no god but God" and that Muhammad is Allah's human messenger. The inscription rejects the Christian doctrine of the Trinity, insisting that Jesus was a prophet and that Allah "has no associates." The inscription thus conveys an unequivocal message that Islam is a superior new monotheism that supersedes both Judaism and Christianity.

MAKING CONNECTIONS

DOME OF THE ROCK AND THE MOSQUE OF SELIM II

The Dome of the Rock fulfilled Caliph Abd al-Malik's goal of using architecture to make a bold religious and political statement. Almost 900 years later, the Ottoman Sultan Selim II and his chief architect Sinan built the Mosque of Selim II (Image 84) to accomplish similar goals. Selim II utilized his towering new mosque to impress European visitors with the greatness of Ottoman Empire. Sinan utilized the mosque to disprove claims that no Muslim architect could match the Byzantine Christian church Hagia Sophia (Image 52).

Diego Delso

IMAGE 186

Great Mosque (Masjid-e Jameh)

Isfahan, Iran

Islamic, Persian, Seljuk, Safavid Dynasties

c. 700-present

Stone, brick, wood, plaster, and glazed ceramic tile

The Great Mosque of Isfahan occupies a special place in the history of Islamic architecture. Its deep blue floral mosaics, ornamental MUQARNAS, and elegant calligraphy embody the beauty of Persian decorative arts. At the same time, the builders of the Grand Mosque introduced a FOUR-IWAN PLAN that gave birth to an important architectural tradition in mosque design.

A LONG, COMPLEX HISTORY

The Great Mosque of Isfahan is the biggest and oldest congregational or Friday mosque in Iran. Its long and complex history stretches back to the eighth century C.E. During the mid-11th century C.E., the Seljuk Turks rebuilt the mosque and made Isfahan the capital of their short-lived dynasty. About 500 years later, the Safavid Sultan Shah Abbas launched an ambitious building program. Under his leadership Isfahan once again became a capital city, and the Great Mosque once again became a center of religious activity and artistic innovation.

The process of construction and renovation did not end with the fall of the Safavid dynasty. The Great Mosque now covers over 200,000 square feet. Seen from the air, it appears inseparable from the adjacent streets, homes, and warehouses. The Great Mosque is an unmistakable presence in a community where people live, work, and worship Allah together.

A FOUR-IWAN MOSQUE

Worshippers enter the Great Mosque by passing into a large rectangular courtyard surrounded by a two-story arcade. The courtyard provides a transitional zone between the outside secular world and the spiritual world inside the mosque. Each of the four courtyard sides contains a centrally located IWAN. As shown in Image 186, an iwan is a monumental barrel-vaulted hall with a wide-open arched entrance. The four facing iwans create an elegant architectural composition, inviting imitation. Thus the FOUR-IWAN PLAN devised at the Great Mosque in Isfahan became a prototype for mosques in Persia and across the Muslim world.

The four iwans all function as passageways. However, each vault contains different dimensions and decorative motifs. This variety was intentional. Isfahan architects did not try to achieve perfection, since this quality can only be attributed to God.

The south-facing iwan served as the qibla iwan, pointing worshippers toward Mecca. The iwan features splendid 15th-century mosaics, two flanking minarets, and distinctive cusped niches called MUQARNAS. Sometimes described as "honeycomb vaulting," the muqarnas provide a striking multi-faced surface, reflecting light and casting shadows.

TWO RIVAL DOMES

The qibla iwan leads to a domed interior space, originally reserved for the sultan and his retinue. In 1086, royal vizier

Nizam al-Mulk ordered the construction of a grand dome above the prayer hall. The new dome featured a double shell with a bulbous outer dome rising above the inner dome. Viewed from the outside, the dome's 170-foot-high peak is the highest point in Isfahan. It provides a vivid symbol of Islam while also serving as a distinctive landmark for both residents and passing travellers.

Although Nizam's dome is now a source of pride, it originally inspired jealousy. The vizier's rival and successor, Taj al-Mulk, vowed to construct a new dome directly across from the quibla dome. Erected in just two years, the new structure is widely recognized as the finest brick dome in Persia. Although smaller than Nizam's dome, Taj's dome incorporates a particularly pleasing set of harmonious mathematical proportions.

A REPRESENTATION OF PARADISE

The Qur'an contains vivid descriptions of the eternal gardens of Paradise. Many features of the Great Mosque are symbolic representations designed to inspire visions of Paradise. For example, each of the four courtyard iwans represents a branch of the river that irrigates Paradise. The ever-present floral mosaic decorations allude to lush gardens, full of flowers and fragrance.

MAKING CONNECTIONS

MOSQUE PLANS

Three plans dominate mosque architecture. The Great Mosque of Isfahan developed a design in which four iwans face each other across a central courtyard. The Great Mosque of Cordoba (Image 56) utilized a HYPOSTYLE HALL design in which rows of columns support the roof and guide worshippers toward the qibla wall. Finally, the Mosque of Selim II (Image 84) employed a CENTRAL PLAN, in which a dome covers a large open space for communal prayers.

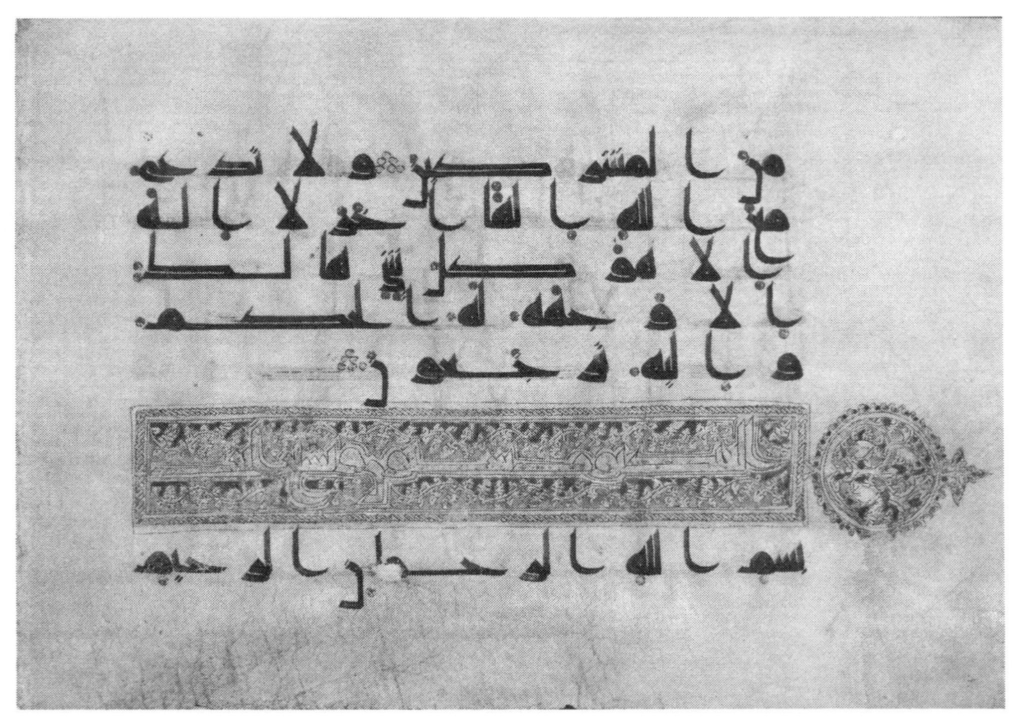

Photo Credit: The Pierpont Morgan Library & Museum / Art Resource, NY

IMAGE 187

Folio from a Qur'an

Arab, North Africa or Near East

Abbasid

c. 9th to early 10th century C.E.
Ink, color, and gold on parchment

The Qur'an is the sacred book of Islam. Muslims believe it contains the word of God as revealed through the archangel Gabriel to the Prophet Muhammad. Image 187 is a fragment from an early 10th-century Qur'an. It provides insight into the process by which Muhammad's followers transformed orally transmitted words into a fixed written text.

THE QUR'AN: FORMATION AND ORGANIZATION

According to Muslim tradition, Muhammad received divine revelations between the years 610 C.E. and his death in 632. Because very few of the Prophet's early companions were able to write, they memorized his messages. Shortly after Muhammad's death, the first Muslim caliph instructed trusted followers to compile their oral recollections into a fixed written form.

As Islam spread beyond the Arabian Peninsula, it became necessary to establish a standard text to preserve the sanctity of Muhammad's message. In about 650 C.E., Muhammad's surviving companions collected his divine revelations and compiled them into an authorized manuscript known as the Qur'an.

The word Qur'an comes from the Arabic verb "to recite." The Qur'an is not a narrative account of Muhammad's life or a recital of his teachings. It is instead Allah's own words, organized into 114 suras, or chapters, arranged from the longest to the shortest.

THE IMPORTANCE OF CALLIGRAPHY

Gabriel conveyed the divine revelations to Mohammad in Arabic. As a result, the language acquired enormous prestige and created a linguistic bond among all Muslims. It also magnified the pressure on scribes and copyists to accurately and artistically render the words of the Qur'an. As a result CALLIGRAPHY, or the art of beautiful writing, became a revered art form in the Islamic world.

KUFIC SCRIPT

Kufic was the first calligraphic script to gain prominence. Its name derives from Kufa, a town along the Euphrates River that became one of the earliest centers of Islamic learning in Iraq. The Kufic script features short vertical strokes, elongated horizontals, and angular letters.

The process of creating a Qur'an required years of arduous training and painstaking craftsmanship. Since the text of the Qur'an is traditionally read aloud, scribes included diacritical marks to serve as visual guideposts. For example, the red dots represent vowels, thus helping readers distinguish among different letters with similar shapes. A pyramid of six gold discs marks the end of a verse.

Each of the 114 suras is named after its theme. For example, Image 187 is taken from Sura 29, "The Spider." The name is derived from an analogy in which skeptics are likened to spiders who build flimsy homes rather than taking secure protection with Allah. Scribes highlighted the sura's title by writing it in gold ink and surrounding it with a rectangle decorated with undulating gold vines. A distinctive rounded palmette extends into the margin, providing readers with an additional visual signpost.

MAKING CONNECTIONS

ABBASID QUR'AN AND *LINDISFARNE GOSPELS*

The Abbasid Qur'an and the *Lindisfarne Gospels* (Image 55) both present sacred texts inscribed on expensive parchment. The Kufic script in the Qur'an is read from right to left, while the Latin text in the *Lindisfarne Gospels* is read from left to right. Both works required an expensive and lengthy creative process. Muslim scribes created the Abbasid Qur'an for a wealthy patron. In contrast, a Christian bishop named Eadfrith created the *Lindisfarne Gospels* for fellow monks living in a remote monastery located off the northeastern coast of England. Unrestricted by religious injunctions against representing human and animal forms, Eadfrith's complex interlace designs include birds, snake-like creatures, a cat that has just devoured eight birds, and portraits of all four Gospel writers.

Captainm

IMAGE 188

Basin (*Baptistère de St. Louis*)

Muhammad ibn al-Zain

c. 1320–1340 C.E.

Brass inlaid with gold and silver

Mamluk sultans ruled Egypt and Syria from 1250 until the Ottoman conquest in 1517. Mamluk patrons sponsored a flourishing artistic culture, renowned across the medieval world for master craftsmen who created exquisite works in glass, textile, and metal. Art historians recognize the brass basin depicted in Image 188 as a masterpiece of Islamic metalwork. One of the world's most famous Islamic works, its surprising history raises a number of puzzling questions.

ORIGINAL FUNCTION

The brass basin contains a number of clues offering tantalizing hints about its possible function. The work is inlaid with gold and silver and stands nine inches high with a diameter of twenty inches. A master metal craftsman named Muhammad ibn al-Zain proudly signed the work six times! This combination of expensive materials, size, and a highly skilled craftsman all suggest that a wealthy Mamluk patron commissioned the work.

Scholars have excluded possible sacred functions. Islamic sacred art is ANICONIC because it forbids the use of human and animal representations. Contrary to this injunction, the brass basin contains friezes depicting numerous human figures and animals. In addition, while al-Zain carefully included his own signature, he failed to add traditional Islamic inscriptions normally found on objects intended for spiritual functions. Given these considerations, art historians believe that a wealthy Mamluk patron may have used the basin as either a magnificent banqueting piece or as a vessel for ceremonial hand washing.

DECORATION

Muhammad ibn al-Zain covered the basin's exterior and interior surfaces with rich imagery. The vessel's wide central outside register depicts a finely crafted procession of 20 Mamluk officials. Each of these characters wears distinctive clothing and carries symbols that identify his rank. Four roundels with mounted horsemen interrupt the procession of dignitaries. Narrow registers above and below the central band display a lively series of unicorns, elephants, camels, antelopes, and leopards.

THE FRENCH CONNECTION

The basin provides an example of an object created for one ceremonial context that was later repurposed for a much different context. Records reveal that on September 14, 1606, the French royal family used the basin as a baptismal font for the future king Louis XIII. Scholars do not know how or why the basin reached France. They do know that despite its commonly used name *Baptistère de St. Louis*, the basin was created between 1320 and 1340 and thus did not exist during the reign of Saint Louis, a revered French king who died in 1270.

MAKING CONNECTIONS

THE *BAPTISTÈRE DE ST. LOUIS* AND THE PYXIS OF AL-MUGHIRA

Highly skilled Islamic craftsmen created the *Baptistère de St. Louis* and the Pyxis of al-Mughira (Image 57) as luxury objects for royal patrons. Images of humans and animals cover both of these secular works. Both of these world-famous works of art can be seen in the Louvre's new galleries of Islamic art.

Harvard Art Museums / Arthur M. Sackler Museum, Bequest of Abby Aldrich Rockefeller, 1960.190. Imaging Department © President and Fellows of Harvard College

IMAGE 189

Bahram Gur Fights the Karg

Folio from the Great Il-Khanid *Shahnama*

Islamic, Persian, Il-Khanid

c. 1330–1340 C.E.

Ink and opaque watercolor, gold, and silver on paper

The Persian poet Ferdowsi devoted just over 30 years to writing the *Shahnama* or "Book of Kings." Completed in 1010 C.E., the *Shahnama's* 50,000 couplets celebrate the exploits of ancient Persian heroes and kings. During the 1330s, a powerful Mongol vizier authorized a project to transform Ferdowsi's epic poem into a splendid illustrated manuscript now known as the Great Il-Khanid *Shahnama*. Image 189 features the Persian hero Bahram Gur as he performs the legendary feat of slaying a monstrous horned wolf known as a Karg.

"THIS CAN'T BE DONE"

According to the *Shahnama*, the great Persian warrior Bahram Gur visited India to learn more about its people and culture. An Indian ruler named Shangal immediately recognized Bahram Gur as a great warrior who could rid his land of a fearsome Karg. Fearing for their leader's life, Bahram Gur's attendants warned their impetuous prince, "Your majesty, this is beyond any man's courage...tell Shangal this can't be done." Undeterred by their plea, Bahram Gur singlehandedly attacked the Karg. His "brain full of fury," Bahram Gur first weakened the beast with a hail of arrows and then used his sword to sever the monster's head.

A STYLISIC BLEND

A team of skilled artists scribed, illustrated, and bound the pages of the Great Il-Khanid *Shahnama* at the royal workshop in Tabriz. Located along the Silk Road, Tabriz became a cosmopolitan hub where innovative artists learned about European and Chinese artistic traditions. Their finished pages were just over 16 inches long and about 12 inches wide. Art historians call these illuminated or decorated pages MINIATURES because of their small size compared with paintings on walls or wood panels.

Bahram Gur's commanding figure dominates the painting. The artists portray him as a rugged Central Asian warrior, sumptuously dressed in a European garment. However, he triumphs over the Karg in a landscape influenced by Chinese artistic conventions, including knarled trees twisted with age, rugged rocks, and overlapping forms that create spatial recession.

"MIRROR FOR PRINCES"

The Great Il-Khanid *Shahnama* served important political functions. As alien rulers, the Mongols felt a need to justify their political legitimacy. The illustrated *Shahnama* provided a link between the new Mongol dynasty and Persia's enduring culture. The Great Il-Khanid *Shahnama* also functioned as an important instructional tool by providing what contemporaries called a "mirror for princes." Bahram Gur's heroic deeds encouraged young nobles to emulate Bahram Gur's courageous behavior

MAKING CONNECTIONS

THE GREAT IL-KHANID *SHAHNAMA* AND THE *VIENNA GENESIS*

The Great Il-Khanid *Shahnama* and the *Vienna Genesis* (Image 50) both use illuminated miniature paintings to illustrate stories from revered ancient texts. In addition, both works combine stylistic elements from different artistic traditions. For example, the *Vienna Genesis* scene featured in Image 50 juxtaposes images of a classical nude figure and fully-clothed portraits of Rebecca, typical of Early Christian art.

Courtesy Wikimedia.

IMAGE 190

The Court of Gayumars

Folio from Shah Tahmasp's *Shahnama*

Sultan Muhammad

c. 1522-1525 C.E.

Ink, opaque watercolor, and gold on paper

The *Shahnama* is an epic poem celebrating the exploits of Persia's ancient heroes and kings. Beginning with the Great Il-Khanid *Shahnama* in the 1330s (see Image 189), Persian rulers commissioned many illustrated copies of the *Shahnama*. During the early 1500s the first Safavid ruler, Shah Ismail, authorized a luxurious manuscript with fine paper enriched by large gold-sprinkled borders and lavish illustrations. Scholars often describe Image 190 as the greatest masterpiece in this renowned literary work.

SULTAN MUHAMMAD

Shah Ismail's new *Shahnama* required the intensive labor of two generations of Persia's most talented artists. When Shah Ismail died, his son Shah Tahmasp I oversaw the monumental project. The new Safavid ruler turned to Sultan Muhammad, an acknowledged master, to paint the opening folio featured in Image 190.

Scholars praise Sultan Muhammad as the greatest artist of the Safavid period. He successfully blended the best elements of Persian painting by using vivid colors and densely packed details within a balanced and harmonious composition. Shah Muhammad's masterful ability to draw minute but realistic details suggests his use of a fine brush which at times utilized squirrel hairs!

GAYUMARS—THE FIRST KING

The *Shahnama* begins by describing Gayumars as "the first man to be king and to establish the ceremonies associated with the crown and throne." His prosperous people lived in the mountains and "dressed in leopard skins." Blessed with a divine radiance called *farr*, Gayumars commanded the respect of humans and all creatures. Indeed, "men and beasts from all parts of the earth came to do him homage and receive laws from his hands."

Sultan Muhammad illustrated this famous description by placing Gayumars at the apex of his composition. The legendary first king rules from a lush mountain paradise filled with colorful vegetation. Sultan Muhammad surrounded Gayumars with a great semicircle of figures that includes his son, grandson, and a host of courtiers. As referenced in the *Shahnama*, everyone wears leopard pelts.

Gayumars rules a peaceable kingdom where humans and animals all live in harmony. Even wild beasts and tame animals peacefully co-exist. Sultan Muhammad used this opening picture of utopia to convey a political message intended to inspire his royal patron: a wise and benevolent ruler will enjoy complete authority over human society and nature.

MAKING CONNECTIONS

THE COURT OF GAYUMARS AND BAHRAM GUR FIGHTS THE KARG

The Court of Gayumars and *Bahram Gur Fights the Karg* (Image 189) both illustrate famous scenes from the *Shahnama*. Working two centuries apart, teams of highly skilled artists created two very different portraits. *The Court of Gayumars* features an elegant and benevolent monarch who presides over a harmonious kingdom. In contrast, *Bahram Gur Fights the Karg* features a rugged warrior who combats and defeats a monstrous and destructive wild beast.

IMAGE 191

The Ardabil Carpet

Maqsud of Kashan

1539-1540 C.E.

Wool and silk

Muslims prize carpets for their role in helping worshippers fulfill their duty of performing five daily prayers. During the 1530s, Shah Tahmasp I commissioned a matching pair of carpets for the funerary shrine of Shayik Safi al-Din Ardabili, a revered 14th-century Sufi religious leader. Located in Ardabil, the shrine quickly became a major pilgrimage site. Image 191 highlights one of the original carpets. Now known as the Ardabil Carpet, this masterpiece is the world's oldest dated carpet.

AN INTEGRATED DESIGN

The Ardabil Carpet required a team of eight to ten highly skilled weavers about three years to complete. The final carpet covers a space approximately 35 feet long and 18 feet wide. The border contains an inscription naming Maqsud of Kashan as the official responsible for the overall project. The carpet's dense wool pile contains 25 million knots, or about 350 knots per square inch. This density enabled Kashani's team to implement an ambitious, integrated design using ten different colors and countless intricate artistic details.

A huge yellow sunburst medallion dominates the carpet's central space. The center of the medallion contains a roundel shaped like a geometric pool, similar to those found in the Alhambra (Image 65) in Spain. This image of a pool of water is a powerful symbol, evoking a sense of the abundance and pleasures awaiting Muslims in Paradise.

A ring of 16 pointed oval shapes surrounds the central medallion. Each of the carpet's four corners repeats a quarter-size composition similar to that of the central design. A fantastic array of swirling flowers, leaves, and vines fills the remaining space.

TWO LAMPS OF UNEQUAL SIZE

Lamps are an essential part of a mosque or Islamic shrine. In addition to providing a source of light, they remind worshippers of a Qur'anic verse proclaiming, "Allah is the Light of the heavens and all the earth." The Ardabil Carpet includes depictions of two different-sized lamps hanging in the vertical axis above and below the central medallion. Some scholars contend that the different sizes represent an optical illusion, intended to persuade worshippers sitting near the small lamp that it is the same size as the larger, distant lamp. However, other scholars contend that the difference in size is a deliberate flaw, intended to illustrate the belief that perfection is a quality reserved for Allah alone.

MAKING CONNECTIONS

THE ARDABIL CARPET AND *THE COURT OF GAYUMARS*

The Ardabil Carpet and the miniature painting *The Court of Gayumars* (Image 190) were both created in royal Safavid workshops in Tabriz. Although they are works of exceptional beauty and design, the Western tradition historically labeled textiles and illuminated manuscripts "decorative arts" and arbitrarily assigned them to an inferior status relative to "fine arts" such as painting and sculpture. However, the Ardabil Carpet and *The Court of Gayumars* are now recognized as extraordinary works of art created by teams of gifted artists.

Content Area 8

SOUTH, EAST, AND SOUTHEAST ASIA

SOUTH, EAST, AND SOUTHEAST ASIA

Content Area 8 includes 21 works created between 300 B.C.E. and 1969 C.E. The artists, architects, and sculptors in these regions produced a wide variety of exceptional works.

Our unit presents the 21 works in this content area in the chronological order provided in the College Board's AP Art History Framework. This organization will enable you to quickly find a specific work of art.

The College Board encourages teachers and students to arrange the works in a wide variety of meaningful topical categories. Here are several possible arrangements:

INDIAN ART

Image 192: Great Stupa at Sanchi
Image 200: Lakshmana Temple
Image 202: Shiva as the Lord of Dance
Image 208: *Jahangir Preferring a Sufi Shaikh to Kings*
Image 209: Taj Mahal

CHINESE ART

Image 193: Terra cotta warriors
Image 194: Funeral banner of Lady Dai
Image 195: Longmen caves
Image 201: *Travelers among Mountains and Streams*
Image 204: The David Vases
Image 206: Forbidden City
Image 212: *Chairman Mao en Route to Anyuan*

KOREAN ART

Image 196: Gold and jade Crown
Image 205: Portrait of Sin Sukju

JAPANESE ART

Image 197: Todai-ji
Image 203: *Night Attack on the Sanjô Palace*
Image 207: Ryoan-ji
Image 210: *White and Red Plum Blossoms*
Image 211: *Under the Wave off Kanagawa*

SOUTHEAST ASIAN ART

Image 198: Borobudur
Image 199: Angkor Wat and Angkor Thom

BUDDHIST MONUMENTS

Image 192: Great Stupa at Sanchi
Image 195: Longmen caves
Image 197: Todai-ji
Image 198: Borobudur
Image 207: Ryoan-ji

HINDU ART AND ARCHITECTURE

Image 199: Ankor Wat and Angkor Thom
Image 200: Lakshmana Temple
Image 202: Shiva as the Lord of Dance

CHINESE, JAPANESE, AND KOREAN PAINTING AND PRINTMAKING

Image 201: *Travelers among Mountains and Streams*
Image 203: *Night Attack on the Sanjô Palace*
Image 205: Portrait of Sin Sukju
Image 210: *White and Red Plum Blossoms*
Image 212: *Chairman Mao en Route to Anyuan*

ASIAN PORTRAITURE

Image 205: Portrait of Sin Sukju
Image 208: *Jahangir Preferring a Sufi Shaikh to Kings*
Image 212: *Chairman Mao en Route to Anyuan*

THE NATURAL WORLD

Image 196: Gold and jade Crown
Image 201: *Travelers among Mountains and Streams*
Image 204: David Vases
Image 207: Ryoan-ji
Image 210: *White and Red Plum Blossoms*
Image 211: *Under the Wave off Kanagawa*

POWER AND AUTHORITY

Image 193: Terra cotta warriors
Image 196: Gold and jade Crown
Image 203: *Night Attack on the Sanjô Palace*
Image 205: Portrait of Sin Sukju
Image 206: Forbidden City
Image 208: *Jahangir Preferring a Sufi Shaikh to Kings*
Image 209: Taj Mahal
Image 212: *Chairman Mao en Route to Anyuan*

DR Travel Photo and Video / Shutterstock.com

IMAGE 192

Great Stupa at Sanchi

Madhya Pradesh, India

Buddhist, Mauryan, late Sunga Dynasty

c. 300 B.C.E-100 C.E.

Stone masonry, sandstone on dome

STUPAS are large hemispherical domes that originally functioned as monuments containing the relics of kings or heroes. They later became associated with the sacred relics of the Buddha. Image 192 invites you to explore the Great Stupa at Sanchi. It is one of the oldest surviving stone structures in India and an architectural prototype for other Buddhist stupas that followed it.

A BRIEF HISTORY

The Mauryan emperor Ashoka the Great ruled almost the entire Indian subcontinent from about 272 to 231 B.C.E. Shortly after taking power, Ashoka conquered the once-prosperous kingdom of Kalinga in a bloody war claiming at least 100,000 lives. As the triumphant emperor toured the battlefield, the dying soldiers' anguished cries filled him with remorse. Shortly afterwards he renounced war and embraced Buddhism's peaceful philosophy.

Ashoka acted on his new faith by distributing Buddha's ashes to stupas he erected across India. The newly built stupa at Sanchi crowned a hilltop in northern India. Ashoka chose the location even though it had no connection to any known event in Buddha's life. However, Sanchi did offer a secluded site for meditation and proximity to a prosperous nearby town.

Ashoka's Great Stupa suffered some damage in the chaos following the breakup of the Mauryan Empire. However, a new wave of religious fervor supported a vigorous renewal project. Restorers doubled the Great Stupa's original size and encased the enlarged structure in stone. The Great Stupa achieved its present state sometime around 75-50 B.C.E. During the next centuries, it functioned as a major pilgrimage site and also served as an integral part of a thriving Buddhist community.

The Great Stupa's golden age did not endure. Buddhism slowly declined in India as a resurgent Hindu faith attracted more and more followers. As Buddhism disappeared, the monuments at Sanchi fell into a state of disrepair and were eventually completely forgotten. In 1818 a British officer discovered the neglected site. His find triggered a wave of treasure hunters who plundered the ancient monuments. During the early 20th century, a team of professional archaeologists and Buddhist scholars finally regained control over the Great Stupa and its surrounding structures. Today the Great Stupa at

Sanchi is the centerpiece of a restored complex containing priceless religious monuments.

THE *TORANAS*

Pilgrims approaching the Great Stupa first encounter an 11-foot-high circular railing. They then stand beneath one of four 35-foot-high *TORANAS*, or gateways, punctuating the railway at each of the four cardinal points. Each *torana* consists of two square pillars supporting three horizontal crossbars.

Deeply carved relief sculptures cover the entire surface of each *torana*. The carvings depict pivotal events from Buddha's life such as his birth, enlightenment, and famous First Sermon. However, the sculptors did not depict Buddha's actual image. Instead, they substituted symbols such as parasols, an empty throne, a pair of footsteps, or a riderless horse.

The sculptors adorned the East Gate with the figure of a sensuous female fertility figure called a *yakshi*. The *yakshi* demonstrates her power as a source of life by touching a nearby mango tree, thus causing it to burst into bloom.

The *yakshi* and other elaborate *torana* carvings are among the finest works of Buddhist art in India. Taken together, they help visiting pilgrims to understand Buddha's life and teachings. For example, the blooming tree reminds worshippers of the flowering lotus, an important symbol of enlightenment.

THE GREAT STUPA—FORM AND SYMBOLISM

As pilgrims pass under a *torana*, they leave the secular world and enter a sacred space protecting Buddha's relics. With a height of 54 feet and a diameter of 120 feet, the Great Stupa presents an imposing form. Its dome supports a square platform called a *harmika*. An axial pole known as a *yasti* occupies a sacred location at the center of the *harmika*. It represents the AXIS MUNDI, or pivot of the universe. The *yasti* bears three umbrella-shaped discs representing the Three Jewels of Buddhism: the Buddha, the Law, and the monastic gathering of monks.

Pilgrims cannot enter the Great Stupa since it is a solid structure. Instead, worshippers meditate and chant as they follow a path allowing them to CIRCUMAMBULATE, or walk around, the stupa. Their circular journey brings them into close proximity with the sacred relics buried inside. The ritual also brings the devout into harmony with the journey of the Earth as it rotates around the Sun.

Ashoka and his successors built the Great Stupa to support their faith and to obtain spiritual benefits or *karma*. Buddhists believe that making a contribution to a stupa will enable the devout to escape poverty in their next lives and also avoid being reborn in an undesirable location. The Great Stupa at Sanchi contains inscriptions by over 600 monks and laypersons who contributed to the monument in hope of receiving these rewards.

MAKING CONNECTIONS

THE GREAT STUPA AT SANCHI AND THE CHURCH OF SAINTE-FOY

The Great Stupa at Sanchi and the Church of Sainte-Foy (Image 58) are both important pilgrimage sites. The two sacred spaces use sculpture to provide religious instruction. For example, the tympanum at the Church of Sainte-Foy presents entering pilgrims with vivid depictions of the rewards of heaven and the torments of hell. Like the pilgrims at the Great Stupa, devout visitors follow a prescribed path, enabling them to view the jewel-encrusted reliquary holding Sainte Foy's relics. However, while the reliquary of Sainte Foy is on public display, the Buddha's ashes are buried in the core of the Great Stupa where they cannot be seen.

Jmhullot

Sirirat / Shutterstock.com

IMAGE 193

Terra cotta Warriors

Mausoleum of the first Qin emperor of China

Qin Dynasty

c. 221–210 B.C.E.

Painted terracotta

On March 29, 1974, a small group of farmers digging a well in a drought-parched field near the city of Xi'an discovered fragments of a clay figure. Subsequent archaeological excavations revealed that the pottery fragments were actually part of an extraordinary army of 8,000 life-sized terracotta warriors. Each year over 1.5 million tourists visit China's Museum of the Terracotta Warriors where they view the world famous scene in Image 193. Amazingly, the museum covers a four-acre site that is a tiny part of a 22-square-mile underground burial complex built by China's First Emperor, Qin Shi Huangdi.

THE FIRST EMPEROR

The ruler who would become China's First Emperor began his royal career as King Zheng, a 13-year-old ruler of Qin, a state on the northwestern fringe of the Chinese world. The young monarch lived in a chaotic political environment where seven states waged perpetual war against one another. The young but ruthless ruler forged an invincible army that attacked its foes "like a stone smashing eggs." By 221 B.C.E., the now 35-year-old conqueror unified the warring kingdoms into a single empire. King Zheng triumphantly took a new name that better reflected his power and majesty–Qin Shi Huangdi, the First Emperor of China.

The First Emperor conquered China with a ferocious army and held it together with a centralized system of government. Qin Shi Huangdi first implemented a uniform system of weights, coins, and measurements. He then built a network of roads to unify the formerly independent parts of his new empire. And finally, he ordered the construction of a Great Wall to protect the empire's northern border from marauding nomads.

Qin Shi Huangdi did more than defeat rival states and build a unified empire; he also attempted to conquer death. The First Emperor believed in an afterlife where people could continue their lives. He viewed death as another form of life. Obsessed with his quest for immortality, Qin Shi Huangdi ordered over 700,000 workers to construct a subterranean domain that would parallel his worldly existence. This mortuary complex survived his death in 210 B.C.E. Over 2,000 years later, a group of Chinese farmers accidentally discovered the first fragments of the First Emperor's previously hidden underground world.

AN UNPARALLELED PROJECT

Archaeologists have thus far uncovered an army of 8,000 life-sized terracotta warriors. Stationed in three underground vaults, this vigilant force stands in a precise formation ready to protect the First Emperor. Astonishingly, no two warriors are identical! Their shoes, hairstyles, facial features and uniform colors all vary.

The ancient craftsmen created more than an army of terracotta warriors. Archaeologists have also unearthed ten-foot-long bronze chariots drawn by teams of four bronze horses. The First Emperor equipped his soldiers with thousands of bronze weapons including spears, crossbows, and swords. Recent finds also include recreational items such as lifelike bronze waterfowl and agile acrobats ready to entertain the First Emperor and his court.

The production of this unprecedented number of figures demanded massive manpower and a complex organization. Workers had to be fed, clothed, and housed. Kilns required a steady supply of firewood and a sticky red clay strong enough to support large figures. Archaeologists have discovered 87 different names stamped on the terracotta warriors. They believe that a team comprised of one master craftsman and ten apprentices could produce about a dozen individualized warriors a year. When multiplied by 87 teams, this process could fabricate about 1,000 warriors a year.

AN UNOPENED TOMB

The First Emperor transcended all the political boundaries of his age. But he could not prevent death. Qin Shi Huangdi died in 210 B.C.E. and was buried in a sealed tomb covered by a huge earthen mound 140 feet high.

Although Chinese archaeologists have yet to excavate the burial mound, ancient records provide tantalizing clues about what may lay inside. According to Sima Qian, a reliable Han dynasty historian, the tomb is "filled with models of palaces, pavilions, and offices as well as fine vessels, precious stones, and rarities." His account indicates that the tomb contains replicas of rivers made with mercury flowing through hills and mountains made of bronze. Wonders also included a ceiling decorated with precious stones representing the sun, moon, and stars.

Modern scientific investigations seem to corroborate Sima Qian's description. Thousands of soil tests have revealed high concentrations of mercury. In addition, remote-sensing technology has confirmed the existence of underground chambers.

The contents of Qin Shi Huangdi's unopened tomb remain a mystery. When it is finally opened, the tomb may reveal the unbelievable treasures described by Sima Qian. But it is also possible that the terracotta warriors may not have protected the First Emperor's treasures from tomb robbers who left behind a looted ruin.

MAKING CONNECTIONS

QIN SHI HUANGDI AND PHAROAH KHUFU

Qin Shi Huangdi and Pharaoh Khufu of Egypt both believed in an afterlife where they would continue to rule. Determined to continue living in royal splendor, these two omnipotent rulers devoted enormous resources to constructing vast burial complexes. Like Qin Shi Huangdi, Khufu did not intend to rule alone in his afterlife. His Great Pyramid (Image 17) was part of a complex that included a temple for personal worship, smaller pyramids for his queens, and tombs for prominent members of his court. However, unlike the First Emperor, Khufu felt secure and did not construct an army to protect him in the afterlife.

Changsha: Hunan Provincial Museum

IMAGE 194

Funeral banner of Lady Dai

Han Dynasty, China

c. 180 B.C.E.

Painted silk

In 1972, Chinese archaeologists excavated three tombs buried beneath a small hill on the outskirts of present-day Changsha. The tomb contained the remains and treasured possessions of Li Cang, a high-ranking Han Dynasty official, his wife Lady Dai, and their son. Lady Dai's perfectly preserved corpse lay within the innermost of four nested coffins. The T-shaped silk banner depicted in Image 194 covered her innermost coffin. This elaborate banner is an early masterpiece of Chinese pictorial art offering important insights into Han Dynasty ideas about the afterlife.

THE BANNER'S OVERALL DESIGN

Lady Dai's contemporaries believed in a close relationship between the human and the supernatural worlds. The over six-foot-long and three-foot-wide T-shaped banner uses three horizontal registers, or panels, to illustrate Lady Dai's ascent to the heavenly realm as a sequential journey. Her path to immortality begins with an underworld portrayed in the lowest register. Her soul then rises to an earthly realm where it becomes the centerpiece of mourning and departure rituals. The top register depicts the heavenly Land of the Immortals, where Lady Dai will reside for eternity.

THE UNDERWORLD

The Han artist uses the bottom panel to provide a glimpse of the underworld. It is a place where souls undergo their first metamorphosis. The subterranean world is a watery realm inhabited by serpents and turtles. A muscular central figure stands on the backs of fish and serpents as he supports a white rectangle thought to represent the Earth.

THE MOURNING HALL SCENE

Two rituals take place in an earthly realm above the underworld. The first occurs in a mourning hall where five men in two opposing rows face an object placed on a low stand. Many scholars believe that the soft, round object represents Lady Dai's body wrapped in the layers of silk cloth that covered her corpse. The mourners fulfill their ritual duty by offering Lady Dai's spirit food and wine.

The mourning hall scene does not take place in a flat space. The Han artist uses the mourner's overlapping bodies to convey a sense of depth. In addition, the artist creates an illusion of space by drawing the ritual vessels in the foreground larger than those in the background.

THE DEPARTURE SCENE

The next earthly scene features a recognizable portrait of Lady Dai leaning on a cane found inside her tomb. The artist positions her as the central figure in a departure scene located near the center of the banner. Three maids attend Lady Dai as she bids farewell to two kneeling figures.

Some scholars believe that the two kneeling figures may be emissaries from the heavenly realm.

The 10-inch-tall image of Lady Dai is the earliest known painted portrait of a specific person in Chinese art. It bears a very close correspondence to Lady Dai's actual corpse. Thick layers of charcoal and clay insulated Lady Dai's body from the decaying effects of oxygen and bacteria. As a result, her remarkably well-preserved facial features are easily identifiable.

TWO INTERTWINED DRAGONS

Dragons are mythical creatures that play an important role in Chinese art. According to Chinese legends, dragons can freely move between heaven and earth. The two intertwined dragons help unify the central register. Their long tails pass through a round bi disk, a traditional symbol representing the heavens. This visual motif links the mourning and departure scenes while reinforcing the idea that the dragons will help Lady Dai ascend to the heavenly realm.

THE REPRESENTATION OF HEAVEN

Lady Dai's quest for immortality ends in a heavenly realm shown in a wide register across the T's horizontal crossbar. Two deities known as the Greater and Lesser Lords of Fate guard the entrance to the heavenly realm. The gods hold records detailing Lady Dai's life. Fortunately, she passes this test and becomes an immortal celestial riding on the wings of a dragon.

The Han depiction of heaven differs greatly from the images of paradise in Islamic art. While Muslim artists include visual references to water and lush gardens, the Han artist decorates the heavenly realm in Lady Dai's banner with references to famous legends. For example, a large red sun containing a black raven occupies the top right corner. A mulberry tree just beneath the sun holds multiple smaller red suns. This image alludes to a legendary story describing how ten rising suns threatened to scorch fields and ruin crops. The archer Yi saves the day by shooting all the suns but one. He then receives the elixir of immortality as a reward. In the left corner a mythical White Hare can be seen sitting near a silvery crescent moon where he grinds the elixir of immortality.

MAKING CONNECTIONS

THE FUNERAL BANNER OF LADY DAI AND THE LAST JUDGMENT OF HU-NEFER

The quest for eternal life preoccupied both the ancient Chinese and the ancient Egyptians. The painted silk Funeral Banner of Lady Dai and the painted parchment scroll of the Last Judgment of Hu-Nefer (Image 24) both use continuous narration to depict aspects of how their cultures view the spiritual journeys of high-ranking individuals. While Lady Dai seems to easily pass into the heavenly realm, Hu-Nefer faces a stern test to determine if he will be rewarded with eternal life or be punished by having a ferocious beast devour his heart.

Charlie

Meiqianbao / Shutterstock.com

IMAGE 195

Longmen caves

Luoyang, China

Tang Dynasty

493-1127 C.E.

Limestone

The Longmen Caves are carved into limestone mountains on both sides of the Yi River, about ten miles south of the ancient Chinese capital of Luoyang. The complex includes more than 2,300 caves, shrines, and niches. These contain almost 110,000 stone statues depicting the Buddha, in sizes ranging from a few inches to larger than a five-story building. The Fengxian Temple complex depicted in Image 195 is Longmen's largest and most important sculptural group.

THE FENGXIAN TEMPLE

The Tang Empress Wu Zetian commissioned the Fengxian Temple in 672 C.E. Completed just three years later, the semicircular complex contains eight sculptural figures grouped around a central 56-foot-high statue of a seated Buddha. A symmetrical arrangement includes a pair of disciples, bodhisattvas, heavenly kings, and guardian figures. The saintly disciples and bodhisattvas encourage worshippers to seek enlightenment, while the fierce heavenly kings and guardian figures stand ready to protect the Buddha and his attendants.

THE VAIROCANA BUDDHA

As Buddhism spread across the Silk Road from India to China, its followers developed new ways of representing Buddha. The early Shakyamuni Buddha stressed how the historical Buddha's life and teachings helped individuals achieve enlightenment. In contrast, the Vairocana Buddha is not a man who actually lived. He is instead a merciful, godlike figure who could help the entire human race achieve salvation.

The size and iconography of the Fengxian Temple's statue of the Vairocana Buddha reflect Buddha's status as a celestial being. The statue's colossal size is designed to impress upon visitors that they are in the presence of a divine being. Buddha's lotus pose and calm demeanor encourage meditation. His topknot, or *ushnisha*, symbolizes the spiritual power of the Buddha's enlightenment. Buddha's elongated earlobes signal his ability to hear and compassionately respond to human suffering.

A POLITICAL STATEMENT

The Fengxian Temple is more than an artistic achievement; it is also a sophisticated example of how art can be used as political propaganda. The sculptors may have deliberately based their portrait of the Vairocana Buddha upon the Empress Wu Zeitan. The wily empress became China's preeminent ruler after her husband suffered a debilitating stroke. Wu's generous financial support for the Fengxian Temple may have had a political motive: the image of Buddha as a supreme deity surrounded by a loyal court provided a model that legitimized her own position in the Tang government.

MAKING CONNECTIONS

THE LONGMEN CAVES AND THE BAMIYAN COMPLEX

The Longmen Caves and the Bamiyan complex (Image 182) both provided secluded sites, inspiring meditation and the renunciation of worldly desires. In addition, the two sites promoted a Buddhist practice of carving monumental statues into the face of mountain cliffs.

IMAGE 196

Gold and jade Crown

Silla Kingdom

Korea

5th to 6th century C.E.

Metalwork

The Silla Kingdom ruled southeastern Korea during the Three Kingdom period from 57 B.C.E. to 688 C.E. The kingdom's kings and queens ruled from their capital city at Gyeongju. The royal court's glittering wealth awed visiting Chinese emissaries, who described Gyeonju as "the city of gold." Modern archaeological excavations have uncovered treasures that more than justify this description. Image 196 features a gold and jade crown that offers insights into the complex roles of Silla's ruling monarchs.

A SURPRISING DISCOVERY

Silla's ruling elite believed that death marked the beginning of a new afterlife. They therefore buried their kings and queens in royal tombs covered by an impenetrable layer of heavy river boulders and massive mounds of dirt. These mounds protected their golden treasures from grave robbers.

Archaeologists uncovered the crown displayed in Image 196 buried inside a massive double tomb containing the remains of a Silla king and queen. The king's tomb contained weapons and a silver and gilded crown. Contrary to expectations, the queen's tomb contained a richly decorated gold and jade crown.

The 11-inch-high crown contains a number of distinctive features. A group of three tree-like vertical projections dominates its center. Two antler-shaped projections extend on either side of the central group. Silla's legendary craftsmen further embellished the crown by adding comma-shaped jade ornaments.

MULTIPLE FUNCTIONS

The royal crown's thin gold bands are very fragile. At first, scholars concluded that the crown functioned as a burial ornament because it could not withstand repeated use. However, ancient records indicate that the Silla kings and queens played the role of a shaman or spiritual leader. When worn on ceremonial occasions, the golden crown symbolized the ruler's responsibility to ensure a favorable relationship with the spiritual world.

THE IMPACT OF BUDDHISM

Chinese Buddhist monks brought Buddhist religious ideas to Silla. In 527 C.E., Silla adopted Buddhism as its state religion. This decision had a significant impact upon burial practices and art. Cremation replaced burial tombs, while Buddhist temples sprang up across the kingdom. As a result, the era of golden burials ended as craftsmen turned their attention to meeting the growing demand for images of the Buddha and his bodhisattvas.

MAKING CONNECTIONS

THE *AXIS MUNDI*

The *AXIS MUNDI* is a point of connection between heaven and earth. Many cultures have sacred objects to express this concept. The branch-like projects on the Silla crown represent the idea of a world tree connecting the celestial and terrestrial worlds. The Lanzon at Chavin de Huantar (Image 153) and the *yasti* atop the Great Stupa at Sanchi (Image 192) provide additional examples of sacred objects designed to provide a link between heaven and earth.

© Vanni Archive / Art Resource, NY

© Vanni Archive / Art Resource, NY

Keith Levit / Alamy Stock Photo

IMAGE 197

Todai-ji

Nara, Japan

743 C.E; rebuilt c. 1700 C.E.
Sculpture–bronze and wood
Architecture–wood with ceramic-tile roofing

Todai-ji is a Buddhist temple complex located in the city of Nara, Japan. The complex includes one of the world's largest wooden buildings, a monumental bronze statue of Buddha weighing more than one million pounds, and two fierce guardian figures carved by acclaimed Japanese sculptors.

SHINTOISM AND BUDDHISM

The early Japanese honored thousands of local gods and spirits. Their varied customs and beliefs combined to form a belief system called Shinto, meaning "the way of the gods."

During the sixth century C.E., Buddhism gradually spread from China and Korea to Japan. However, the Japanese did not give up their Shinto customs. Instead, Shintoism and Buddhism comfortably coexisted. As a result Buddhist temples honored Shinto traditions.

EMPEROR SHOMU AND THE CONSTRUCTION OF TODAI-JI

Shomu became the 45th emperor of Japan in 724 C.E. He embraced Buddhism as a spiritual force that could unify the Japanese people and help consolidate his power. Almost twenty years later, Shomu launched an unprecedented project to construct a Buddhist temple complex in his newly established capital in Nara. The emperor's plan called for a vast Great Buddha Hall, or Daibutsuden, that would house a colossal bronze statue of the Vairocana or cosmic Buddha.

The size of the project posed formidable challenges. Carpenters required over 80 massive cypress pillars to support a building measuring 288 feet long, 169 feet wide, and 156 feet high. The need for bronze posed an even greater challenge. In 743 C.E., Shomu issued a decree exhorting his subjects to "melt any and all bronze available in the country." His appeal worked. During the next nine years, skilled craftsmen cast a 53-foot-high bronze statue of the Vairocana Buddha.

Emperor Shomu recognized that the Great Buddha Hall and its monumental statue formed the spiritual heart of the Todai-ji complex. On April 9, 752, he led a solemn procession of Buddhist monks and foreign dignitaries in a lavish "eye-opening" ceremony. Crimson fabrics covered the Great Buddha Hall's floor as candlelight illuminated clouds of incense rising above the statue of Buddha. An honored monk from India then carefully painted Buddha's eyes, thus bringing the statue to life.

THE INFLUENCE OF SHINTOISM

Despite Emperor Shomu's devotion to Buddhism, Todai-ji illustrates the continuing influence of Shinto traditions. In Shintoism, spirits known as *kami* are thought to dwell in trees and other natural forms. In order to avoid offending these spirits, Japanese carpenters did not pound nails into the wood. Instead they relied upon a system of complex wooden joints. The surrounding gardens at Todai-ji also reflect the complementary interplay of Shintoism and Buddhism. Shintoism views deer as messengers of the gods. As a result, spotted Sika deer are allowed to freely roam the Todai-ji grounds.

THE NIO GUARDIAN FIGURES

The Todai-ji complex built by Emperor Shomu suffered periodic damage from earthquakes, fires, and typhoons. Even worse, a destructive civil war swept across Japan, leaving Nara and Todai-ji in ruins. In 1185 a military leader known as a shogun seized power and restored order.

Shoguns and their fierce samurai warriors disdained refined elegance and instead prized bravery, honor, and strength. Japan's new leaders turned to a group of master sculptors known as the Kei school to help restore Todai-ji. Led by Unkei and Keikei, the Kei sculptors carved a pair of Nio guardian figures to occupy large niches in the Todai-ji's rebuilt Great Southern Gate. Standing almost 28 feet tall, the guardians feature bulging muscles, swirling drapery, and scowling faces. The fearsome warriors appear ready to spring into action to repel evil spirits and other unwanted intruders.

AN ENDURING MONUMENT

Unkei and Keikei installed the pair of Nio guardian statues in 1203. Although their work remains intact, the Great Buddha Hall suffered extensive damage in 1567. The Daibutsuden that stands today dates primarily from 1709 and is two-thirds the size of the original building. The bronze statue of Vairocana Buddha also suffered damage and required recasting. The 500-ton statue continues to welcome devout pilgrims. Buddha's raised right hand displays the famous abhaya mudra, a gesture meant to dispel fear and promise divine protection to worshippers who follow the path of righteousness.

MAKING CONNECTIONS

NIO GUARDIAN FIGURES AND ASSYRIAN LAMASSU

Objects with the same function can differ greatly in appearance. The Nio guardian figures are towering wooden warriors guarding the entrance to the Todai-ji temple complex. In contrast, the Assyrian lamassu (Image 25) are three-ton alabaster statues of winged bulls guarding the entrance to Sargon II's palace in Khorsabad. Although they differ in appearance, both works are intended to project project fearsome power as they perform their common function as guardians.

R.M. Nunes / Shutterstock.com

Isvara Pranidhana / Shutterstock.com

IMAGE 198

Borobudur

Central Java, Indonesia

Sailendra Dynasty

c. 750-842 C.E.

Volcanic stone masonry

Borobudur is located on the island of Java in modern Indonesia. Its long and surprising history begins with a brief period of intense activity followed by centuries of neglect and then a recent era of rediscovery and restoration. Over one million visitors tour Borobudur each year, making it Indonesia's most popular historical monument. Despite its popularity and years of intense scholarly study, Borobudur retains many baffling mysteries.

A MONUMENT LIKE NO OTHER

Historians now recognize that Java contributed rice and hardwood to an extensive trading network connecting ports in Malaysia, China, and India.

This exchange brought Java both wealth and Buddhist ideas. The influx of Buddhist scholars and pilgrims contributed to a period of intellectual activity. A family known as the Sailendras, or "Lords of the Mountains," embraced Buddhism and sponsored the construction of Borobudur.

Scholars do not know why the Sailendras chose to build Borobudur. But they do know that the architects designed the largest and most unique Buddhist monument in the world. Borobudur measures about 400 feet on each side of its base and rises about 98 feet to the sky. It begins with a series of six concentric terraces that rise like steps to a giant central STUPA. Built without mortar, the monument does not include a roof, vault, or central sanctuary. Nonetheless, Borobudur does contain 1,460 relief panels and 504 life-size statues of the Buddha.

LOST AND FOUND

Java's brief era of monumental construction began in 750 C.E. and abruptly ended by 930 C.E. Scholars do not know why the Sailendras' support came to a sudden and complete end. Over time, Borobudur's original meaning ceased to be relevant, and the monument slipped into obscurity.

In 1814, Sir Thomas Stamford Raffles, the British lieutenant-governor of Java, dispatched an expedition to search the tropical plains of Java for a legendary "hill of statues." After hacking through the jungle, the astonished expedition found the fabled ruins of a forgotten lost world.

Discovering Borobudur did not guarantee the monument's survival. Souvenir hunters and looters pillaged the site, and colonial authorities allowed the construction of a bamboo teahouse atop the central stupa. Restoration efforts finally began in the 20th century. Between 1974 and 1983, a major project financed by the Indonesian government with the assistance of international experts successfully saved Borobudur. The reopened monument now stands as one of the world's supreme architectural and cultural achievements.

THE GALLERIES: BUDDHA'S JOURNEY

Pilgrims begin their spiritual journey at Borobudur by viewing a series of 720 panels illustrating *Jataka* or "Birth Stories" that recount acts of self-sacrifice by Buddha in his earlier incarnations. For example, in one well-known story the Buddha was reborn as a woodpecker. One day he chanced upon a lion who suffered excruciating pain from a bone caught in his throat. The woodpecker opened the lion's mouth with a bit of wood and then walked in to remove the bone. Although the woodpecker was very hungry, the lion refused to share his meal. This taught the woodpecker an important lesson: the reward for a good deed is the pleasure of helping someone who may not reciprocate.

The 500 *Jataka* stories helped Buddha accumulate the wisdom he would need for his final earthly existence as Prince Siddhartha Gautama. The panels then recount the familiar story of how the historical Buddha travels beyond his palace walls and encounters the harsh reality that life is suffering. Siddhartha comes to understand that suffering is caused by unfulfilled desire. By extinguishing desire he achieves enlightenment and becomes the Buddha.

THE GALLERIES: SUDHANA'S JOURNEY

The gallery panels next depict the story of Sudhana, a merchant's son who begins a search for enlightenment. During his spiritual quest, Sudhana encounters 52 teachers from all walks of life. For example, he learns about compassion for the ill from a doctor and about simple happiness from children at play. Sudhana ultimately learns that life is a journey with many paths leading to small but important truths.

THE ROUND TERRACES AND AN EMPTY STUPA

Pilgrims must walk about three miles to view all the relief panels. They then emerge from the confines of narrow corridors to enter three open circular terraces. Each terrace offers a view of the surrounding countryside. These panoramic vistas offer a liberating feeling of spaciousness. The circular terraces contain 72 bell-shaped stone stupas. Each 12-foot-tall stupa holds a sculpted figure of a Buddha. These statues promote a sense of spiritual calmness that encourages meditation.

The celestial Buddha prepares pilgrims for the climax of their spiritual journey—a single, empty stupa. The stupa's emptiness represents perfection. This absence of form requires no further explanation. Having climbed the holy man-made mountain, pilgrims have attained enlightenment and can return to their homes to help others acquire the insights and wisdom they learned from Borobudur.

MAKING CONNECTIONS

BOROBUDUR AND CHARTRES

Borobudur and Chartres cathedral (Image 60) are both monumental expressions of the vision and daring engineering of their patrons and architects. Borobudur's relief panels and Chartres' glowing stained glass windows provide spiritual instruction for devout worshippers. Pilgrims thus emerge from these great symbols of Buddhism and Christianity with a renewed sense of spiritual enlightenment.

Bjørn Christian Tørrissen

Ham Phitchaya / Shutterstock.com

IMAGE 199

Angkor, the temple of Angkor Wat and the city of Angkor Thom

Cambodia

Khmer Dynasty

c. 800-1400 C.E.

Stone masonry, sandstone

Between 802 and 1431 C.E., a dynasty of Khmer kings ruled a vast empire from Angkor, a large metropolitan area now located within Cambodia. This region contained Angkor Wat, the largest religious monument ever built. Located nearby, the city of Angkor Thom features the Bayon temple with its memorable faces of the Buddha. These two temples reflect the power of the god-kings who commissioned them, the brilliance of the architects who designed them, and the faith of the people who built them.

THE GOD-KINGS OF THE KHMER EMPIRE

Jayavarman II founded the Khmer Empire in 802 C.E. He promptly proclaimed himself a *devaraja* or "god-king." Jayavarman II and his successors concentrated their building activity at Angkor. Each ruler constructed a temple designed to exhibit his political power and religious authority. In 1113 C.E., a ruthless young prince named Suryavarman II shattered the empire's peaceful succession of rulers when he ambushed and killed the reigning king.

After taking power, Suryavarman II turned to architecture and art to demonstrate his legitimacy as a ruler who enjoyed divine approval. Previous Khmer kings dedicated their temples to the Hindu god Shiva. In contrast, Suryavarman II deliberately selected Vishnu as his divine protector. A new temple dedicated to Vishnu would function as a sacred place where the god and Suryavarman II would exercise undisputed power.

VAST SCALE AND A SYMBOLIC DESIGN

Suryavarman's bold decision launched an ambitious building project, dwarfing all previous Angkor temples. Now known as Angkor Wat, the massive monument required five to ten million sandstone blocks, cut from a quarry about 20 miles from the building site. An extensive system of canals enabled elephants and water buffaloes to tow about 300 to 400 stone blocks a day. Workers used these stones to build a series of towers and rectangular galleries. In addition, they surrounded the temple's three-mile perimeter with a deep moat.

From a distance, the completed temple looked like a colossal mass of stones. On closer inspection, Angkor Wat's priest-architects designed a MANDALA or earthly model of the cosmic world. The five soaring towers represent the peaks of Mount Meru, the mythical home of Vishnu and the other Hindu gods. The temple's outer walls correspond to the mountains at the edge of the world, while the surrounding moat symbolizes the great oceans beyond.

Unlike previous Khmer temples, Angkor Wat faces west, the traditional direction of death. Many scholars believe that Suryavarman II may have built Angkor Wat as a mausoleum. Like Shih Huangdi's burial city (Image 193) and Hatshepsut's mortuary temple (Image 21), Angkor Wat may have served as a gateway to the afterlife.

EPIC STORIES IN BAS-RELIEF

Teams of highly skilled Khmer sculptors decorated the temple walls with an extensive collection of bas-relief friezes. The 220-foot-long friezes illustrate legendary Hindu epics and battles featuring Suryavarman II's victorious armies. Like the Palette of King Narmer (Image 13) and the Benin wall plaque (Image 169), Khmer bas-reliefs use HIERARCHICAL SCALE to indicate a figure's importance.

Angkor Wat's most renowned frieze illustrates a great Hindu epic story known as the *Churning of the Ocean of Milk*. In this story, gods and demons vie for immortality. Vishnu saves the universe from catastrophe by cleverly encouraging the rivals to work together. A spectacular bas-relief depicts 92 demons and 88 gods pulling on a serpent wrapped around Mount Mandara. Their back-and-forth action rotates the mountain, thus churning the surrounding ocean. After furiously pulling for 1,000 years, their churning action finally produces the elixir of immortality. Aided by Vishnu, the gods defeat the demons and restore the balance of good and evil.

JAYAVARMAN VII AND ANGKOR THOM

Suryavarman II died in 1150 C.E. During the century following his death, Angkor rapidly developed into a sprawling metropolitan area, connected by an intricate network of roads and canals. Jayavarman VII ascended to the Khmer throne in 1181. During the next four decades, he converted to Buddhism and sponsored a number of massive building projects.

Jayavarman VII designed Angkor Thom as his political and religious capital. A new state temple, called the Bayon, dominated the city. The complex included towers displaying gigantic stone faces, benignly gazing toward each cardinal point. The faces may represent all-seeing and all-knowing images of Buddha or perhaps Jayavarman VII himself!

COLLAPSE AND REBIRTH

A long line of Khmer god-kings transformed Angkor into one of the world's greatest cities. However, their success may have contained the seeds of the city's sudden collapse. Angkor's steadily rising population placed increasing pressure on the land's ability to supply food. At that same time, the city's complex but fragile canal system required constant repair. And finally, the combination of Angkor's growing weakness and great wealth proved an irresistible target for its hostile neighbors.

In 1431, Thai armies attacked and conquered Angkor. For reasons that remain unexplained, the Khmers abandoned their city. During the next 400 years, the relentlessly encroaching jungle covered Angkor's crumbling monuments. A new era of rediscovery began in 1860, when a French naturalist accidently discovered the ruins of Angkor Wat. The process of restoring and understanding Angkor has continued to the present day.

MAKING CONNECTIONS

ANGKOR WAT AND THE LAKSHMANA TEMPLE

Angkor Wat and the Lakshmana Temple (Image 200) share a common symbolic form. Both temples are MANDALAS, or architectural representations of the Hindu cosmos. Five towers representing the peaks of Mount Meru crown each temple. The main tower in both temples is an AXIS MUNDI, symbolically connecting the earth with the heavens.

Vera Tropynina / Shutterstock.com

IMAGE 200

Lakshmana Temple
Khajuraho, India

Hindu, Chandella Dynasty

c. 930-950 C.E.
Sandstone

The Chandella kings ruled northern and Central India from the 9th to the 12th centuries. During this time they commissioned over 80 structures for their capital city at Khajuraho. The Lakshmana Temple is one of 24 surviving structures. Begun by King Yashovarma and consecrated by his son in 954 C.E., the Lakshmana Temple embodies the central characteristics of Hindu temple architecture.

FUNCTION AND FORM

The Lakshmana Temple is a home for Vishnu, a central Hindu deity who is revered as the preserver of the universe and the restorer of moral order. The temple is thus a sacred space where devotees can approach the divine. Its design encourages reflection and the attainment of the essential spiritual knowledge that all life is connected.

The Lakshmana Temple is constructed out of sandstone blocks. It sits on a raised platform accessed by stairs, separating the outside secular world from the spiritual world inside. The shrine measures 85 feet in both height and length. Located at the corner of the temple platform, four freestanding subsidiary shrines flank the main shrine.

A tower known as a *shikhara*, or "mountain peak," forms the Lakshmana Temple's most prominent visible feature. The main *shikhara* and the four subsidiary shrines evoke images of Mount Meru, the five-peaked mythical mountain home of the Hindu gods.

EXTERNAL SCULPTURE

Worshippers approach the Lakshmana Temple from the east. They begin their visit by CIRCUMABULATING, or walking around, the entire structure. This practice represents a demonstration of piety that prepares pilgrims for entering the sacred spaces inside the temple.

As they begin their clockwise circumambulation, worshippers first encounter a statue of the elephant-headed Ganesha. The beloved son of Shiva and Parvanti, Ganesha is the Lord of Beginnings who removes obstacles to success and prosperity. Paying respect to Ganesha prepares worshippers for their spiritual journey ahead.

The temple's exterior walls contain three horizontal registers displaying over 600 carved figures. These elaborate decorations begin with a row of majestic elephants, symbolizing the mighty Chandella kings. They are followed by seemingly endless processions of marching soldiers, mounted hunters, and lively musicians. There are no freestanding sculptures. Architecture and sculpture are integrated, thus demonstrating the essential Hindu truth that many become one.

EROTIC SCULPTURE

As devotees circumambulate the temple, they encounter exquisite portraits of graceful nymphs. These sensuous figures dance, play musical instruments, and engage in sexual acts. Scholars have proposed different theories to explain the erotic images. One argument holds that sensuality is a fundamental human experience that brings joy and creates life. Other arguments contend that the erotic images are best understood as visual reminders of the Hindu belief that the universe is driven by the union of male and female forces.

THE *GARBHAGRIHA*

After circumambulating the Lakshmana Temple, worshippers continue their search for spiritual knowledge by entering the temple. They walk through a series of richly decorated halls before approaching the *garbhagriha*. This inner sanctum, or "womb-chamber," is the temple's symbolic and physical core. Unlike the large congregational spaces in Christian cathedrals and Islamic mosques, the square, windowless *garbhagriha* is designed for the intimate worship of a divine icon.

MAKING CONNECTIONS

THE LAKSHMANA TEMPLE AND THE PARTHENON

The Lakshmana Temple and the Parthenon (Image 35) share a number of characteristics. Ancient Greek and Hindu temples were not places where a congregation regularly met to worship and listen to a sermon. Instead, both the Lakshmana Temple and the Parthenon are relatively small structures that contain an interior room housing a revered icon. Exquisitely carved sculptural friezes adorn both temples. And finally, each structure reflects the glory and growing power of its builders.

National Palace Museum

IMAGE 201

Travelers among Mountains and Streams

Fan Kuan

c. 1000 C.E.

Ink and colors on silk

Monumental landscape painting emerged as China's premier art form during the early Song Dynasty (960–1279 C.E.). *Travelers among Mountains and Streams* is an iconic work by Fan Kuan, a recognized master of the genre known as *shan shui hua*, or "mountain-water painting." The work utilizes a monochromatic palette and SHIFTING PERSPECTIVE to create a harmonious composition, filled with intricate and meaningful details. Many art historians rank this nearly seven-foot hanging scroll as one of the greatest works in Chinese art.

FAN QUAN AND DAOISM

Fan Kuan rejected urban life and a career working as a court painter. Instead, he preferred retreating to the rugged landscape surrounding Mount Hua, a natural setting where he could closely observe streams cascading over rocks, clouds drifting across the sky, and mists forming in a valley.

Fan Kuan's spiritual communion with nature reflects his strong commitment to Daoist principles. DAOISM is an ancient Chinese philosophy based upon following a path known as the *Dao*, or way. For Fan Kuan and other Daoists, following the *Dao* meant submitting to the enduring and unchanging principles of nature. Like other Daoists, Fan Kuan spurned fame, riches, and power. He spent his later years living in remote mountain temples, where he found a deeper spiritual reality by seeking harmony with the rhythms of nature.

A LANDSCAPE PAINTED IN INK MONOCHROME

Travelers among Mountains and Streams gives visual expression to Fan Kuan's Daoist ideals. The scroll's long length invites viewers to go on a visual journey where mountains and water coexist in harmony. The journey begins in a foreground comprised of a low-lying group of boulders. Although the boulders are realistically drawn, they are not in color. Like other Chinese landscape artists, Fan Kuan forgoes color pigments in favor of the demanding medium of ink monochrome on silk. He deftly varies the thickness and wetness of his brushes to create an astonishing array of textures that portray the nuances of nature.

SHIFTING PERSPECTIVES ON A VISUAL JOURNEY

Fan Kuan believed that nature was too vast to be viewed at one time or from one point of view. Rather than confine his viewers to a single, fixed viewpoint, he used a technique called SHIFTING PERSPECTIVE to provide multiple vantage points. This technique encourages a visual journey that embraced the work's overall composition and its many intricate details.

Our visual journey begins along a path in the lower right corner where two barely visible men lead a mule train laden with wood. The path guides our eyes to the left, where a tiny traveler crosses over a bridge spanning a waterfall. The figure is following a path leading to a half-concealed temple nestled on the side of a wooded knoll. A majestic mountain in the background dwarfs the diminutive human figures, suggesting the permanence of nature and the impermanence of human actions. Fan Kuan reinforces this

Daoist view of the relationship between humans and the natural world by tucking his own signature in the foliage above the mule train.

Fan Quan uses mist to veil the transition from the temple to the towering mountain dominating the background. The mist and mountain convey a sense of timeless grandeur. A long slender waterfall further emphasizes the mountain's awesome presence. Fan Kuan demonstrates his deft use of shifting perspective by slanting the mountaintop shrubbery toward the viewer. This unique perspective adds visual variety and depth to the mountain's craggy face.

FAN QUAN AND NEO-CONFUCIANISM

During Fan Kuan's lifetime, Song Dynasty philosophers restored Confucian ideas about social harmony. Known as NEO-CONFUCIANISM, this belief system places great emphasis upon *li*, a concept expressing the search for underlying patterns and order.

Travelers among Mountains and Streams provides viewers with more than a Daoist landscape; it also deepens the Neo-Confucian search for *li*. Influenced by this Neo-Confucian idea, Fan Kuan did not depict a specific mountain. Instead, he creates a harmonious natural setting expressing the essence of "mountain-ness." His orderly image of the timeless relationship between mountains, foothills, and streams captures the Neo-Confucian ideal of a harmonious natural order. When applied to human society, Fan Kuan's landscape implies that an equally harmonious relationship should also exist between an emperor and his subjects. Similarly, Fan Kuan's image of a central mountain flanked by two lesser peaks references the Neo-Confucian notion of an emperor supported by his loyal ministers.

MAKING CONNECTIONS

TRAVELERS AMONG MOUNTAINS AND STREAMS AND *HUNTERS IN THE SNOW*

Fan Kuan's *Travelers among Mountains and Streams* and Pieter Brugel the Elder's *Hunters in the Snow* (Image 83) present strikingly different landscape paintings. Fan Kuan's painting is a vertical presentation that utilizes ink monochrome and SHIFTING PERSPECTIVES to create a natural world where nature overwhelms the insignificant impact of miniscule humans. In contrast, Brugel's painting is a horizontal presentation that utilizes colorful oil pigments and LINEAR PERSPECTIVE to create a setting populated by energetic people, whose buildings and activities are transforming their natural setting.

Gift of R. H. Ellsworth Ltd., in honor of Susan Dillon, 1987, The Metropolitan Museum of Art

IMAGE 202

Shiva as the Lord of Dance (Nataraja)

Hindu

India (Tamil Nadu), Chola Dynasty

11th century C.E.
Cast bronze

Image 202 portrays the Hindu god Shiva as Nataraja, the "Lord of the Dance." Shiva has not taken this form to entertain us. Created and designed in southern India during the Chola period (880–1279 C.E.), the statue portrays Shiva performing the *Tandava*, a dance believed to be the source of the cycles of creation, preservation, and destruction. The statue provides an extraordinary iconographic representation of many central tenets of the Hindu faith.

A COSMIC RING OF FIRE

Shiva's dance occurs in the center of a cosmic ring of fire. The ring is a perfect circle, symbolizing the Hindu belief that time is an endless cycle with no beginning, no middle, and no end.

A SET OF MULTIPLE ARMS

Shiva's four arms allow the god to fully display his awesome powers. His upraised left hand holds a five-pointed divine flame that will destroy the universe. But Shiva's powers are not just destructive. His upraised right hand holds a drum, providing rhythm to the god's dance and also marking the beat of life and thus the first stage of creation. Destruction and creation are balanced against each other, and both are governed by Shiva.

Shiva's second right hand employs a MUDRA, or hand gesture, intended to speak directly to the god's frightened followers. The "fear not" mudra bestows peace and protection by signaling to his devotees, "Be not afraid, for those who follow the path of righteousness will have my blessing." Shiva's second left hand extends toward the god's left foot, beneath which worshippers may take refuge from the visible world.

A DWARF OF IGNORANCE

Shiva's right foot is shown crushing Apasmara, a dwarf demon who personifies illusion and ignorance. Blinded by illusions, humans fail to see a divine truth: all living things are part of the interconnected rhythm of Shiva's dance. Shiva's triumph over the dwarf of human ignorance inspired Hindu holy men, who hailed Shiva by chanting, "We behold you dancing, source of the world...We take refuge in you! We adore you...who dances the divine dance."

A RELIGIOUS CONTEXT

Skilled Chola craftsmen did not sculpt Shiva Nataraja as an object to be admired in museums or discussed in AP Art History classes. Instead, Image 202 is a sacred object made for a temple, where devout Hindu worshippers could have contact with their god. The experience of encountering this sculpture was not limited to revering it in a temple. Processional parades organized by priests provided an opportunity for Hindu devotees to view Shiva Nataraja and receive blessing from their religious leaders. On these festive occasions, the statue of Shiva Nataraja would be adorned with gold jewelry, flowers, and red and green clothes.

AN ENDURING INFLUENCE

On June 18, 2004, dignitaries from India unveiled a 6.5-foot-tall statue of Shiva Nataraja on the campus of CERN, the European Center for Research in Particle Physics located near Geneva, Switzerland. What relevance did a statue designed over 1,000 years ago have for a high-tech facility where physicists use powerful scientific instruments to probe the nature of subatomic particles? Fritzof Capra, an Austrian-born American physicist, provided insight into the connection between an ancient religious statue and modern physics when he explained:

"Every subatomic particle not only performs an energy dance but also is an energy dance; a pulsating process of creation and destruction... For the modern physicist, Shiva's dance is the dance of subatomic matter. As in Hindu mythology, it is a continual dance of creation and destruction involving the whole cosmos; the basis of all existence and of all natural phenomena."

Shiva's dance thus reveals an underlying universal harmony that forms the basis of all existence.

MAKING CONNECTIONS

BRONZE CASTING

The Greek, Roman and Chola sculptors all used the LOST-WAX METHOD to cast their bronze statues. However, even classical masterpieces such as the Doryphorus (Image 34) were hollow. In contrast, the bronze statues of Shiva are solid. This feat required great precision to prevent bubbles and cracks. No other group of sculptors replicated this feat until the modern age.

Photograph © Museum of Fine Arts, Boston

Photograph © Museum of Fine Arts, Boston

IMAGE 203

Night Attack on the Sanjô Palace

Kamakura Period, Japan

c. 1250-1300 C.E.

Handscroll (ink and color on paper)

An unknown Japanese artist painted the *Night Attack on the Sanjô Palace* sometime between 1250 and 1300 C.E. The work is a nearly 23-foot-long and 16-inch-high illustrated handscroll known as an EMAKI. Image 203 portrays a triumphant warrior who has just taken part in a brief but violent attack on the Sanjô Palace in Kyoto. Although the attack on the Emperor's palace was an insignificant skirmish, the painting is an enduring masterpiece of Japanese art and a gripping portrayal of the horrors of war.

A MASTERPIECE OF THE YAMATO-E STYLE

Chinese art and architecture had a significant impact on Japanese culture during the Nara period from 645-784 C.E. For example, the architectural and sculptural styles at Todai-ji (Image 197) reflect Chinese influences. In 794 C.E., the imperial family moved from Nara to Kyoto. The royal court in Kyoto soon developed a distinctive artistic style known as YAMATO-E, or "Japanese painting."

Yamato-e artists portrayed subjects that appealed to Japan's powerful military leaders. The *Night Attack on the Sanjô Palace* thus abandons the introspective Daoist philosophy found in Chinese works such as *Travelers among Mountains and Streams* (Image 201). Instead, it provides an action-packed portrayal of war and violence.

The *Night Attack* also illustrates the new artistic vocabulary employed by Yamato-e artists. For example, the artist removes the Sanjô Palace's walls to provide viewers with an elevated or "bird's eye" view of the horror and chaos taking place, as flames envelop the imperial residence. The chieftain featured in Image 203 also illustrates the new Yamato-e style. Like the other warriors he is a depersonalized figure with few facial features. By contrast, his armor and weapons received detailed attention.

A PALACE OF POETRY AND BETRAYAL

The Sanjô Palace provided an opulent home for former Emperor Go-Shirakawa, his son Emperor Nijo, and their court. Noble ladies demonstrated their refined taste by wearing thick layers of multi-colored silk kimonos.

Their court life included endless rounds of elaborate ceremonies, lavish banquets, and poetry contests describing full moons, autumn leaves, and spring flowers.

While the royal ladies and their lovers hatched frivolous romantic plots, battle-hardened chiefs from the increasingly powerful Taira and Minamoto clans began to view the royal court with disdain. The *Night Attack on the Sanjô Palace* begins with an inscription explaining that a trusted high court official named Fujiwara no Nobuyori plotted to betray Go-Shirakawa.

"SET FIRE TO THE PALACE"

Nobuyori commanded a force of about 500 fierce samurai warriors. He and his ally, Minamoto no Yoshitomo, launched a surprise night attack at 2:00 a.m. They refused Go-Shirakawa's urgent plea to negotiate and brusquely ordered him to "hasten into the Imperial carriage." Nobuyori then ordered his men to "set fire to the Palace."

The capture of Go-Shirakawa and the order to burn the Sanjô Palace set in motion a chaotic sequence of events. The artist uses CONTINUOUS NARRATION by placing the Imperial carriage, Nobuyori, and Yoshitomo in multiple scenes. The dramatic technique unifies the flow of action.

"IT WAS MORE THAN TERRIBLE"

The painting provides an unfolding series of gruesome scenes. Mounted samurai warriors thunder across the scroll, unleashing a hail of arrows on the palace's overmatched defenders. As the fire blazes out of control, merciless warriors decapitate once-proud aristocrats and then parade their heads on poles.

The escalating violence trapped the panic-stricken court ladies. When the desperate women rushed out to avoid the fire, they met a barrage of arrows. Terrified by the arrows and the flames, they jumped into wells, where they suffocated each other. The artist provides a poignant picture of the dead ladies still wearing their layered robes. The scroll's inscription underscored the tragic scene by stating, "It was more than terrible."

THE AFTERMATH

The artist concludes his scroll with a portrait of a victorious commander leaving the palace. However, Nobuyori's victory proved to be fleeting. Taira no Kiyomori, the powerful head of the Taira clan, rescued Go-Shirakawa and beheaded Nobuyori. But the story does not end there. Kiyomori died during a bloody war with the Minamoto clan. Yoshitomo's son Yoritomo then became Japan's first shogun, or military dictator.

MAKING CONNECTIONS

NIGHT ATTACK ON THE SANJÔ PALACE AND THE BAYEUX TAPESTRY

The *Night Attack on the Sanjô Palace* and the Bayeux Tapestry (Image 59) have important similarities and differences. Both works use CONTINUOUS NARRATION to portray a complex cast of characters. The artists provide detailed visual evidence about the arms, armor, and tactics used by both fighting forces. The two works carefully depict how these deadly weapons contribute to brutal scenes of death and destruction. The Norman conquest of England proved to be a milestone event with lasting historic consequences. In contrast, the *Night Attack on the Sanjô Palace* proved to be a minor skirmish in a complex war.

Sir Percival David Collection; © The Trustees of the British Museum / Art Resource, NY

IMAGE 204

The David Vases

Yuan Dynasty, China

1351 C.E.

White porcelain with cobalt blue underglaze

Blue-and-white porcelain is one of China's most celebrated innovations. The David Vases featured in Image 204 are among the world's best known and most important examples of this prized ceramic product. The two vases are named for Sir Percival David, a British collector of rare Chinese ceramics. They are key links in a fascinating story that connects Mongol conquerors, Chinese ceramicists, and Persian cobalt mines.

THE DEVELOPMENT OF CHINESE PORCELAIN

Clay for making pottery fired below 1,000 °C can be found in most countries. However, Chinese ceramics quickly became the most advanced in the world. China is especially rich in deposits of kaolin, the key ingredient when porcelain is fired at about 1,350 °C. Porcelain is whiter, more translucent, and more glass-like than pottery fired at lower temperatures.

During the early to mid-14th century, skilled ceramicists working at imperial kilns in Jingdezhen learned how to create a pure white, translucent porcelain. This provided an ideal surface for a brilliant cobalt blue pigment that had to be imported from Persia. But reaching Persia required a long and sometimes dangerous journey that made cobalt a coveted commodity, with a value about twice that of gold.

THE MONGOLS AND PORCELAIN

Ruthless Mongol armies, led by Genghis Khan and his sons, played an unexpected role in promoting China's production of blue-and-white porcelain. Between 1206 and 1279, the Mongols successfully conquered, terrorized, and unified a vast empire stretching from China to Persia. Paradoxically, these destructive conquests promoted economic prosperity, by ensuring a long period of peace and stability along the Silk Road connecting China and Persia. As a result, Persian cobalt could reach Chinese kilns in Jingdezhen, where skilled ceramicists used it to produce blue-and-white porcelain.

AN INFORMATIVE INSCRIPTION

The David Vases are an artistic consequence of what historians call the "Pax Mongolica" or Mongolian Peace. Each of the 2.5-foot-tall vases contains a lengthy inscription filled with precise historic details. For example, we learn that a man named Zhang Wenjiin dedicated the vases on Tuesday, May 13, 1351. He offered them as a donation to a Daoist temple. The vases are intended to honor a revered 13th century Chinese general who had recently become recognized as a god. Zhang Wenjiin expressed his hope that the new god will protect and bless his "whole family."

DRAGONS AND PHOENIXES

The David Vases feature two key mythological beasts—a dragon and a phoenix. The artist-craftsmen at Jingdezhen wrapped an elongated dragon around the center of each vase. As China's traditional symbol for the emperor, the dragon represents high rank, power, and good fortune. In Chinese mythology, a dragon symbolizes abundance because of its ability to bring rain to parched lands. The blue clouds trailing each dragon may be a reference to this creature's miraculous power.

The artist-craftsmen placed a phoenix along the bottom portion of each vase's neck. Known as the "king of birds," the phoenix symbolizes good fortune because it only appears in times of peace and prosperity. The phoenix is also a symbol for the empress. Each vase pairs a phoenix with a dragon. Taken together, these auspicious symbols stand for a perfect marriage.

MAKING CONNECTIONS

THE DAVID VASES AND *SUNFLOWER SEEDS*

The David Vases and Ai Weiwei's *Sunflower Seeds* (Image 250) have very different forms. While differing in appearance, the two vases and the 100 million sunflower seeds share two striking similarities: both were made out of porcelain by skilled ceramicists working in Jingdezhen. Ai Weiwei recognized Jingdezhen's historic importance as the center of Chinese porcelain production. He deliberately chose to employ artisans in small-scale workshops to underscore their link with the great tradition of Chinese porcelain production.

Courtesy Wikimedia.

IMAGE 205

Portrait of Sin Sukju (1417–1475)

Imperial Bureau of Painting

c. 15th century C.E.

Hanging scroll (ink and color on silk)

Sin Sukju served the Joseon Dynasty kings with great distinction. The monarchs rewarded their loyal scholar-official by declaring him a "Meritorious Subject" who deserved an official portrait. Shown in Image 205, Sin Jukju's portrait fills a 5.5-foot-long and 3.7-foot-wide silk scroll. The portrait does more than capture Sin Sukju's likeness—it also provides valuable insights into Korean artistic conventions and cultural practices.

THE JOSEON DYNASTY AND NEO-CONFUCIANISM

In 1392, a new line of Korean rulers ended the period of Mongol domination by establishing the Joseon or "Fresh Dawn" Dynasty. The first Joseon kings more than lived up to their name. They purged corrupt practices, expanded the kingdom's northern border, and fostered a cultural renaissance.

Influenced by reform-minded Confucian scholars, the Joseon kings used NEO-CONFUCIAN principles to promote a harmonious society. Neo-Confucianism stressed the importance of rulers who practiced virtuous living and performed complex rituals. In return, law-abiding subjects demonstrated loyalty to their kings. Neo-Confucianism also placed great emphasis upon filial piety, the honor and respect owed to one's elders and ancestors.

SIN SUKJU, A MERITORIOUS SUBJECT

The Joseon kings actively promoted an elite class of scholar-officials who exemplified the Neo-Confucian code of behavior. Sin Sukju's career thrived in this merit-based system. He quickly established himself as an eminent scholar who contributed commentaries on the royal painting collection and an accomplished linguist who helped create a Korean phonetic alphabet now known as *Hangul*.

Sin Sukju's talents also extended to diplomacy and politics. The king entrusted him to head sensitive diplomatic missions to the Chinese and Japanese royal courts. At the same time, Sin Sukju became a powerful politician who served as First State Councilor from 1461 to 1466 and from 1471 to his death in 1475.

"EXACTLY AS THEY ARE"

Meritorious Subjects such as Sin Jukju received a number of prized awards. For example, Sin Sukju's award included a quantity of gold and silk and the distinction of having his name and services engraved on a great bell. In addition, Sin Sukju received an even more coveted honor—sitting for a full-length silk portrait.

A talented but unknown artist, working for the prestigious Imperial Bureau of Painting, painted the portrait of Sin Sukju shown in Image 205. The artist followed conventional practice by depicting Sin Sukju seated in a chair. He wears an official robe, a black silk hat, and leather shoes resting on a footstool. At the same time, the artist followed a strict requirement to portray his models "exactly as they are." A team of critics closely evaluated the portrait to ensure a high standard of representation. In contrast to the idealized Roman imperial statue of Augustus Prima Porta (Image 43), Sin Sukju's portrait presents a serious and experienced senior official. Sin Jukju's resplendent official robe features a distinctive gold-embroidered rank badge. The Joseon court used a hierarchy of highly visible status symbols. For example, the king's badge featured a five-clawed dragon. Sin Sukju's insignia displayed a pair of peacocks, symbols of authority reserved for a civil official of the first rank.

POLITICAL AND FAMILY FUNCTIONS

Sin Sukju's portrait represented a great personal achievement. At the same time, it performed a number of important functions for the Joseon Dynasty and for Sin Sukju's family. The Joseon kings used portraits to reward loyalty, underscoring the connection between scholar-officials and the crown. When displayed in a shrine, a long line of portrait scrolls provided an impressive visual image of dynastic continuity. The portraits thus served as a form of political propaganda, expressing the unity of the country and the power of the royal court.

Sin Jukju's portrait functioned as more than a political tool; it also played an important role for his family. Filial piety demanded that the living respect their ancestors. Hung in a family shrine, Sin Sukju's portrait ensured everlasting respect while serving as a focus of continuing ancestor rituals. Because of this vital function, modern Korean families are reluctant to allow treasured family portraits to participate in museum exhibits.

MAKING CONNECTIONS

THE PORTRAIT OF SIN SUKJU AND THE HEAD OF A ROMAN PATRICIAN

The Portrait of Sin Sukju and the Head of a Roman Patrician are both realistic portrayals of powerful men. The two images convey a seriousness of purpose, or *gravitas*, that demonstrates the value the Joseon Dynasty and the Roman republic placed upon civic duty. And finally, both the Korean and Roman cultures stressed the role of portraits in honoring esteemed ancestors.

06photo / Shutterstock.com

travellight / Shutterstock.com

IMAGE 206

Forbidden City

Beijing, China

Ming Dynasty

15th century C.E. and later

Stone masonry, marble, brick, wood, and ceramic tile

In 1404 the new Ming emperor Zhu Di moved the Chinese capital from Nanjing ("southern capital") to Beijing ("northern capital"). Two years later the ruthless but gifted emperor marshaled enormous resources to build a massive complex of palaces, administrative buildings, and residences. During the next five centuries, 24 Chinese emperors called the great city within a city their home. But the palace's forbidding moat and high walls excluded almost all the emperor's subjects. They called Zhu Di's grandiose palace the Forbidden City.

IN HARMONY WITH THE UNIVERSE

Emperor Zhu Di ordered his architects to build a palace "in harmony with the Universe." The Chinese believed that a Supreme Being lived in a 10,000-room "palace in the sky." As the Son of Heaven, the Chinese emperor was more than just a mortal ruler; he was also a divine being whose presence formed a link between the earthly and celestial worlds. Zhu Di's grand new imperial hub thus served as both the political and religious center of the Ming empire and the axis of the Universe where "earth and sky meet."

One million workers and 100,000 skilled engineers and artisans built the Forbidden City in just 14 years. A rectangular moat with a high wall separated the 250-acre compound from the bustling city outside. Conceived on a grand scale, the Forbidden City contained 90 palaces, 980 buildings, and according to legend, 9,999 rooms—one less than the Supreme Deity's palace.

Zhu Di's architects used time-honored traditions to appease the gods and ensure good fortune. They arranged the main entrance gates and imperial halls along a long axis running north to south. All of the buildings face south, the direction from which benevolent spirits come. The crimson color of the buildings symbolizes the light of the North Star, while the yellow-tiled roofs take their color from the Sun.

The Chinese attached great significance to special numbers. For example, they considered nine a particularly auspicious number, because of its similar sound to their word for eternal. Given this favorable connection, artisans carefully placed a row of nine fanciful earthenware creatures on rooftops where they could ward off malevolent spirits. The row always included a dragon, as a beneficial creature symbolizing the emperor and bringing much-needed rain.

THE HALL OF SUPREME HARMONY—"ALL UNDER HEAVEN"

The Hall of Supreme Harmony dominated the Forbidden City's great north-south axis. Imperial architects spared no expense to create a magnificent building that awed visitors. The Hall of Supreme Harmony stood high atop a white marble terrace overlooking a 600-foot-wide courtyard. Carpenters shaped the long and sturdy trunks of Nanmu evergreen trees into massive columns that supported the huge roof. It required four years to transport the 100-foot-tall trees from mountain forests 1,000 miles south of Beijing.

The audience chamber inside the Hall of Supreme Harmony served as the empire's symbolic center. Gold and jade bells rang as the emperor ascended his gilded Dragon Throne. Wearing a yellow silk dragon robe, the emperor commanded the imperial armies, presided over royal weddings, and supervised New Year's Day festivities. As he performed these official duties, the emperor sat at the center of the Universe, ruling "all under heaven."

THE INNER COURT—A GOLDEN CAGE

The Forbidden City consisted of an Outer Court, dominated by the Hall of Supreme Harmony, and an Inner Court, where the imperial family lived. The Inner Court included a large array of palaces, pavilions, courtyards, and even a spacious Imperial Garden. Hundreds of concubines and thousands of eunuchs worked and lived in the Inner Court. Their luxurious surroundings concealed a harsh reality–the Forbidden City became a golden cage they could rarely leave.

Strict rules and rituals dominated life in the Inner Court. For example, royal concubines had to conform to specific height and weight guidelines. They even had to pass a smell test! Royal meals conformed to rigid rules. The kitchen staff regularly presented the emperor with a bountiful breakfast buffet that included 40 different dishes.

FROM A FORBIDDEN CITY TO A POPULAR MUSEUM

The Forbidden City's high walls and auspicious symbols could not stop the waves of revolutionary change sweeping across China. In 1911, the Nationalist People's Party led by Sun Yat-sen overthrew the last Qing emperor. Thirteen years later, China's new leaders transformed the Forbidden City into a public museum. With over 15 million people visiting it each year, the Palace Museum is now China's most popular tourist destination.

MAKING CONNECTIONS

THE FORBIDDEN CITY AND THE PALACE AT VERSAILLES

Zhu Di and Louis XIV successfully marshaled enormous resources to create magnificent palace complexes. The Forbidden City and the Palace at Versailles (Image 93) both expressed the basic political reality that the emperors of China and the kings of France ruled as absolute monarchs. The meticulous rituals at the Hall of Supreme Harmony and the Hall of Mirrors provided a visual display of power and grandeur. In China, Zhu Di and his successors ruled "all under Heaven." In France, Louis XIV confidently boasted, "L'etat, c'est moi" ("The state, it is I").

IMAGE 207

Ryoan-ji

Kyoto, Japan

c. 1480 C.E.

Current design most likely dates to the 18th-century rock garden

Ryoan-ji is a Zen temple in northwestern Kyoto, Japan. It covers about 120 acres with a beautiful pond, magnificent views of nearby mountains, and a renowned Zen rock garden. The garden's deceptively simple gravel-and-rock arrangement is one of the masterpieces of Japanese culture and one of the most photographed gardens in the world.

ZEN BUDDHISM

The Ryoan-ji rock garden has become an internationally recognized symbol of Zen Buddhism. The word Zen means "meditation" or "concentration." The practice originated in India and China before spreading to Japan in the late 12th and early 13th centuries. Followers of Zen Buddhism believe that meditation is the primary tool to help them achieve a heightened sense of self-awareness. A rock garden provides a setting where devotees can achieve a sudden insight that deepens into more profound self-realization.

DISTINCTIVE FEATURES

The history of the Ryoan-ji rock garden contains many mysteries. Scholars believe that the original rock garden dates to the late 1400s. However, its current form can only be traced back to the late 18th or early 19th centuries. The creators of these gardens remain unknown.

During its long history, the Ryoan-ji rock garden retained many distinctive features. It never offered visitors flowers to admire, paths to walk on, or benches to sit on. Like a painting or sculpture, the rock garden requires viewers to consider it from a distance.

The Ryoan-ji rock garden presents a deceptively simple form. It is located within an enclosed courtyard measuring 30 feet by 78 feet. The garden contains 15 stones of different sizes, artfully placed in five isolated groups—one with five stones, two with three stones, and two with two stones. A small moss border surrounds these island groups. Carefully raked white gravel fills the remaining space. A nearly six-foot-high oil-earthen wall, made up of clay mixed with rapeseed oil, frames the garden on two sides. The wall prevents the sun's glare from reflecting off the garden's white gravel.

Devotees view the rock garden from the veranda outside the abbot's hall. The stone islands are strategically placed so that only 14 of the 15 rocks can be seen from any single vantage point. Although the garden initially appears to look like a sandbox, its enigmatic arrangement invites quiet meditation.

WHAT DID THE ARTIST HAVE IN MIND?

No one knows the artist's intent when he designed the Ryoan-ji rock garden. This has not stopped viewers from proposing a number of interpretations. For example, many visitors believe that the garden represents mountain peaks rising above the clouds, islands basking in the sun, or even a mother tiger leading her cubs across a stream.

Although they provide interesting possibilities, these interpretations do not deepen our understanding of Zen Buddhism's philosophical quest for self-enlightenment. The best Japanese art is suggestive rather than declarative. Viewed from this perspective, the 15 stones may suggest self-important but deluded individuals. In Buddhist thought, life is an illusion in which people are always moving yet going nowhere. Blinded by illusion, humans endlessly walk in shadows, futilely searching for light.

The rocks and small pieces of gravel in the Ryoan-ji garden can provide insight into the human condition. Like the garden rocks, we will all became insignificant pieces of gravel. Quiet meditation in the Ryoan-ji rock garden can guide devotees to the important insight that the cycle of life rests upon impermanence. This condition can only be broken by intensive self-awareness about one's true nature.

MAKING CONNECTIONS

RYOAN-JI AND *TRAVELERS AMONG MOUNTAINS AND STREAMS*

The Ryoan-ji rock garden and *Travelers among Mountains and Streams* (Image 201) have obvious differences. The rock garden occupies a three-dimensional space, while Fan Kuan's painting is a two-dimensional silk scroll. Philosophically, the rock garden reflects Zen Buddhist influences, while Fan Kuan's masterpiece reflects Neo-Confucian thought. However, these differences conceal striking similarities. The Daoist view of the insignificance of humans amidst the dominance of nature influenced both works. In addition, the two works use SHIFTING PERSPECTIVE to encourage viewers to lose themselves in quiet contemplation.

Freer Gallery of Art and Arthur M. Sackler Gallery, Smithsonian Institution, Washington, D.C.: Purchase, Charles Land Peter Endowment, F1942.15a

IMAGE 208

Jahangir Preferring a Sufi Shaikh to Kings

Bichitr

c. 1620 C.E.

Watercolor, gold, and ink on paper

Image 208 invites viewers to examine a famous miniature painting by Bichitr, an early 17th-century court artist for the Mughal emperor Jahangir. Although the work is just 18 inches high and 13 inches wide, it includes a complex blend of Mughal, Persian, and European styles. Bichitr's combination of realistic portraits and allegorical symbols provides a window into a unique period of Indian history.

THE MUGHAL DYNASTY

An Islamic dynasty known as the Mughals ruled most of India from 1526 to 1857. Under Akbar the Great, the Mughal court became a vibrant artistic center. Akbar contributed to this cultural renaissance by adopting a tolerant attitude toward India's diverse religious groups.

Although blessed with great success, Akbar experienced increasing anxiety over his lack of a male heir. The deeply troubled emperor turned for help to a revered Islamic mystic named Shaikh Salim Chishti. The Sufi holy man blessed Akbar and confidently foretold the imminent birth of a son. Shortly thereafter, Akbar's Hindu wife gave birth to a young prince. The grateful royal couple named their son Salim to honor the Sufi sage.

JAHANGIR, THE "WORLD-SEIZER"

Salim ascended the Mughal throne in 1605. He inherited a vast empire that reportedly took caravans two years to cross. Determined to take advantage of his seemingly limitless opportunities, Salim chose the name Jahangir, meaning "World-Seizer," as the "title which best suited my character."

Jahangir failed to live up to his ambitious title. He soon became a vain and fickle ruler who alienated his supporters and tortured his opponents. His frightened courtiers burst into applause when Jahangir issued trivial orders or recited uninspiring verses of poetry.

Although Jahangir proved to be a disappointing political leader, he earned a reputation as an avid and knowledgeable art patron. He enthusiastically widened commercial and artistic contacts with Europe. The influx of European paintings exposed his gifted court artists to naturalistic portraits and symbolically rich allegories. Bichitr skillfully used both of these stylistic elements to glorify Jahangir.

Jahangir did not commission works of art for public display. Instead, he bound miniatures such as Image 208 into a *muraqqa*, or album, for private viewing. Sometime around 1620 C.E., Bichitr received a royal directive to create a miniature featuring a flattering allegorical portrait of Jahangir and a subordinate group of spiritual and royal figures.

A SPIRITUAL MESSAGE

Bichitr's carefully drawn portrait of Jahangir dominates the composition. The seated emperor is much larger than the other figures. A halo comprised of a golden sun and silver moon surrounds Jahangir, demonstrating that he is the source of all light. In the upper right corner a Renaissance-style cupid covers his eyes to protect them from the halo's blinding radiance.

Jahangir sits on a jeweled circular throne resting above a European hourglass. Two clothed cupids hold the hourglass and inscribe an inscription wishing that the emperor would live for a thousand years. But the sands of time are inexorably running out. Bichitr's carefully designed allegorical image conveys a spiritual message that Jahangir must turn his attention from this world to the next.

Jahangir understands the inevitable passage of time. He ignores an unidentified Ottoman sultan and the English King James I. Instead, Jahangir focuses his full attention on Shaikh Husain, a Sufi holy man. Jahangir presents the sage a sumptuous leather-bound book held together by gold clamps. The gift recognizes the important role Husain's predecessor played in correctly predicting Jahangir's birth. The image also underscores Jahangir's commitment to spiritual wisdom over worldly power.

BICHITR

Jahangir extended Bichitr the rare honor of including his self-portrait in the painting. Bichitr recognized the privilege but also understood his own humble status. Although his portrait in the lower left corner is closest to the viewer, he ignored the rules of realistic perspective by modestly drawing himself as the miniature's smallest figure. A close inspection reveals that Bichitr is holding a small painting depicting two horses and an elephant. This painting-within-a-painting also includes a self-portrait showing Bichitr deeply bowing as a sign of his gratitude for these costly imperial gifts.

In another display of honor tempered by humility, Bichitr placed his signature across the top of the richly decorated footstool located to the left of the hourglass. Bichitr understood that Jahangir would step on his name as he rose to his throne. This deliberate symbolism underscores the artist's understanding of his inferior status.

MAKING CONNECTIONS

JAHANGIR PREFERRING A SUFI SHAIKH TO KINGS AND *THE COURT OF GAYUMARS*

Jahangir Preferring a Sufi Shaikh to Kings and *The Court of Gayumars* (Image 190) share a number of important characteristics. Both Bachitr and Sultan Muhammad packed meticulously drawn details into small pictorial spaces. For example, the two works include intricate floral designs skillfully painted with jewel-like colors. Although Bachitr's composition owes much to Persian aesthetics, his contact with European paintings prompted him to include features such as cupids and an allegorical hourglass.

Suraj rajiv

IMAGE 209

Taj Mahal

Agra, India

Masons, marble workers, mosaicists, and decorators working under the direction of Ustad Ahmad Lahori

1632-1653 C. E.

Stone masonry and marble with inlay of precious and semiprecious stones; gardens

The Mughal emperor Shah Jahan built the Taj Mahal on the banks of the Yamuna River in Agra. The exquisite white marble mausoleum is the final resting place of Shah Jahan's beloved queen Mumtaz Mahal. The great shrine is an unchallenged architectural masterpiece and a recognized symbol of India. For millions of visitors it is also a symbol of love and great beauty. The Indian poet Rabindranath Tagore expressed this feeling when he described the Taj Mahal as "a teardrop of love on the cheek of time."

SHAH JAHAN AND MUMTAZ MAHAL

The origins of the Taj Mahal can be traced back to a chance encounter in a palace bazaar between a handsome Mughal prince and a beautiful daughter of a royal prime minister. The story is told that as Prince Khurran strolled from stall to stall, his eyes suddenly met those of Arjumand Banu Begam. The two fell in love, and the next day Khurran asked his father, the emperor Jahangir, for permission to marry Arjumand. Although Jahangir granted his son's request, the couple had to wait for astrologers to agree upon an auspicious wedding date.

The long-awaited royal wedding took place on March 27, 1612. To show his esteem, Jahangir bestowed the bride with a new name—Mumtaz Mahal, "The Chosen One of the Palace." As the years passed, Prince Khurran won acclaim as a victorious general, while court poets praised Mumtaz for her beauty, intelligence, and compassion. Following Jahangir's death in 1628, Khurran eliminated his rivals, seized power, and took a new name—Shah Jahan, "The King of the World."

Fortune smiled on the royal couple, but not for long. In 1631, Mumtaz accompanied Shah Jahan on a grueling military campaign. While her husband subdued the rebels, Mumtaz experienced unexpected complications as she gave birth to her 14th child. Stunned by the news, Shah Jahan rushed to her bedside. Although he commanded unbounded power, the emperor could not save the love of his life. As Mumtaz lay dying she whispered a final wish, asking Shah Jahan to build a monument that would forever convey the purity of love. The brokenhearted emperor agreed, and within a year workers began to construct the Taj Mahal.

MORE THAN A TOMB

Shah Jahan summoned gifted master craftsmen and expert calligraphers from across his vast empire. The royal architect Ustad Ahmad Lahori directed as many as 20,000 workers. This commitment of enormous resources enabled Shah Jahan to complete the mausoleum in 1643 and the entire complex in 1653.

The Taj Mahal is more than just a burial place; it is also a symbolic image on earth of the heavenly mansion awaiting Mumtaz Mahal in Paradise.

THE GARDEN

The Taj Mahal's garden serves an important function by representing the Qur'an's description of Paradise as a garden watered by rivers of water, milk, wine, and honey. The garden uses a Persian design known as *chahar bagh* to evoke this vision. The plan features two intersecting canals, whose four parts symbolize the Four Rivers of Paradise. The Taj Mahal's marble canals meet at a raised pond, representing the pool where the faithful quench their thirst when they arrive in Paradise.

KEY ARCHITECTURAL FEATURES

Shah Jahan's architects reserved white marble for the mausoleum. Although very costly, the pure white marble enabled the emperor to identify the Mughal dynasty with deeply rooted Hindu and Islamic traditions. Ancient Hindu texts recommended using white stone for buildings used by Brahmins, the priestly caste standing at the apex of Indian society. At the same time, Islamic tradition strongly associated white with purity and spirituality.

A commitment to perfect symmetry shaped the Taj Mahal's balanced and harmonious form. The building's four identical facades all contain a central IWAN, or arched opening, flanked by two levels of smaller iwans. Four identical minarets frame the tomb.

An onion-shaped dome crowns the white marble tomb. Four Indian pavilions known as *chhatris* or "umbrellas" surround the great dome. This elegant composition resembles a giant pearl floating above the building. The shape recalls the Prophet Muhammad's vision of the throne of God as a pearl surrounded by four pillars. As a devout Muslim, Shah Jahan believed God would sit in judgment before allowing him to reunite with his beloved wife.

KEY DECORATIVE FEATURES

The Taj Mahal combines striking architectural forms with dazzling decorative features. Master calligraphers inscribed flowing black Arabic letters on the Taj Mahal's white marble walls. For example, the tomb's four iwan arches invite viewers to contemplate the entire text of the Qur'an's 36th sura. Traditionally read to the dying, its reassuring verses speak of God's bountiful gifts and promises of eternal life in Paradise for the faithful.

The Taj Mahal's decorative program also includes a technique known by its Italian name, *PIETRA DURA*. Although it is not known how knowledge of *pietra dura* reached India, it is known that its beautiful designs won Shah Jahan's enthusiastic support. His highly skilled craftsmen first carved floral shapes into the marble. This created a setting for laying hundreds of carefully fitted semiprecious stones. The resulting stone flowers offer a strong visual contrast to the real but ephemeral flowers in the outside gardens.

INSEPARABLE IN DEATH

Shah Jahan positioned Mumtaz Mahal's cenotaph in the precise center of the Taj Mahal. When he died in 1666, his son placed the deceased emperor's cenotaph beside that of Mumtaz. The two cenotaphs are in fact elaborately decorated empty boxes. The real sarcophagi containing their remains lie in a crypt directly below. This arrangement places Mumtaz to Shah Jahan's left, the side of his heart. Inseparable in life, the royal couple remain inseparable in death.

MAKING CONNECTIONS

BILATERAL SYMMETRY

Shah Jahan's architects used the principle of BILATERAL SYMMETRY to divide the Taj Mahal complex into equal halves. Their choice was not accidental. Bilateral symmetry is often associated with monumental projects commissioned by absolute rulers. For example, Louis XIV's Versailles Palace (Image 93) and Zhu Di's Forbidden City (Image 206) provide imposing examples of rulers who used bilateral symmetry to project their power.

MOA Museum of Art

IMAGE 210

White and Red Plum Blossoms

Ogata Korin

c. 1710-1716 C. E.

Ink, watercolor, and gold leaf on paper

Ogata Korin's artistic career began in Kyoto, Japan in the late 1690s and lasted for less than two decades. During this short period, he created striking images for screen paintings, ceramics, textiles, and lacquerware. Art historians recognize *White and Red Plum Blossoms* as Korin's supreme artistic achievement and a masterpiece of Japanese art.

OGATA KORIN, AN ARTISTIC LATE BLOOMER

Korin enjoyed a youth filled with luxury and aesthetic refinement. His family owned a stylish clothing store where wealthy clients purchased expensive fabrics. Korin's father left him a sizeable inheritance. However, he pursued a frivolous lifestyle and squandered his fortune. Facing financial ruin, Korin turned to art. He soon established himself as a gifted painter, whose work reflected the taste of Japan's increasingly prosperous middle class.

A STREAM AND TWO PLUM TREES

The Japanese traditionally welcome flowering plum trees as harbingers of spring. Art historians believe Korin explored this popular subject in the years just before his death in 1715. He painted the memorable image *White and Red Plum Blossoms* on a pair of two-panel folding screens. Each screen measures almost 62 inches wide and just under 68 inches high.

A stream flows across the center of Korin's two panels. At first broad, the stream rapidly narrows as it recedes into the distance. Korin uses stylized curls to represent a swirling current. His dark and gently twisting ripples suggest the passage of time and the changes in his own life.

The abstract stream passes between two plum trees. A young and vigorous red plum stands to the right. Its brilliant red blossoms decorate branches that reach upward, suggesting the unlimited opportunities of Korin's youth. In contrast, the white plum tree is much older. Delicate white blossoms decorate its thin branches, suggesting the wisdom Korin has acquired as a mature artist.

Korin places his abstract river and realistic trees in a space dominated by a gold background. Like the Byzantine mosaics featured in Image 51, the gold background denies a sense of time and place. Instead, it creates a dreamlike setting that invites viewers to contemplate the ephemeral beauty of nature and the inevitable passage of time.

ARTISTIC TECHNIQUES

Korin achieved his distinctive interplay of abstraction and realism by employing artistic techniques known as *TARASHIKOMI* and *MOKKOTSU*. He used *tarachikomi* by dipping paint or ink onto his initial layer of wet paint. The pigments then merge and blur, giving his painting depth and a quality of unpredictability. Korin's skillful use of *tarashikomi* added visual interest and variety to his work.

Korin enhanced the striking appearance of his trees by adding *mokkotsu* to create vibrant red and white blossoms. Instead of filling in the outline of a flower, Korin painted each form without extensive lines. This natural look conveys each flower's sparkling color and vitality.

THE RINPA STYLE

Ogata Korin's works employ distinctive brush techniques and stylistic preferences for vivid colors, bold abstract designs, motifs drawn from nature, and the extensive use of gold and silver. This combination of characteristics influenced several generations of Japanese artists known collectively as the RINPA School. The name Rinpa derives from the last syllable of Korin's name ("rin") and the Japanese word "pa," meaning school. Although Rinpa artists shared similar interests, they did not constitute a formal school such as the Kei School of sculptors, who carved the fierce guardian figures at Todai-ji (Image 197).

MAKING CONNECTIONS

WHITE AND RED PLUM BLOSSOMS AND *THE KISS*

Both *White and Red Plum Blossoms* and *The Kiss* (Image 128) use gold backgrounds. This stylistic feature enables Korin and Klimt to create shallow spaces in which the past, present, and future all mingle in a single moment. In addition, both artists successfully combine abstract and representational images to create memorable compositions.

H.O. Havemeyer Collection, The Metropolitan Museum of Art, Bequest of Mrs. H. O. Havemeyer, 1929

IMAGE 211

Under the Wave off Kanagawa

Also known as the *Great Wave*
From the series *Thirty-six Views of Mount Fuji*

Katsushika Hokusai

1830-1833 C.E.

Polychrome woodblock print; ink and color on paper

Katsushika Hokusai was born in 1760 in Edo, a Japanese city now known as Tokyo. During a prolific career that stretched from the 1790s to his death in 1849, Hokusai created over 10,000 woodcuts and between 30,000 and 40,000 drawings. However, his global fame rests on a single polychrome woodblock print popularly known as the *Great Wave*. This image of a towering wave threatening to overwhelm oarsmen in three fragile skiffs has fascinated, inspired, and challenged viewers since it first appeared in the early 1830s.

HOKUSAI AND THE "FLOATING WORLD"

An artistic style known as UKIYO-E dominated Japanese popular culture during Hokusai's lifetime. *Ukiyo-e* artists focused on creating images of a transient urban "floating world," populated by Kabuki actors and beautiful geishas. Hokusai broadened the range of *ukiyo-e* subjects to include a rich panorama of Japanese life, ranging from playful sparrows to fierce warriors. Although he achieved prominence as an accomplished *ukiyo-e artist*, Hokusai dismissed his work: "Until the age of 70, nothing I drew was worthy of notice."

HOKUSAI AND MOUNT FUJI

In 1830, Hokusai turned to portraying Mount Fuji, a subject he deemed "worthy of notice." Located 62 miles southwest of Edo, the majestic cone-shaped mountain played an important role in shaping Japan's national identity. Like Buddhist and Shinto worshippers, Hokusai venerated Mount Fuji as an immortal and indestructible part of his homeland. Indeed, the word "fu-shi" literally means "no death."

The early 19th century witnessed a boom in popular travel within Japan. Many tourists included Mount Fuji as a featured destination. Hokusai alertly recognized the commercial potential of inexpensive woodcut prints of Mount Fuji. A tourist could purchase a souvenir print for the price of a cup of noodle soup. Motivated by his inspired idea, Hokusai began a series of 36 woodcut prints that would all include an image of Mount Fuji. Named after the 36 immortals of Japanese classical poetry, the *Thirty-six Views of Mount Fuji* would ensure Hokusai an honored place in art history.

HOKUSAI AND NEW ARTISTIC INFLUENCES

Hokusai lived in a country that resisted outside influences. During the late 1630s, Japan's Tokugawa shoguns instituted a policy that forbade foreigners from entering Japan. For two centuries, Japanese authorities allowed just one exception: a few Dutch ships could briefly dock at the port of Nagasaki.

Strict laws prohibited Dutch merchants from crossing a narrow bridge to the mainland. But the restrictions did not stop Dutch art prints and new chemical dyes from reaching Japanese artists. Hokusai carefully studied how Dutch master painters used LINEAR PERSPECTIVE to create the illusion of depth on a flat picture plane. He also purchased a dark blue chemical pigment called Prussian blue. First synthesized in Prussia, the dye provided an ideal color for the sky and water scenes in his series on Mount Fuji.

AN UNFORGETTABLE COMPOSITION

The *Great Wave* is the most famous scene from *Thirty-six Views of Mount Fuji*. It presents viewers with a striking and unforgettable composition. A massive, deep blue rogue wave dominates the left side of Hokusai's image. The cresting wave's thunderous force poses an imminent danger to oarsmen huddled in three narrow skiffs.

Hokusai's dramatic composition does not neglect Mount Fuji. A small wave-peak in front of the great wave repeats Mount Fuji's form. Hokusai uses linear perspective to draw the viewer's eye to the legendary snow-capped mountain positioned near the center of a low horizon line.

AN AMBIGUOUS MESSAGE

Hokusai's dramatic image presents viewers with a visual cliffhanger. The valiant oarsmen face an uncertain fate. The viewer does not know if they will succumb to the wave's overwhelming force or skillfully evade the danger.

The *Great Wave* does more than create dramatic tension; it also serves as a visual metaphor for Japan's increasingly anxious state of mind. Although the island nation remained isolated, Hokusai's exposure to Dutch art served notice that Japan could not indefinitely resist joining the global trading network. The massive wave can thus be viewed as a symbol of the growing perils facing Japan. In this context, Hokusai uses Mount Fuji as a reassuring source of stability.

THE GREAT WAVE SWEEPS ACROSS THE WORLD

The changes Hokusai sensed swept across Japan in the years following his death in 1849. Less than a decade later, Japan opened its ports to foreign trade. Within a short time, ships carried prints by Hokusai and other Japanese artists to Paris and other centers of Western art. Manet, van Gogh, and Cassatt (Image 121) all responded enthusiastically to the JAPONISME style of using flat planes of color and partial views to depict scenes of everyday life. It is possible that Cezanne's famous sequence of paintings of Mont Saint-Victoire (Image 125) were a homage to Hokusai's *Thirty-six Views of Mount Fuji*.

MAKING CONNECTIONS

THE *GREAT WAVE* AND *TRAVELERS AMONG MOUNTAINS AND STREAMS*

The *Great Wave* and *Travelers Among Mountains and Streams* (Image 201) explore the relationship between humans and the natural world. Both works depict humans as an insignificant presence in settings dominated by nature. However, the travelers in Fan Kuan's hanging scroll live in harmony with their magnificent landscape. In contrast, the oarsmen in Hokusai's woodcut print face a perilous encounter with a relentless natural force. Fan Kuan created his scroll for individual contemplation, while Hokusai created his woodcut as part of a commercial endeavor for a mass audience.

Private Collection, © The Chambers Gallery, London / Bridgeman Images

IMAGE 212

Chairman Mao en Route to Anyuan

Artist unknown; based upon an oil painting by Liu Chunhua

c. 1969 C.E.
Color lithograph

Image 212, *Chairman Mao en Route to Anyuan*, presents AP Art History students with a puzzling but instructive paradox. On the one hand, the painting was reproduced an astounding 900 million times, making it the most duplicated image in human history. On the other hand, the painting and its artist, Liu Chunhua, are almost unknown outside of China. In fact, Liu Chunhua does not even have an English-language Wikipedia page! However, a close inspection of the work yields surprising insights into Chinese history and the uses of art.

MAO ZEDONG

Mao Zedong stands as one of the most important leaders of the 20th century. His long list of accomplishments includes organizing the Chinese Communist Party, founding the People's Republic of China, and governing the new country as Chairman of the Communist Party of China from 1949 until his death in 1976. But Mao also pursued misguided policies that produced calamitous consequences for the Chinese people. In 1966, he launched the Great Proletarian Cultural Revolution, urging China's youth to "learn revolution by making revolution." Millions of high school and college students responded by forming military-like units called Red Guards. Armed with Chairman Mao's thoughts, the Red Guards aimed to purge old customs and traditional ideas from Chinese society. They demonstrated their revolutionary zeal by denouncing professors, government officials, factory managers, and even their own parents. The Red Guards did not limit their actions to verbal tirades. They also burned classic Chinese books and destroyed priceless works of art as they ransacked museums.

LIU CHUNHUA

Mao's call for revolutionary change inspired Liu Chunhua, a 24-year-old Red Guard studying at the Central Academy of Industrial Arts in Beijing. Liu "longed to use my paints and brushes to portray our great leader." His opportunity came when the sponsors of a Mao art exhibit called upon Liu to create an oil painting depicting Mao on his way to inspire a strike at the famous Anyuan coal mines. Although he had never been taught oil painting, Liu enthusiastically embraced his assignment.

The Cultural Revolution motivated artists to create "Mao paintings" glorifying the legendary party leader. Like other artists, Liu turned to SOCIALIST REALISM, an artistic style pioneered in the Soviet Union. Socialist Realist artists focused upon painting positive portraits of youthful heroes overcoming obstacles to build a classless society. The bold new oil-on-canvas works marked a departure from traditional Chinese ink-on-silk hanging scrolls, such as Fan Kuan's *Travelers among Mountains and Streams* (Image 201).

Liu understood the historic importance of the Anyuan Strike. Inspired and organized by Mao and other Chinese Communist Party leaders, 20,000 miners and 1,500 railway workers walked off their jobs on September 14, 1922. They demanded higher wages, better working conditions, and above all recognition for their workers club or union. Management capitulated just five days later, producing a landmark victory for the workers and the newly formed Chinese Community Party.

"LIKE A RISING SUN"

Liu deliberately placed a youthful and idealized image of Mao in the center of his painting. Mao advances toward the viewer "like a rising sun bringing hope to the people." This heroic image reinforced Mao's most admired qualities. His clenched left fist provides a vivid reminder of Mao's iron will. The old umbrella under his right arm emphasized Mao's plain living and willingness to endure adverse weather conditions as he travelled great distances to promote the revolutionary cause.

Liu focused particular attention on Mao's facial expression. Although he faces a daunting challenge, Mao projects an aura of confidence and determination. Liu later explained that he strove "for an expression of Chairman Mao's broad proletarian outlook, his youthful vigor, his complete dedication to the affairs of the country."

Liu achieved his goal of creating an indelible image of "the heroic spirit of Chairman Mao in his youth." Party officials quickly recognized the work's importance as a tool for shaping public opinion. They used color lithography to produce an estimated 900 million copies of a ubiquitous image that became the Cultural Revolution's most iconic work of art.

A NEW MANDATE OF HEAVEN

The Cultural Revolution deliberately and often destructively rejected Chinese artistic traditions. As an ardent member of the Red Guards, Liu did not view *Chairman Mao en Route to Anyuan* as a traditional artistic vehicle to promote meditation. Instead he created it instead to inspire veneration for a great Chinese leader.

Despite the Cultural Revolution's commitment to change, Liu's painting conveys a message deeply rooted in Chinese history. The Chinese believed that legitimate rulers enjoyed divine approval known as the Mandate of Heaven. Mao's successful leadership during the Anyuan strike provided convincing evidence that he was destined to receive the Mandate of Heaven.

MAKING CONNECTIONS

ART AS PROPAGANDA

PROPAGANDA is the deliberate use of biased information to promote a particular individual, political cause, or point of view. Varvara Stepanova's *Illustrations from the Result of the First Five-Year Plan* (Image 137) closely parallels Liu's *Chairman Mao en Route to Anyuan*. Both works use propagandist techniques to glorify totalitarian rulers. Designed to illustrate the success of Stalin's First Five-Year Plan, Stepanova's photomontage includes an oversized image of Vladimir Lenin, the founder of the Soviet Union. Like Liu, Stepanova ignores the use of violence and terror to promote communist ideology.

Content Area 9

THE PACIFIC

THE PACIFIC

Content Area 9 includes 11 works created between 1600 B.C.E. and 1953 C.E. The artists, architects, weavers, and sculptors in Oceania produced a wide variety of exceptional works.

Our unit presents the 11 works in this content area in the chronological order provided in the College Board's AP Art History Framework. This organization will enable you to quickly find a specific work of art.

The College Board encourages teachers and students to arrange the works in a wide variety of meaningful topical categories. Here are several possible arrangements:

MICRONESIA

Image 213: Nan Madol
Image 217: Female deity
Image 221: Navigation chart

MELANESIA

Image 218: Buk (mask)
Image 220: *Tamati Waka Nene*
Image 222: *Malagan* display and mask

POLYNESIA

Image 214: Moai on platform (*ahu*)
Image 215: 'Ahu 'ula (feather cape)
Image 216: Staff god
Image 219: *Hiapo* (tapa)
Image 213: Presentation of Fijian mats and tapa cloths to Queen Elizabeth II

MASKS

Image 218: Buk (mask)
Image 222: *Malagan* display and mask

THE POWER OF BELIEF

Image 214: Moai on platform (*ahu*)
Image 217: Female deity
Image 218: Buk (mask)
Image 222: *Malagan* display and mask

SACRED OBJECTS AND RITUAL PERFORMANCES

Image 216: Staff god
Image 217: Female deity
Image 218: Buk (mask)
Image 222: *Malagan* display and mask

CLOTH AND CLOTH MAKING

Image 219: *Hiapo* (tapa)
Image 223: Presentation of Fijian mats and tapa Cloths to Queen Elizabeth II

IMAGES OF POWER AND AUTHORITY

Image 213: Nan Madol
Image 214: Moai on platform (*ahu*)
Image 220: *Tamati Waka Nene*

APPLIED ART

Image 219: *Hiapo* (tapa)
Image 220: *Tamati Waka Nene*
Image 221: Navigation chart

OBJECTS OF POWER AND AUTHORITY

Image: 215: 'Ahu 'ula (feather cape)
Image 223: Presentation of Fijian mats and tapa cloths to Queen Elizabeth II

Robert Harding / Alamy Stock Photo

IMAGE 213

Nan Madol

Pohnpei, Micronesia

Saudeleur Dynasty

c. 1100-1600 C.E.

Basalt boulders and prismatic columns

Nan Madol is an abandoned city located on Pohnpei, a remote Micronesian island northeast of New Guinea. The ancient ruins reveal an engineering marvel. They comprise almost 100 stone and coral fill platforms, built atop artificial islets connected by narrow canals and protected by high seawalls. At its peak between 1200 and 1600 C.E., Nan Madol served as the ceremonial and political center for the ruling Saudeleur Dynasty. The surviving ruins pose still-unanswered questions about how architects built these remarkable stone structures.

THE SAUDELEUR DYNASTY

According to a well-known Pohnpeian legend, the Saudeleur Dynasty began with the arrival of Olisihpa and Olosohpa, twin brothers who were sorcerers from another island. Aided by flying dragons, the brothers levitated huge boulders to construct an altar dedicated to an important god of agriculture. After Olisihpa died of old age, Olosopha married a local woman and founded the Saudeleur Dynasty.

Olosopha's successors quickly asserted their authority over the entire island. They rewarded an aristocratic class with land and then demanded tribute of fresh fish and fruit from the large class of landless commoners. This stratified social structure supported the earliest known example of a centralized political system in the western Pacific.

BUILDING NAN MADOL

Pohnpei's remote island location meant that its Saudeleur rulers did not have to devote scarce resources to maintaining a strong military. Instead, they concentrated upon building a unique capital city complex for themselves. Recent uranium series dating indicates that major building projects began between 1180 and 1200 C.E.

Many unresolved mysteries still surround the construction of Nan Madol. Work crews carved basalt stones from volcanic plugs. They somehow transported boulders, ranging between five and fifty tons, from the mountain quarries to the coral reef lagoon at Nan Madol. Engineers and their workers accomplished this remarkable feat without the benefit of large animals, pulleys, or metal levers. Archaeologists believe Pohnpei crews used palm trunks to lever the massive stones into position.

Like the architects at Great Zimbabwe (Image 167) and Machu Picchu (Image 161), the Nan Madol builders did not use concrete. Instead, they utilized a distinctive crisscrossing pattern of horizontal basalt logs called STRETCHERS laid on top of perpendicular basalt logs called HEADERS. Then they used coral to fill in the floor and middle layers. A series of thick seawalls protected Nan Madol from Pacific storm surges. This enormous building project required centuries to complete.

LIFE IN NAN MADOL

The name Nan Madol means "spaces between." It refers to the canals that link the islets. However, the city's 1,000 inhabitants described their home as *Soun Nan-leng*, the "Reef of Heaven." For the city's elite group of rulers, Nan Madol must have indeed seemed like a heavenly reef. They enjoyed living in luxurious palaces surrounded by obedient servants. In order to control potential rivals, the Saudeleurs forced local chiefs to move to Nan Madol where their activities could be closely monitored. Five centuries later, Louis XIV used the same strategy at his newly opened Versailles Palace (Image 93).

Nan Madol contained more than palaces for the rich and powerful; it also included a variety of specialized islets. For example, some islets contained facilities for holding sacred eels, constructing canoes, and preparing coconut oil for ceremonial anointing at important rituals. The Saudeleurs reserved the largest and most prominent islet for a massive royal mortuary compound. A group of specially trained priests conducted elaborate ceremonies within this walled enclosure.

THE COLLAPSE OF SAUDELEUR POWER

The Saudeleur Dynasty ruled Pohnpei for at least five centuries. According to local oral history, increasingly oppressive rulers placed an unbearable burden upon the people. Even worse, the Saudeleurs offended the Thunder God. Aided by this powerful deity, the people rebelled. Although the last Saudeleur ruler desperately tried to cling to his power, the insurrection finally toppled the dynasty in 1628.

The new rulers of Pohnpei lived in Nan Madol for a short time before moving inland and abandoning the city. The Saudeleurs left future generations no written records or artistic carvings. Now partly covered by the jungle, Nan Madol's crumbling basalt ruins stand as impressive but silent monuments to a mysterious city built upon coral reefs.

MAKING CONNECTIONS

NAN MADOL AND THE GREAT PYRAMIDS

Absolute rulers committed significant resources to build Nan Madol and the Great Pyramids (Image 17). The Saudeleurs and pharaohs demonstrated little regard for the welfare of their people. Instead, they used their monuments to glorify themselves and preserve their entombed remains. Architects at Nan Madol and Giza both transported massive stones without the aid of pulleys or mechanical levers. Their engineering techniques remain a mystery that still puzzles archaeologists.

Alberto Loyo / Shutterstock.com

IMAGE 214

Moai on platform (*ahu*)

Rapa Nui (Easter Island)

c. 1100–1600 C.E.

Volcanic tuff figures on basalt bases

Rapa Nui is one of the most remote inhabited spots on the globe. This tiny island is located in the South Pacific, more than 1,200 miles east of Pitcairn Island and 2,300 miles west of Chile. The prehistoric people who lived on this isolated island carved and moved almost 900 enormous stone statues. Known as MOAI, these monolithic figures have baffled generations of archaeologists who have attempted to resolve their many mysteries.

THE GREAT MONOLITHS OF RAPA NUI

According to Rapa Nuian oral histories, Polynesian explorers led by Hotu Matu'a discovered and settled Rapa Nui. The colonizers may have reached the island as early as 800 C.E. However, recent radio carbon dating places their arrival closer to 1200 C.E. Regardless of when they arrived, the settlers brought a well-established tradition of carving wooden and stone figures. But sculptures on no other Pacific island can match with the extraordinary size or number of the moai found on Rapa Nui.

The process of creating a moai began at a quarry located on the side of one of the island's three extinct volcanoes. Skilled carvers used stone tools to "awaken" the statues from the compressed volcanic ash. The average moai stood 12 feet tall and weighed 13 tons.

These imposing stone figures are all standing males. Large rectangular heads comprise one-third of each moai. The stylized heads include prominent foreheads, large staring eyes, long straight noses, and elongated earlobes. The moai have slender arms pressed close to each side. These huge blocky figures lack legs.

WALKING WITHOUT LEGS

The Rapa Nuians now faced a daunting challenge: how would they move the multi-ton moai from the quarry to specially prepared platforms, called *ahu*, located up to a dozen miles away? Modern investigators have proposed two competing possibilities. One group speculates that the Rapa Nuians used wooden sleds to push the horizontal statues along prepared paths. A second group offered a novel idea inspired by an ancient oral tradition—the stone giants walked to their platforms!

Archaeologists Terry Hunt and Carl Lipo did not dismiss the Rapa Nuian oral traditions. Instead, they conducted a carefully designed test. Hunt and Lipo began by commissioning a design firm to build an exact replica of a five-ton and ten-foot-tall moai. They then conducted a series of experiments in which 26 volunteers used ropes to rock, or "walk," the upright moai they named Hotu Matu'a. After a number of trials and errors, the teams learned how to use rhythmic pulls and twists to successfully move Hotu Matu'a along a prepared path. The experiment offered convincing evidence that the moai had indeed "walked without legs."

LIVING FACES

The journey from the quarry to an *ahu* platform did not complete the project. After erecting a moai, islanders inserted eyes of white coral with inlaid pupils of red or black rock. They sometimes capped the statue's head with topknots made of red stone weighing as much as ten tons.

Rapa Nui's early settlers called the completed statues *aringa ora* or "living faces." Endowed with a spiritual force called *MANA*, the moai represented honored ancestors. The vast majority of the moai did not face the ocean. Instead, they faced inland, intently watching over their descendants.

DECLINE AND REVIVAL

Archaeologists believe the Rapa Nuians carved most of the moai between 1200 and 1600 C.E. Like the contemporary European builders of Gothic cathedrals, they invested significant resources into a project deemed vital to the spiritual welfare of their community. Yet by 1680, the island plunged into a civil war. For reasons that remain unclear, the Rapa Nuians overturned all of their statues.

European explorers discovered Rapa Nui on Easter Sunday, 1722. As in North and South America, their arrival brought culture shock, exploitation, and worst of all deadly diseases. During the 1860s, Peruvian slave raiders kidnapped 1,500 Rapa Nuians, or about one-third of the island's population. Almost all of the Rapa Nuian captives died working in guano mines. A tiny group of survivors returned to their homes, only to infect the population with smallpox. Known as the Great Death, the epidemic reduced Rapa Nui's population to just 111 people. The island's moai now outnumbered the human population.

After centuries of decline, Rapa Nui is now experiencing a revival. A growing population and a dramatic increase in tourism have spurred economic growth. Over 100,000 tourists now visit the island to gaze in awe at the restored stone monuments.

MAKING CONNECTIONS

THE MOAI AND *THE KISS* BY BRANCUSI

The moai's anonymous sculptors and Constantin Brancusi share the common goal of trying to capture the essence of their subjects. To accomplish this objective, they both eliminated all unnecessary details. As a result, neither the moai nor *The Kiss* (Image 129) are realistic portraits of distinct individuals. For example, both works lack legs and specific facial features. Instead, the Rapa Nui sculptors used monumental block-like heads to portray the enduring power of their ancestors, while Brancusi used his much smaller block-like figures to portray the enduring power of love.

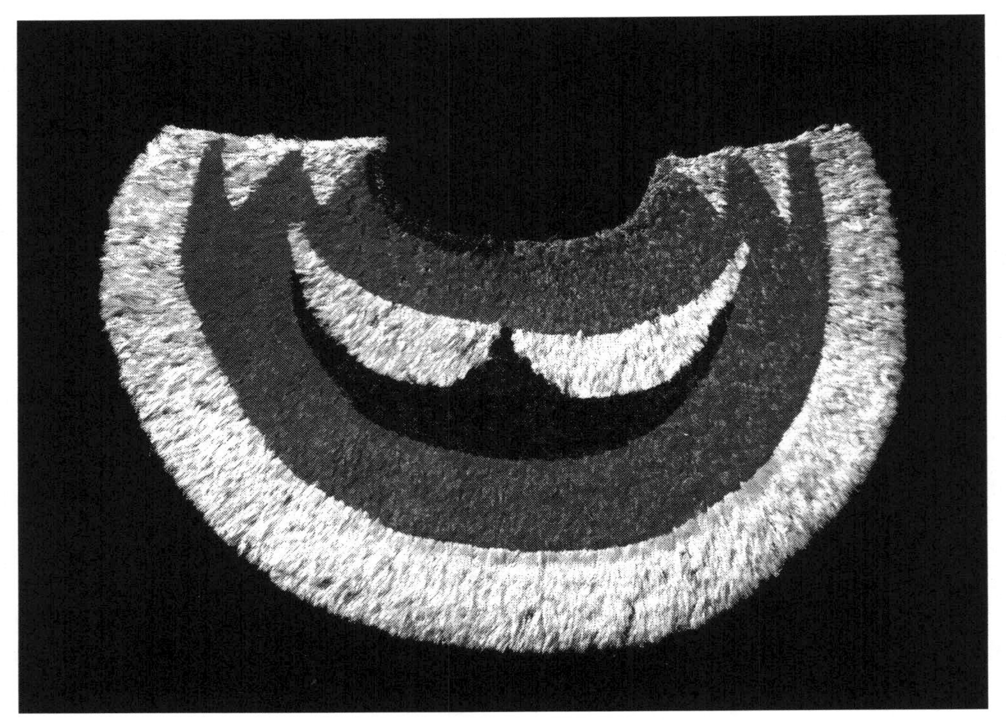

IMAGE 215

'Ahu 'ula (feather cape)

Hawaiian

Late 18th century C.E.

Feathers and fiber

A hereditary ruling elite known as the *ali'i* dominated Hawaii's social, political, and artistic life. Executed in brilliant sacred colors, the elaborate feathered cape featured in Image 215 signalled its owner's royal status. The cape served as more than an expensive status symbol; it also embodied key Hawaiian ideas about the continuing presence of ancestors and the protective power of their gods.

SHARKS THAT WALKED ON LAND

Hawaiian proverbs describe their elite rulers as sharks that walked on land. Genealogy assumed great importance in a culture that valued hereditary titles. A prized 'ahu 'ula created a vital link between the living and their ancestors.

The 'ahu 'ula manifests a great spiritual force called *MANA*. As a treasured royal possession, a feathered cape acquired more and more *mana* as it passed from one generation to the next. Worn by an eminent chief, an 'ahu 'ula conveyed a majestic image of awe-inspiring power that intimidated rivals and impressed followers.

BIRDS, FEATHERS, AND *MANA*

Throughout history, rulers have used coveted raw materials to display their power. For example, the obas of Benin commissioned brass plaques (Image 169), and the kings of Silla commissioned gold and jade crowns (Image 196). Similarly, Hawaiian chiefs turned to their most precious raw material—the feathers of rare birds.

Hawaiians viewed birds as spiritual messengers, capable of flying between the earthly and heavenly realms. This link between birds and gods made feathers sacred objects that could only be worn by members of the *ali'i*. Hawaiians assigned special symbolic value to specific colors. For example, red feathers represented royalty while yellow feathers indicated a prosperous future.

Creating a feathered cloak required a long and painstaking process. Skilled trappers caught tiny birds by snaring them midair with nets or by using decoy birds to lure them onto branches coated with a sticky substance. They then harvested a few prized feathers from each bird before releasing it. The relatively small cloak featured in Image 215 required thousands of feathers.

Specially trained male weavers attached tiny overlapping clusters of feathers to a plant fiber foundation. Each cloak had a distinctive geometric pattern, associated with a particular lineage. As weavers knotted cords, they recited prayers and chanted ancestral names. This ritual helped imbue the cloak with additional protective *mana*.

MULTIPLE FUNCTIONS

A completed 'ahu 'ula served a variety of functions. It signaled the wearer's high status at religious festivals and other important ceremonial occasions. Hawaiian chiefs also wore their dazzling feathered capes and similarly feathered helmets into battle. And finally, chiefs used their 'ahu 'ulas as ceremonial gifts. For example, when Chief Kalani' opu' u met the British explorer Captain James Cook, he took off his resplendent feathered cloak and wrapped it around his distinguished visitor's shoulders. The cloak is a celebrated cultural treasure that is now on display at the Bishop Museum in Honolulu, Hawaii.

MAKING CONNECTIONS

THE HAWAIIAN 'AHU 'ULA AND MOTECUHZOMA II'S FEATHER HEADDRESS

The Hawaiian chiefs and Aztec emperors prized rare bird feathers as symbols of their authority and links to their gods. Both cultures assigned high status to skilled feather artists. Motecuhzoma II's headdress (Image 158) featured 400 closely spaced iridescent green quetzal tail feathers. Like their Hawaiian counterparts, Aztec emperors used their elaborate headdresses as prestigious gifts. For example, Motecuhzoma II gifted his headdress to the Spanish conquistador Hernan Cortes. The original headdress can now be seen in the Museum of Ethnology in Vienna, Austria. An exact replica is on display in the National Museum of Anthropology in Mexico City, Mexico.

IMAGE 216

Staff god

Rarotonga, Cook Islands, Central Polynesia

Late 18th to early 19th century C.E.

Wood, tapa, fiber, and feathers

Rarotonga is located in the Cook Islands, northeast of New Zealand. Wood carvers working on the tiny volcanic island created a distinctive style of art. Image 216 is the only surviving example of a large wrapped staff god. The image offers a tantalizing but elusive glimpse into Rarotongan religious beliefs and the artistic roles of men and women.

TANGAROA AND THE LONDON MISSIONARY SOCIETY

The Rarotongan people believed that Tangaroa was the first god. He lived in a round shell shaped like an egg. Nothing existed but the shell and the outside world. Finally, Tangaroa broke his shell and called out, "Who's there?" But he neither saw nor heard any life. Tangaroa then began to create a family of gods.

The Rarotonga crafted many objects to honor Tangaroa. The 12-foot-long staff god illustrated in Image 216 may represent Tangaroa's head, spine, and body. The people of Rarotonga prominently displayed and worshipped their staff gods in outdoor courtyards.

Members of the London Missionary Society arrived in Rarotonga in 1827. Within a short time, they convinced the people to embrace Christianity and abandon their traditional religion. Encouraged by the missionaries, the people destroyed many of their staff gods. This profound change in the island's religious beliefs disrupted artistic production. As a result, much traditional knowledge has been irrevocably lost.

A LARGE HEAD AND SMALL FIGURES

The Rarotonga staff god consists of an elongated body topped by an elaborately carved head that may represent Tangaroa. The creator god's outsized head comprises about one-third of the wood carving. The god's smooth head features stylized large eyes along with a pointed chin and tightly closed mouth.

Rarotongan carvers positioned a line of smaller figures just below Tangaroa's head, This combination of small figures placed alongside a large figure is a characteristic motif of Polynesian art. Scholars believe the placement of the small figures suggests that they are positioned along vertebrae, symbolizing genealogical continuity. The line of alternate male and female images could represent Tangaroa's children. The frontal females may represent women in childbirth, while the males shown in profile may represent important ancestors. Taken together, this image reinforces

Tangaroa's important role as a god of fertility.

A LONG SHAFT WRAPPED IN BARKCLOTH

Thick layers of barkcloth conceal the remainder of the staff god. The wrapping served a variety of functions. First and foremost, it protects and contains the deity's spiritual force, or *MANA*. If for any reason the islanders removed the wrapping, the deity would leave, rendering the staff god useless. In addition, the barkcloth provides the god with clothing, since it would be inappropriate for a deity to be seen naked.

MALE AND FEMALE CONTRIBUTIONS

The process of creating a staff god required a unique combination of distinctive male and female contributions. Male carvers created the staff god's head, miniature figures, and wooden core. They also carved a large phallus, originally placed at the end of the figure. The phallus may have represented Tangaroa's role as a divinity responsible for creation and thus sexual reproduction. However, the phallus symbols offended the missionaries and they forced the islanders to remove them.

Highly skilled women weavers also played a vital role by creating the barkcloth that covered the staff god's central core. Producing barkcloth required a demanding series of steps. See Image 219 for a discussion explaining how weavers on Niue created barkcloth.

MAKING CONNECTIONS

THE IMPORTANCE OF *MANA* IN OCEANIC ART

Mana is a key Oceanic concept indicating a special power or spiritual force that can be invested in objects or people. For example, the staff god's *mana* was so great that it required a protective cover of barkcloth. *Mana* can also be associated with important leaders. For example, the Maori chief Tamati Waka Nene (Image 220) also possessed great *mana*.

Werner Forman Archive / Bridgeman Images

IMAGE 217

Female deity

Nukuoro, Micronesia

c. 18th to 19th century C. E.

Wood

The Nukuoro Atoll is a ring of 46 tiny islets that surround a lagoon in Micronesia. First inhabited between 800 and 1000 C.E., the atoll's abundant crops and rich sea life have nourished a population of about 400 people. Despite its remote location and small population, the atoll has supported generations of exceptionally creative carvers, who sculpted widely admired wooden figures of their gods and deified ancestors. Image 217 provides an example of Nukuoro's unique artistic tradition.

SPIRIT HOUSES

Five clans dominated religious life on Nukuoro. Each clan maintained its own religious building and cult objects. The entire population worshipped in a large community spirit house called an *amalau*.

Today we appreciate works of Pacific art for their aesthetic beauty. However, like other Pacific islanders, the people of Nukuoro created their statues to be used and not just viewed. For example, Image 217 may have occupied a special spot along one of the walls of the rectangular *amalau*. Priests adorned the statue with flowers and special headdresses. They expressed gratitude to their gods and ancestors by organizing festive parades to celebrate a bountiful harvest.

A RARE FEMALE DEITY

An unknown Nukuoroan master sculptor carved Image 217 sometime before 1830. He used the light but sturdy wood from a breadfruit tree. Although Nukuoro statues range in height from one to seven feet, they all follow an established artistic canon.

The female deity portrayed in Image 217 stands under 16 inches tall. The sculptor skillfully draws the viewer's eye upward to the statue's head, the seat of its *MANA*, or spiritual energy. Her ovoid or egg-shaped head lacks distinctive facial features. The Nukuoro artist followed a canon that did not use representational proportions. For example, the figure's truncated legs support an elongated torso. Simple incised lines suggest the statue's chest and pubic area.

The Nukuoro statues convey a sense of strength, designed to awe viewers. Only 37 of the statues still exist. Their simplified abstract form deeply impressed early modern sculptors such as Constantin Brancusi (Image 129) and Alberto Giacometti.

MAKING CONNECTIONS

NUKUORO FEMALE DEITY AND ATHENIAN PEPLOS KORE

The Nukuoro female deity and the Athenian Peplos Kore (Image 28) present strikingly different portraits of female deities. Although both sculptors employed vertical poses, the draped Kore conveys a more rounded, naturalistic female form. The Kore's Archaic smile and soft flesh give the statue a much more lifelike appearance than the Nukuoro female deity.

IMAGE 218

Buk (mask)

Torres Strait

Mid-to late 19th century C.E.
Wood

The shallow waters of the Torres Strait separate Australia and the Melanesia island of New Guinea. The strait includes a maze of reefs, extensive beds of seagrass, and 274 small islands. Scholars believe that skilled artists living on the island of Wabuiag created the complex mask depicted in Image 218. The mask's distinctive appearance makes it one of the most admired works of Oceanic art.

A COMPLEX CONTRUCTION

Torres Strait mask makers created works like Image 218 for centuries. They began the painstaking construction process by heating individual plates from the shells of hawksbill sea turtles and then bending them into a desired shape. After completing this critical step, artists pierced holes along the outer edge of each plate. This enabled them to use fiber to stitch the plates together and assemble them into a three-dimensional sculptural image. The maskmakers completed the construction process by adding decorative shells, feathers, and hair to accentuate the eyes, mouth, and wig.

A COMPOSITE FORM

Image 218 presents a ceremonial mask called buk. This unique work is a distinctive combination of a human face crowned by a soaring frigate bird. The human face may represent a revered ancestor or a legendary cultural hero. For example, many Torres Strait masks celebrate the exploits of Kwoian, a great warrior renowned for his many conquests.

The frigate bird may serve as Kwoian's personal totem or emblem. The black seabird's striking features include a distinctive forked tail, an elongated hooked beak, and a long wingspan. Like eagles in American art and culture, the soaring frigate suggests great strength and nobility.

MULTIPLE FUNCTIONS

Scholars believe masks like the buk featured in Image 218 played an integral role in the ceremonial life of the Torres Strait islanders. Important uses included male initiation and funerary rites as well as rituals associated with hunting and warfare. The mask also enhanced increase rites performed to assure bountiful harvests and an abundant supply of fish and game.

Male dancers performed during elaborate ceremonies illuminated by campfire lights. The performers wore masks, fitted over their heads like a helmet. The steady beat of sacred drums provided a rhythm for dancers wearing grass costumes. This combination of awe-inspiring masks and pounding drums must have impressed, instructed, and even terrified onlookers.

MAKING CONNECTIONS

BUK AND TRANSFORMATION MASKS

Skilled artists created the buk and transformation (Image 164) masks to facilitate access to supernatural powers. Both masks feature a composite structure that includes human faces and powerful animals. The frigate bird in the buk mask and the eagle in the transformation mask gave their wearers access to totemic spiritual powers.

Hiapo, Niue. (1886). Auckland War Memorial Museum Tāmaki Paenga Hira. 30088.

IMAGE 219

Hiapo (tapa)
Niue

c. 1850–1900 C.E.
Tapa or barkcloth
Freehand painting

Niue is a small Polynesian island country, located 1,500 miles northeast of New Zealand. Its position near Tonga, Samoa, and the Cook Islands exposed it to increasingly frequent encounters with traders and Christian missionaries. During the second half of the 19th century, Niuean women created a distinctive style of barkcloth or tapa, illustrated by the fine lines and intricate geometric designs in Image 219.

MAKING BARKCLOTH

The art of making barkcloth fabric is a distinctive part of Pacific culture. The process is performed almost entirely by women. Unlike the silk and wool Ardabil carpet (Image 191) and the camelid fiber and cotton All-T'oqapu tunic (Image 162), barkcloth is not a woven material. Instead, it is manufactured from the soft inner bark of the paper mulberry tree.

The arduous process of creating fine barkcloth requires many steps. Once harvested, the mulberry tree's outer bark is separated from its inner fiber. A process of soaking and repeated beating with a heavy wooden mallet transforms the inner fiber into thin, flat strips of barkcloth. In a procedure called felting, these pieces are beaten together and combined into long, plain sheets.

Once the felting is completed, the widened barkcloth is ready for dying. Skilled women stamp, stencil, or paint designs onto the cloth. Dyes come from earth pigments and a variety of berries and plants. The final result is a beautiful and sophisticated work of art.

A DISTINCTIVE BUT ELUSIVE NIUEAN STYLE

Hiapo is the word for barkcloth, or tapa, in the Niuean language. Christian missionaries introduced barkcloth to Niue in the 1830s. Within 50 years Niueans developed a distinctive decorative style.

Image 219 illustrates a Niuean *hiapo* design. The cloth is 8 feet long and 6.5 feet wide. Talented female artists used a black dye to decorate this *hiapo* by hand. Their intricate pattern includes a complex combination of geometric and botanical motifs, placed within a circular form. The triangles, squares, and diamonds diminish in size as they approach the center.

The meaning and symbolism of these motifs is elusive. In a careful study of Niuean *hiapo*, John Pule and Nicholas

Thomas conclude that, "The written and illustrative source material relating to the culture and history of Niue is unusually sparse and fragmented." This "poverty of facts" continued into the 20th century. Niuean women discontinued production of their distinctive *hiapo* by the early 1900s. No *hiapo* has been made on Niue since the 1930s.

A WIDE RANGE OF FUNCTIONS

Like other Polynesian barkcloths, Niuean *hiapo* performed a wide range of functions. As a highly prized form of clothing, *hiapo* often served as signs of status and prosperity. High-ranking individuals wore their decorated cloths at every important stage of their lives. For example, parents would wrap their newborn children in a *hiapo*, suggesting the close relationship between an individual and his or her clothing. In addition, Niueans wore *hiapo* at ritual ceremonies, exchanged them at rites of passage such as marriages, and used them to wrap sacred objects.

MAKING CONNECTIONS

THE *HIAPO* AND THE ALL-T'OQAPU TUNIC

Highly skilled women created both the Niuean *hiapo* and the Inka All-T'oqapu tunic (Image 162). Each cloth required a significant commitment of time and a major investment of natural resources. Both objects included an intricate pattern of geometric designs whose meaning is no longer fully understood. And finally, *hiapo* were typically created for high-status individuals, while the All-T'oqapu was created for the Inka ruler.

PAINTING / Alamy Stock Photo

IMAGE 220

Tamati Waka Nene

Gottfried Lindauer

1890 C.E.

Oil on canvas

Gottfried Lindauer was born in 1839 in Pilsen, Bohemia. He studied art at the prestigious Academy of Fine Arts in Vienna. Lindauer immigrated to New Zealand in 1874 to avoid compulsory military service and to win commissions for his specialty as a portraitist. Within a short time, he began painting a compelling series of finely detailed images of indigenous Maori leaders. Image 220 captures both the likeness and *MANA* of Tamati Waka Nene, a renowned Maori warrior and peacemaker, whose life story illustrates the tumultuous changes that took place in 19th-century New Zealand.

THE MAORI BEFORE CONTACT

Sometime between 1200 and 1300 C.E., a people later known as Maori discovered and settled New Zealand. They soon divided into tribes linked to a common ancestor. Although they lived in separate tribes, the Maori developed a distinctive culture that included a belief in the importance of *mana* as a force that invested a person with power and prestige. In addition, Maori culture placed special importance on using complex tattoos to adorn their faces.

THE BRITISH ARRIVE

Captain James Cook explored the New Zealand coastline in 1769. By the early 1800s, British traders and missionaries began regular visits to New Zealand. The missionaries introduced the Maori to the spiritual power of Christianity, while the traders introduced the Maori to the military power of guns.

Maori chiefs coveted guns known as muskets. The new weapons soon ignited an intertribal arms race among chiefs determined to gain territory and avenge past grievances. A series of 3,000 battles known as the Musket Wars claimed between 20,000 and 40,000 Maori lives.

British officials attempted to restore order by inviting Maori chiefs to sign a treaty with the Crown. Known as the Treaty of Waitangi, the agreement made New Zealand a British colony. However, the treaty did not end tensions over disputed land purchases. Thousands of British troops finally overpowered the Maori and firmly established the Crown's authority over New Zealand.

TAMATI WAKA NENE—WARRIOR AND PEACEMAKER

The upheavals that shook Maori society during the 19th century had a profound effect on Tamati Waka Nene. During the Musket Wars, Nene distinguished himself as a ruthless and successful warrior. As a result, he became one of New Zealand's most powerful chiefs.

Nene understood the turbulent changes taking place in New Zealand. For example, he protected the Wesleyan missionaries and was baptized into their faith in 1839. He took the name Tamati Waka after Thomas Walker, a prominent British merchant and patron of the Church Missionary Society.

Nene proved to be a successful leader in both war and peace. He played a pivotal role in persuading Maori chiefs to accept the historic Treaty of Waitangi by convincingly arguing that resisting the British presence in New Zealand was futile. During the tense years following the treaty, British officials frequently turned to Nene for advice. When the aging chief died on August 4, 1871, the royal governor praised Nene as a leader who "did more than any other...to establish the Queen's authority and promote colonization."

THE ARTIST AND THE CHIEF

Gottfried Lindauer arrived in New Zealand in 1874, three years after Nene's death. Supported by a wealthy patron, he immersed himself in Maori culture. Lindauer's many life-sized and lifelike portraits form a unique pictorial record of Maori culture during the late 19th and early 20th centuries.

Lindauer began work on a portrait of Tamati Waka Nene in 1890. Although he had never met Nene, Lindauer located a newspaper photograph of the famous chief. He then used the photograph to help guide his portrait. This integration of photography and art characterized many of Lindauer's portraits.

Lindauer chose to portray Nene in traditional Maori garb. The great chief thus wears a fine cloak covered in kiwi feathers. A valuable greenstone earring dangles from his right earlobe. Lindauer reaffirms Nene's status as a warrior by prominently positioning a *tewhatewha* hand weapon in his right hand. The artist devoted particular care to painting Nene's intricate facial tattoo, or *moko*. The swirling tattoo conveys information about Nene's lofty status, impressive clan connections, and powerful *mana*.

MAKING CONNECTIONS

TAMATI WAKA NENE AND GEORGE WASHINGTON

Gottfried Lindauer painted his portrait of Tamati Waka Nene at the same time that the French sculptor Jean-Antoine Houdon carved his statue of George Washington (Image 104). Although the two artists worked in very different mediums, they faced the similar challenge of deciding how to portray famous figures who experienced dramatic changes in their personal identities. For example, Nene was a warrior who learned to negotiate with the British. In contrast, Washington abandoned diplomacy and chose to lead a successful rebellion against the Crown. Lindauer resolved his challenge by portraying Nene as a warrior chief who projected great *mana*. Houdon resolved his challenge by portraying Washington as a retired general who projected great *gravitas*, or personal dignity. The two artists thus created convincing portraits by allowing their subjects to embody esteemed cultural values.

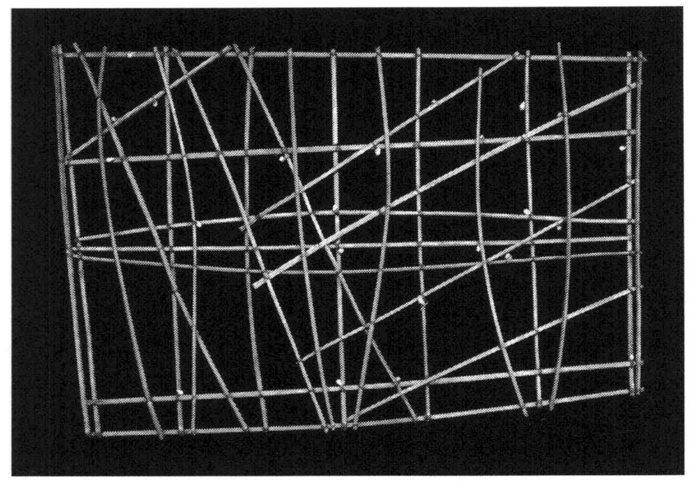

IMAGE 221

Navigation chart

Marshall Islands, Micronesia

19th to early 20th century C.E.

Wood and fiber

The Marshall Islands include tiny dots of land surrounded by the vast waters of the Pacific Ocean. The presence of successful communities on these islands baffled European explorers. Seasoned sea captains could not explain how "primitive" island navigators could discover and explore widely scattered islands without the aid of compasses, sextants, and detailed maps. The seemingly random sticks and shells in Image 221 provide a surprising explanation that offers insights into the unique skills of Marshall Island navigators.

TINY ISLANDS AND A VAST OCEAN

The Marshall Islands are located about 2,300 miles southwest of Honolulu, Hawaii. The island group includes 29 atolls with roughly 1,200 islets, spread across 750,000 square miles of ocean. While outsiders might view the ocean as a barrier, the Marshallese have always viewed it as a unifying part of their daily lives. However, reaching the low-lying islands poses a special problem, since they cannot be seen from a distance. This forced expert Marshallese navigators known as *ri-metos* to develop a unique understanding of the ocean.

READING THE OCEAN

The ability of Marshallese *ri-metos* to navigate across hundreds of miles of open waters stems from their skill in understanding the movement of ocean swells. Weather systems from as far away as Alaska, California, and Antarctica generate swells or moving waves that can travel thousands of miles. Marshallese navigators understood that when a swell strikes a low-lying island, some of the wave's energy reflects back in arcs of water.

A highly experienced *ri-meto* could observe or even feel the pattern of swells bouncing back from an island. This ability to read the ocean enabled a *ri-meto* to fix his nautical position. The master navigator could then steer his vessel into a reflective swell and thus reach the island that caused it.

STICK CHARTS

Master Marchallese navigators created a variety of stick charts to symbolically display their understanding of how islands disrupt swells and create wave patterns. Some of the charts represented a large geographic area while others focused on the waters around specific islands. Still other stick charts functioned as tools to help young apprentices understand the principles of how swells interact with islands.

Ri-metos jealously guarded the knowledge contained in their stick charts. They even threatened to kill anyone who revealed their secrets! Navigators memorized their charts before departing on a voyage. Safely stored with their family, the stick chart remained a prized possession that fathers only shared with their sons.

MAKING CONNECTIONS

A NAVIGATION CHART AND A LUKASA

A Marshall Island navigation chart and a Mbudye Society *lukasa* (Image 177) both store vital information. The objects provide abstract designs that function as mnemonic devices for highly skilled *ri-metos* and Luba "men of memory." The ability to "read" these conceptual guides provides each elite group of specialists with great status and influence.

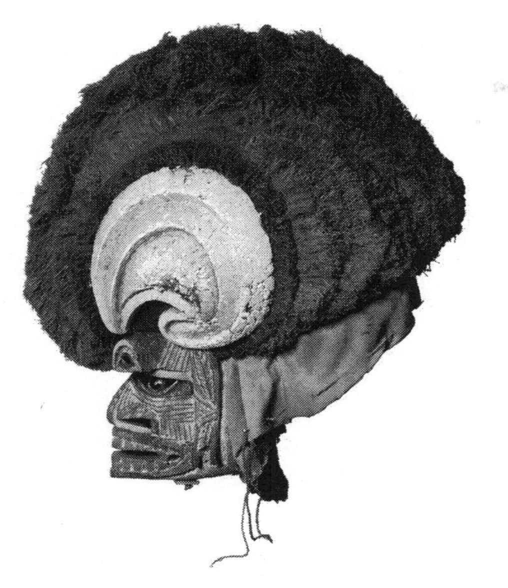

University Museum, Pennsylvania, PA, USA / Photo © AISA / Bridgeman Images

IMAGE 222

Malagan display and mask

Papua New Guinea

c. 20th century C.E.

Wood, pigment, fiber, and shell

New Ireland is a large island province in Papua New Guinea. Islanders are renowned for staging elaborate ceremonies to honor recently deceased clan members. The term *MALAGAN* refers to both the festivities and to sculpture carved for the event. The striking *malagan* carvings and mask illustrated in Image 222 are among the most memorable sculptures in Oceanic art.

PURPOSE AND PREPARATION

The *malagan* ceremony includes a complex set of rituals designed to facilitate the transition of a soul from the world of the living to the realm of the dead. The ceremony does more than just evoke grief for the dead, however. It also includes rites to initiate young men into adulthood. The *malagan* thus reinforces a community's spiritual and social ties.

Malagan activities require months and even years of meticulous planning. Farmers must prepare for large feasts by planting extra crops and raising additional pigs. At the same time, organizers choreograph dances, hire carvers, and build a special ceremonial house.

SPECTACULAR BUT EPHEMERAL

The process of creating *malagan* sculptures begins in secret. Workers cut down trees noted for a soft, lightweight wood that lends itself to detailed carving. They then cover the logs with leaves to protect them from the forbidden eyes of women. Next they carry the concealed wood to a special enclosure, where an expert carver and his assistants spend months crafting a variety of statues.

The completed sculptures remain hidden while guests enjoy days of dancing, feasting, and singing. At a climactic moment, the organizers dramatically unveil a line of statues arranged in front of a newly built ceremonial house. The statues do not represent specific individuals. Instead, they honor spirits associated with supernatural beings and ancestors.

The *malagan* display is created for a spectacular but fleeting moment. Once seen, the exhibit frees the living from their obligation to the dead. The no longer needed sculptures can then be discarded or sold to foreign collectors.

TATANUA MASKS

Specially costumed *tatanua* dancers provide an emotional concluding performance. Derived from the word for spirit or soul, *tatanua* refers to both a dance and to distinctive helmet-like masks. Although no two *tatanua* masks are alike, they all contain prominent open mouths and a prominent asymmetrical hair design. The bald sides represent how a New Ireland man shaves his head to show his grief. The ceremonial dance provides a tangible display of unity and a restored feeling of vitality.

MAKING CONNECTIONS

FUNERAL RITUALS IN NEW IRELAND AND AMONG THE ANCIENT ETRUSCANS

The New Ireland islanders and the ancient Etruscans both used funeral rituals to mark the transition of the deceased from the world of the living to that of the dead. The wall paintings in the Tomb of the Triclinium (Image 32) reveal that Etruscan funerals were festive occasions that included banquets, music, and dances reminiscent of those in the New Ireland *malagan* ceremonies.

Courtesy of Alexander Turnbull Library, Wellington, New Zealand

IMAGE 223

Presentation of Fijian mats and tapa cloths to Queen Elizabeth II
Fiji, Polynesia

1953 C.E.
Multimedia performance, photographic documentation

Queen Elizabeth II visited Fiji and Tonga in December 1953. Both of these small Polynesian islands staged elaborate ceremonies to welcome the Queen. Image 223 shows a procession of Fiji women presenting Elizabeth II with specially prepared mats. Two days later, Queen Salote of Tonga presented the British monarch with an extraordinary tapa. The use of tapa for important ceremonial gifts underscores the role of female artists in the cultural traditions of both islands.

SAME TAPA BUT DIFFERENT NAMES

The art of making tapa or barkcloth is a distinctive part of Polynesian culture. Although the process of manufacturing the fabric is the same, local names for tapa vary from island to island. In Fiji, for example, tapa is called *masi*, whereas in Tonga it is called *ngati*.

Tapa is created from the bark of the paper mulberry tree. Custom dictates that men tend to the trees. However, once men have harvested the trees, only women may turn the soft inner bark into a finished fabric.

Skilled female artisans begin the arduous production process by cutting the soft bark into strips. They then use a heavy wooden mallet to transform the fabric into thin, flat strips. In a procedure called felting, women beat the pieces together to form long plain sheets. Once the felting is completed, female artists imprint a design onto the cloth. They often enhance the fabric by adding extra decorations.

Tapa serves a variety of functions. Artisans use it to make cloth, sheets, capes, and even kites. They also use tapa as a gift for weddings, feasts and important ceremonial events.

FIJI—"A GREAT DAY INDEED"

Queen Elizabeth II arrived at Suva, the capital of Pacific island nation of Fiji on December 17, 1953. The islanders initially welcomed the Queen with silence—a traditional sign of great respect. The silent welcome continued as Elizabeth's motorcade reached Albert Park in the center of Suva. As required by custom, an official presented Elizabeth II with a polished coconut cup filled with kava, a bitter drink made by mixing the pounded roots of a pepper plant with fresh water. The completion of the ceremonial drinking broke the silence and signaled the beginning of an afternoon filled with songs and dances.

A news reporter later described the festivities in Albert Park as "a great day indeed." Scholars do not know when the photographer took the photograph featured in Image 223. The image captures a procession of women wearing beautifully decorated *masi* skirts. The women are carrying rolls of woven mats that they will present to Queen Elizabeth II. Although the picture does not show the mats, we do know that they featured beautiful geometric designs.

TONGA—"THE FRIENDLY ISLANDS"

Queen Elizabeth left Fiji on December 19th. She then flew 460 miles to Nuku'alofa, the capital of Tonga. Living up to Tonga's reputation as "The Friendly Islands," the island kingdom's beloved Queen Salote extended Elizabeth II a warm welcome. The two queens enjoyed a lavish banquet featuring the island's best fresh fruits and fish. They then watched carefully choreographed traditional dances. Queen Elizabeth even "met" Tu'I Malila, the famed female tortoise Captain James Cook gave to the Tongan royal family.

NGATU LAUNIMA

Tongan artists prepared an extraordinary *ngatu launima* for the royal visit. *Ngatu* is Tongan barkcloth, and the term *launima* indicates the piece's length. The specially made *ngatu* reached an impressive length of 74.6 feet with a width of 14.2 feet. The design featured Elizabeth's royal initials, "ERII."

The *ngatu launima* later played a much more somber role in Tongan history. After suffering a long illness, Salote passed away in a New Zealand hospital in 1965. The royal party placed the famed *ngatu launima* under her coffin as a plane returned her body to Tonga. Visitors can now see the historic *ngatu launima* at the Te Papa Museum in Wellington, New Zealand.

MAKING CONNECTIONS

THE ROLE OF FEMALE WEAVERS IN POLYNESIA AND ANCIENT ATHENS

Polynesian and ancient Athenian societies prized their highly skilled female weavers. Female artists created the fine tapa fabric created for Queen Elizabeth's historic visits. Athenian women performed a similar role by creating the peplos that adorned the gold-and-ivory statue of *Athena Parthenos* in the Parthenon (Image 35).

Content Area 10

GLOBAL CONTEMPORARY

GLOBAL CONTEMPORARY

Content Area 10 includes 27 works created between 1980 and 2000. The artists and architects who produced these works represent a wide diversity of nationalities and ethnicities. As participants in the digital age, they often utilized technological advances ranging from video monitors to sophisticated computer programs. Taken together, the Global Contemporary works include a wide variety of styles ranging from sociopolitical critiques to reflections on the natural world.

Our unit presents the 27 Global Contemporary works in the chronological order provided in the College Board's AP Art History Framework. This organization will enable you to quickly find a specific work of art. It is important to stress that the Global Contemporary works cannot be neatly packaged into a few mutually exclusive categories. Indeed, many of the works can be placed in multiple groupings. The College Board encourages teachers and students to arrange the works in a wide variety of meaningful topical categories. Here are 12 possible arrangements:

INSTALLATIONS

Image 224: *The Gates*
Image 229: *The Book from the Sky*
Image 236: *En la Barberia no se Llora*
Image 238: *Electronic Superhighway*
Image 239: *The Crossing*
Image 244: *The Swing (after Fragonard)*
Image 248: *Shibboleth*

POLITICAL PROTEST ART

Image 229: *The Book from the Sky*
Image 233: *Trade (Gifts for Trading Land with White People)*
Image 235: *Rebellious Silence*
Image 237: *Pisupo Lua Afe (Corned Beef 2000)*
Image 248: *Shibboleth*
Image 250: *Kui Hua Zi (Sunflower Seeds)*

IMMERSIVE INVOLVEMENT

Image 225: Vietnam Veterans Memorial
Image 236: *En la Barberia no se Llora*
Image 238: *Electronic Superhighway*
Image 243: *Darkytown Rebellion*
Image 244: *The Swing (after Fragonard)*

FEMINIST ART

Image 231: *Untitled (#228)*
Image 235: *Rebellious Silence*
Image 242: *Lying with the Wolf*
Image 247: *Preying Mantra*

RACE, ETHNICITY, AND IDENTITY

Image 226: *Horn Players*
Image 232: *Dancing at the Louvre*
Image 234: *Earth's Creation*
Image 243: *Darkytown Rebellion*

GLOBAL CULTURAL AND ECONOMIC EXCHANGES

Image 233: Trade *(Gifts for Trading Land with White People)*
Image 244: *The Swing (after Fragonard)*
Image 245: *Old Man's Cloth*
Image 246: *Stadia II*

SCULPTURE

Image 226: Vietnam Veterans Memorial
Image 228: *Androgyn III*
Image 230: *Pink Panther*
Image 237: *Pisupo Lua Afe (Corned Beef 2000)*

ARTISTIC APPROPRIATION

Image 230: *Pink Panther*
Image 231: *Untitled (#228)*
Image 241: *Pure Land*

SITE-SPECIFIC PUBLIC ART

Image 224: *The Gates*
Image 225: Vietnam Veterans Memorial
Image 236: *En la Barberia no se Llora*

LEE SNIDER PHOTO IMAGES / Shutterstock.com

IMAGE 224

The Gates

New York City, New York, U.S.A.

Christo and Jeanne-Claude

1979–2005 C.E.

Mixed-media installation

Known only by their first names, Christo and Jeanne-Claude formed a unique artistic and marital partnership. The duo achieved international recognition for their practice of using specially designed fabric to wrap public places such as the Reichstag in Berlin and the Pont Neuf in Paris. Although often labeled "wrapping artists," Christo and Jeanne-Claude preferred to be known as visual artists. *The Gates* illustrates their vision of transforming a familiar urban park into a dramatic example of environmental art.

VAST BUT EPHEMERAL

Christo and Jeanne-Claude first proposed *The Gates* in 1979. Like all of their installations, *The Gates* did not require government or corporate financial support. Instead, the couple maintained their artistic independence by funding the project from the sale of original drawings, collages, and scale models. Although financing did not present a problem, bureaucratic regulations presented seemingly insurmountable obstacles that delayed the project for 26 years. Mayor Michael Bloomberg ultimately provided crucial support by praising *The Gates* as "one of the most exciting public art projects ever put on anywhere in the world."

The Gates lived up to Bloomberg's enthusiastic endorsement. The vast project began when a small army of 600 workers installed 7,503 vinyl gates along 23 miles of Central Park pathways. They then attached free-hanging saffron-colored nylon panels to the top of each of the 16-foot-tall gates. As Christo and Jeanne-Claude proudly watched, workers unfurled the nine-footlong panels on February 12, 2005.

Although *The Gates* required 26 years to fully realize, the exhibition period lasted for just 16 days. The deliberately short duration period gave the work what Christo calls "a feeling of urgency to be seen." He defends this commitment to brevity by contending, "I think it takes much greater courage to create things to be gone than to create things that will remain."

JOY AND BEAUTY

Christo and Jeanne-Claude insist that their artistic creations are designed to inspire "joy and beauty" rather than to explore deep messages. Jeanne-Claude emphatically stated, "Our art has absolutely no purpose except to be a work of art. We do not give messages."

In February 2005, joy and beauty came to Central Park as over four million visitors enjoyed new ways of seeing and experiencing a well-known landscape. For strollers inside the park, the saffron-colored corridors offered a welcome contrast to New York City's rigid geometrically gridded streets and avenues. When seen from the skyscrapers surrounding the park, *The Gates* seemed like what Christo and Jean-Claude poetically described as "a golden river appearing and disappearing through the bare branches of trees and highlighting the shape of meandering footpaths."

MAKING CONNECTIONS

THE GATES AND *SPIRAL JETTY*

Although *The Gates*'s saffron scaffolds recall tori at a Japanese Shinto shrine, they provide a more direct artistic connection with Robert Smithson's *Spiral Jetty* (Image 151). Both *The Gates* and *Spiral Jetty* are examples of environmental art designed for specific sites. Unlike the industrially manufactured materials Christo and Jeanne-Claude used in *The Gates*, Smithson used black basalt and earth found at the site in the Great Salt Lake. Christo and Jeanne-Claude dismantled *The Gates* after 16 days. In contrast, Smithson allowed natural processes of erosion and flooding to gradually transform his work.

Geir Olav Lyngfjell / Shutterstock.com

IMAGE 225

Vietnam Veterans Memorial

Washington, D.C., U.S.A.

Maya Lin

1982 C.E.
Polished black granite

Maya Lin's parents fled to the United States just before Mao Zedong and his Communist Party took control of China in 1949. Born in 1959, Maya grew up in Athens, Ohio, home of Ohio University. Her father served as Dean of the College of Fine Arts while her mother taught literature classes. Maya's parents instilled a respect for creativity and what she later called an "unspoken push to do something you feel is very important." During her senior year at Yale, a nationwide competition to design a Vietnam Veterans Memorial provided Maya with an unexpected opportunity to do something that was indeed "very important."

THE COMPETITION

The Vietnam War opened deep and painful wounds that divided families, friends, and eventually the entire nation. As the war wound down, veterans returned to a country eager to forget the war and the people who fought in Vietnam. No ticker tape parades, victory celebrations, or larger than life monuments welcomed the returning soldiers.

As time passed, public attitudes gradually changed. In 1979, Jan Scruggs and a group of prominent veterans incorporated the Vietnam Veterans Memorial Fund (VVMF). Within a short time they raised the necessary funds to build a memorial on the National Mall in Washington, D.C. The monument would recognize the sacrifices of the men and women who served in Vietnam.

In October 1980, the VVMF invited artists to submit ideas for what a memorial should look like. The design criteria specified that the memorial would "be reflective and contemplative in character; harmonize with its surroundings; contain the names of those who had died in the conflict or were still missing; and make no political statement about the war."

A panel of eight distinguished sculptors, architects, and landscape designers examined over 1,400 anonymous entries. After careful deliberation, they unanimously selected Entry Number 1026.

MAYA'S MINIMALIST DESIGN

Unknown to the selection panel, Maya Lin, a 21-year-old architecture senior at Yale University, submitted Entry Number 1026. Unlike traditional war memorials,

Lin's proposal included no statues of brave heroes, no glorified statements about war, and no mention of specific battles. Instead, she called for a simple but powerful MINIMALIST design based upon an unadorned geometric form.

Lin proposed a memorial comprised of two polished black granite walls each 246 feet 9 inches long. The walls would be sunk into the ground, with the earth behind them. The V-shaped walls would meet at an apex ten feet high and then taper to a height of eight inches at either end. Lin positioned the walls so that one pointed to the Lincoln Memorial and the other to the Washington Monument. She believed that linking these two monuments would "create a unity between the nation's past and present."

"THE POWER OF A NAME"

The black granite walls contain a chronological list of the 58,286 men and women who died in the Vietnam War from 1959 to 1975. The sequence of names begins at the top of the eastern wall. Upon reaching the farthest end of memorial, the pattern continues from the far western end and continues back to the center. The names thus form a circular chronology in which the beginning and end of the war meet at the same point. The vast number of names conveys a profound awareness of an immeasurable loss.

The polished black surface contributes to the monument's meaning. Lin understood "the power of a name" to evoke "every single memory you have of that person." Her design created a space where visitors could read and touch each name. At the same time, the polished black surface deepened the monument's meaning by reflecting the images of the living and superimposing them on the names of the dead. Lin used this "mirrored effect" to create a private space "for the living and dead to meet."

CONTROVERSY AND COMPROMISE

The selection of her proposal catapulted Lin into the glare of instant national fame and controversy. Critics assailed her unconventional design for its lack of heroic statues. One angry critic bitterly described it as "a black gash of shame and sorrow." After a heated debate, opponents and supporters reached a compromise that added realistic sculptures of brave soldiers and nurses. The two sculptural groups occupy sites near the Memorial Wall but far enough away to preserve the integrity of Lin's artistic vision.

Officials dedicated the Vietnam Veteran's Memorial on November 13, 1982. Jan Scruggs spoke for many when he expressed his hope that the monument would "contribute to a collective healing for the nation." It is now one of the best-known and most viewed works of public art in the United States.

MAKING CONNECTIONS

MAYA LIN AND AUGUSTE RODIN

Both Maya Lin and Auguste Rodin created war memorials that defied conventional expectations and aroused strong opposition. Like Lin's Vietnam Veteran's Memorial, Rodin's *Burghers of Calais* (Image 119) did not place heroic individuals on a raised pedestal. Instead, Rodin created a controversial design by portraying the six burghers of Calais as ordinary people rather than as idealized heroes. Despite initial controversy, both Lin's Vietnam Veterans Memorial and Rodin's *Burghers of Calais* are now recognized as innovative and powerful works that successfully convey a range of human emotions.

The Broad Art Foundation. Photo: Douglas M. Parker Studio, Los Angeles.

IMAGE 226

Horn Players

Jean-Michel Basquiat

1983 C.E.

Acrylic and oil paintstick on three canvas panels

Jean-Michel Basquiat was born in Brooklyn, New York in 1960. Although he was the son of a successful Haitian-born accountant and an art-loving Puerto Rican mother, Basquiat rebelled against his comfortable middle-class upbringing. Ambitious, talented, and temperamental, Basquiat dropped out of high school, left home, and became a well-known graffiti artist. His work soon attracted the attention of influential art dealers. Basquiat quickly became a rising star in New York City's thriving art market. Painted at the height of his career in 1983, *Horn Players* illustrates the unique artistic style that made Basquiat America's most successful black artist.

A METEORIC RISE

Jean-Michel Basquiat's meteoric rise to artistic prominence is without parallel in American art. Basquiat began his career as a graffiti artist when he was just 17. No wall, subway train, or sidewalk was safe from "SAMO," Basquiat's eye catching acronym for "Same Old Shit." The ubiquitous SAMO proudly boasted, "SAMO is all, all is SAMO."

Basquiat's easily recognized graffiti and personal charm earned him invitations to participate in the well-advertised Times Square Show in June 1980 and the New York/New Wave show seven months later. His distinctive paintings caught the attention of New York art dealers eager for an exciting new look. Economic prosperity fueled a booming art market as the number of New York galleries soared from 73 in 1970 to 450 in 1985.

Basquiat's paintings expressed a vibrant artistic spirit. A new and younger generation of affluent art buyers favored the emotionally charged paintings created by NEO-EXPRESSIONIST artists. These painters rejected the abstract coldness of CONCEPTUAL ART. Instead, they favored passionate works that utilized bold colors and recognizable figures. Basquiat's quick brushstrokes, thick jagged lines, and striking compositions catapulted the young artist from rundown streets to prestigious art galleries.

BASQUIAT AND THE *HORN PLAYERS*

The *Horn Players* uses a traditional TRIPTYCH, or three-panel format, to celebrate the work of two of Basquiat's heroes, jazz saxman Charlie Parker and jazz trumpeter Dizzy Gillespie. The two musicians pioneered the transformation of jazz into the fast-paced, improvisational bebop style. The painting illustrates Basquiat's trademark fusion of images and textual references.

Dizzy Gillespie dominates the painting's right wing. Basquiat depicts Gillespie holding a jazz trumpet. Located to the left of his head, the words "DOH SHOO DE OBEE" reference the renowned trumpeter's use of scat or vocal improvisation with nonsense words.

Charlie Parker dominates the painting's left wing. Basquiat depicts Parker holding an alto saxophone emitting hot pink musical notes. Words pay homage to Parker's musical accomplishments and personal life. Repeated five times, the word "Ornithology" (meaning the study of birds) is a sly reference to both Parker's nickname, "Bird," and to the title of his famous bebop composition. Printed above Parker's head, the name "Chan" refers to the musician's longtime companion. Printed below Parker's saxophone, the name "Pree" refers to Parker's infant daughter who died before her second birthday.

Basquiat felt a particular affinity for Charlie Parker's life and work. Both men left home at an early age, lacked formal artistic training, and experienced the burden of racial discrimination. Like Parker, Basquiat developed an energetic, improvisational style that help him create an art of rage and rebellion. The angry, glaring mask in the center of the *Horn Players* triptych may be Basquiat's artistic stand-in for himself.

A TRAGIC END

Basquiat always lived a fast-paced life close to the edge. Although he was a prolific artist who painted almost 700 large-format works on canvas, Basquiat was also addicted to heroin. Repeated attempts at sobriety failed to curb his $1,000 a day habit. The addiction drained Basquiat's health and sapped his creative energy. A heroin overdose ended his brilliant but flawed career. Basquiat died alone in his art studio a few months before his 28th birthday.

CONTINUED FAME

Many art critics predicted that Basquiat's artistic reputation would prove to be a shooting star that streaked across the sky and then disappeared. However, death did not end Basquiat's fame and popularity. His work is now among the most coveted produced by an artist born after 1945. In 2017 "Untitled," Basquiat's powerful depiction of a skull, sold for $110,487,500. The work thus ranks as the sixth most expensive painting ever sold at an auction.

MAKING CONNECTIONS

BASQUIAT AND PICASSO

Basquiat's work references a variety of artists including Leonardo, Edouard Manet, and Pablo Picasso. For example, a close analysis of *Horn Players* reveals several links with Picasso's *Three Musicians*. Both works use a triptych format and flat patches of color to present fragmented figures. Although Picasso did incorporate words in some of his collages, the *Three Musicians* lacks this distinctive Basquiat trait.

IMAGE 227

Summer Trees

Song Su-Nam

1983 C.E.
Ink on paper, 2 feet 5/8 inches high

Song Su-Nam is one of South Korea's foremost late-20th-century artists. During the 1980s, he led the Oriental Ink Movement to revitalize Korean art. *Summer Trees* embodies Song's attempt to reinvent Korean art by combining historic Korean and contemporary Western styles of art.

KOREA'S BATTERED NATIONAL IDENTITY

The 20th century had a traumatic impact upon Korea's national identity. The Joseon dynasty provided Korea with five centuries of political continuity along with a commitment to preserving Confucian cultural and artistic traditions. This long period of stability ended when the Japanese annexed Korea in 1910. The Japanese occupiers threatened to extinguish Korea's language and culture. The Allied victory in World War II ended the Japanese occupation of Korea. However, it did not end the series of catastrophic events that battered Korea's national identity. Cold War rivalry between the Soviet Union and the United States left the Korean peninsula divided between a Soviet-supported government in the north and a pro-Western government in the south. Partition failed to restore stability. In 1950, the North Koreans suddenly invaded South Korea, precipitating a bloody conflict that lasted three years and claimed over 400,000 Korean lives.

THE ORIENTAL INK MOVEMENT

Song Su-Nam's academic and artistic career began during the period of sweeping changes following the Korean War. As modernization transformed South Korea, many artists embraced ABSTRACT EXPRESSIONISM and the use of oil paint. A respected scholar-artist, Song stood at the crossroads between tradition and modernity. Although he did not reject abstraction, Song recognized that ink brush painting held an honored place in Korea's national artistic inheritance. Determined to revitalize Korea's endangered artistic traditions, Song became the leader of the "Sumukhwa" or Oriental Ink Movement.

Song hoped the Oriental Ink Movement would revive INK WASH PAINTING, an East Asian artistic technique that uses black ink in various concentrations. For centuries, Chinese and Korean scholar-gentlemen known as LITERATI used ink's nuanced tones to express their inner spirituality. As a modern Korean *literati*, Song believed that imported oil paints were "too gaudy" for the subtle messages he could convey with ink.

MODERN BUT STEEPED IN TRADITION

Summer Trees represents an attempt to revive ink wash painting in a modern context. The work consists of nine parallel and overlapping vertical stripes of ink. A close inspection reveals a number of small stick-like objects beneath each stripe. The different tones of black and gray provide visual evidence of Song's virtuoso command of ink painting.

Summer Trees can be viewed as an abstract piece of contemporary art. The painting includes no specific references to the summer season or to trees. At the same time, *Summer Trees* is deeply anchored in traditional *literati* motifs. For example, in *literati* works a group of trees often symbolizes a gathering of friends. In addition, the subtle shades of black and gray provide a meditative quality that Song felt had been lost in the modern technological age.

MAKING CONNECTIONS

SONG SU-NAM, HELEN FRANKENTHALER, AND FAN KUAN

Summer Trees can be compared with *The Bay* by Helen Frankenthaler (Image 149) and *Travelers among Mountains and Streams* by Fan Kuan (Image 201). Both *Summer Trees* and *The Bay* are abstract renderings of nature with titles referencing the natural objects that inspired them. While *The Bay* uses acrylic on canvas, both *Summer Trees* and *Travelers among Mountains and Streams* rely on ink to deliver nuanced gradations of shading to convey favored *literati* themes intended to explore nature's beauty and spiritual messages.

Image © The Metropolitan Museum of Art / Image source: Art Resource, NY

IMAGE 228

Androgyn III

Magdalena Abakanowicz

1985 C.E.

Burlap, resin, wood, nails, string

Magdalena Abakanowicz experienced the brutality of World War II and the crushing oppression of a communist government in postwar Poland. Abakanowicz overcame these nightmares and emerged as one of Poland's most original and acclaimed artists. Like many of her works, *Androgyn III* evokes the dehumanizing forces at work during her lifetime.

"I FELT INCREASINGLY HOLLOW"

Magdalena enjoyed a privileged childhood as the daughter of a wealthy aristocratic family that owned an estate 120 miles east of Warsaw. Her carefree life abruptly ended when German forces invaded Poland on September 1, 1939. World War II brought her family horror and ruin. In 1943, Nazi soldiers burst into her home. Paralyzed with fear, Magdalena watched as a drunken soldier shot her mother's arm, severing it below the shoulder. Although she was just 13 years old, the traumatic event had a profound effect on Magdalena's future art. She later recalled, "I felt increasingly hollow. As if my insides had been removed and the exterior, unsupported by anything, shrank, losing its form."

"WE, AS FAMILY, LOST OUR IDENTITY"

The defeat of Nazi Germany did not release the Abakanowicz family from the grip of political upheavals. Led by Joseph Stalin, the Soviet Union quickly turned Poland into a tightly controlled satellite nation. As members of a hated and now persecuted pre-war aristocratic elite, the Abakanowicz family lost everything: "We, as family, lost our identity. We were deprived of our social position and thrown out of society."

BEGINNING A NEW LIFE

Forced to start a new life, Abakanowicz turned to art. The Academy of Fine Arts, Poland's leading art school, recognized Abakanowicz's promise and admitted her. However, Polish officials adopted SOCIALIST REALISM, insisting that artists paint images of smiling workers living in a perfect socialist society. Abakanowicz successfully resisted pressures to conform and instead created her own distinctive sculptural forms.

"CROWDS, INJUSTICE, AND AGGRESSION"

Abakanowicz later acknowledged that her sculptures came "from the experiences of crowds, injustice, and aggression." *Androgyn III* expresses her haunting message about the impact of these forces on the human condition.

Abakanowicz formed *Androgyn III* by first dipping burlap, string, and cotton gauze into resin. She then pressed this mixture into a hardened plaster mold. The resulting figure is a hollow shell lacking arms, feet, and a head. Androgyn III is precariously perched on low stretchers of wooden logs. The hollow and incomplete figure expresses a somber warning about the human condition. "Crowds, injustice, and aggression" have combined to leave humanity devoid of hope and clothed only in an air of desolation.

MAKING CONNECTIONS
MAGDALENA ABAKANOWICZ AND KARA WALKER

Both Magdalena Abakanowicz and Kara Walker created unconventional and incomplete forms to explore the effects of injustice and aggression. Walker's silhouettes depict both the victims and the perpetrators of slavery. The figures in *Darkytown Rebellion* (Image 243) are caught in a tragic web that continues to impact American racial attitudes and stereotypes. Similarly, Abakanowicz's hollow *Androgyn III* underscores human vulnerability to the universal problems of injustice and aggression.

Courtesy of Xu Bing Studio, Photo by Colin Doyle

IMAGE 229

The Book from the Sky

Xu Bing

1987–1991

Mixed-media installation

Xu Bing first exhibited *The Book from the Sky* in the National Gallery in Beijing. Visitors entered a large room where they were literally surrounded by Chinese characters. They walked beneath 50-foot-long printed scrolls hanging from the ceiling, viewed 400 handmade books arranged in neat rows, and tried to read wall panels printed in the style of outdoor Chinese newspapers. The sophisticated museumgoers soon made an unsettling discovery – the exhibit consisted of imaginary words based upon invented characters. Why did Xu Bing devote almost four years to creating this installation? Is the work meaningless? Or is it in fact profoundly meaningful?

XU BING AND THE CULTURAL REVOLUTION

The search for answers to these questions begins with how China's Cultural Revolution affected Xu Bing's life. Xu Bing grew up surrounded by books and scholars. His father chaired the history department at Beijing University while his mother worked as a library administrator. The Cultural Revolution changed everything. Mao Zedong's campaign to radically transform Chinese culture inspired students to form paramilitary units called Red Guards. The Red Guards quickly papered Beijing with posters and banners denouncing intellectuals such as Xu Bing's father as "reactionaries" and "capitalist roaders." In a cruel twist of fate, Xu Bing's school recognized his precocious artistic talent by enrolling him in a propaganda brigade where he designed posters like the ones condemning his father.

The tumultuous Cultural Revolution finally ended with Mao's death in 1976. The new more settled era enabled the 21-year-old Xu Bing to enroll in the prestigious Central Academy of Fine Arts in Beijing. He graduated in 1981 and received a Masters in Fine Arts degree in printmaking six years later. Xu Bing then began the painstaking process of creating the 4,000 characters he would incorporate into *The Book from the Sky*. The completed work established Xu Bing as one of China's foremost artists.

MEANINGLESS OR MEANINGFUL?

The Book from the Sky is a masterpiece of the bookmaker's craft. A specialist in the ancient art of woodcut printing, Xu Bing hand-carved each character. His masterful work helped revive traditional Chinese typesetting, binding, and stringing techniques that had been all but lost.

The Book from the Sky is more than just an aesthetic and technical achievement; it is also a political and philosophical statement. On first glance Xu Bing's installation strikes most visitors as beautiful but nonsensical. Like DADA artists who protested the madness of World War I's assault on human life, Xu Bing protested the Cultural Revolution's assault on language. "To strike the written word," he warned, "is to strike at the very essence of the culture." *A Book from the Sky* is a powerful condemnation of Chinese authorities who inundated their country with meaningless propaganda slogans. Seen from this perspective, Xu Bing's "meaningless" work actually conveys a meaningful and timeless message – freedom of thought is fragile and must be protected.

MAKING CONNECTIONS

LIU CHUNHUA AND XU BING

Liu Chunhua and Xu Bing had strikingly different responses to the Cultural Revolution. Liu joined the Red Guards and used his artistic talent to create *Chairman Mao en Route to Anyuan* (Image 212), a propaganda painting intended to glorify a ruthless ruler. In contrast, Xu Bing opposed the Red Guards and used his artistic talent to create *The Book from the Sky* to warn viewers that unscrupulous political leaders can use political propaganda to distort and manipulate language and therefore thought.

© Jeff Koons. Digital Image © The Museum of Modern Art / Licensed by SCALA / Art Resource, NY

IMAGE 230

Pink Panther

Jeff Koons

1988 C.E.

Glazed porcelain

Jeff Koons is one of the world's most famous, commercially successful, and controversial living artists. Koons does not paint, sculpt, or draw. Instead, he directs a complex collaborative team of highly skilled artists. A renowned perfectionist, Koons applies cutting-edge production techniques to create works like the *Pink Panther* that are inspired by popular culture.

A BLOND BOMBSHELL AND A CARTOON CHARACTER

The *Pink Panther* features the intertwined figures of Jayne Mansfield, a popular Hollywood sex symbol in the late 1950s and early 1960s, and the Pink Panther, a cuddly cartoon character. Mansfield is scantily clad, wearing just a mint green dress. She projects a radiant smile as if posing for photographers.

Mansfield is shown holding the Pink Panther in her left arm. The Pink Panther was originally created for the opening sequence of a 1963 movie. The popular cartoon figure then became the hero of its own television show. The Panther's face conveys a sense of confusion as it seems to wonder why an innocent childhood toy is in the arms of a Hollywood goddess.

BANALITY AND KITCH

The *Pink Panther* is part of a series of 20 sculptures Koons unveiled in 1988. Known collectively as the *Banality Series*, the works were inspired by cartoon characters, gift shop souvenirs, and pop culture celebrities. Although created by skilled workshops in Germany and Italy, the *Banality* figures' high level of craftsmanship did not stop critics from dismissing them as KITCH, commercial art produced for a mass audience.

COMPELLING YET ELUSIVE

The *Pink Panther* presents viewers with a visually compelling juxtaposition of a semi-nude Hollywood sex symbol holding a popular children's cartoon character. Some critics contend that the *Pink Panther* is a critique of America's vapid consumer culture. Others argue that it is a carefully calculated work cynically intended to capitalize on America's love of kitch. While both of these perspectives have validity, the *Pink Panther* is consistent with Koons' ability to create accessible images that elicit a sense of wonder and surprise.

MAKING CONNECTIONS

JEFF KOONS AND ANDY WARHOL

The *Pink Panther* can be compared with Andy Warhol's *Marilyn Diptych* (Image 147). Both works explore the cult of celebrity. In addition, both Koons and Warhol are commercially successful artists who demonstrate a sophisticated understanding of media and advertising.

Courtesy of the Artist and Metro Pictures, New York

IMAGE 231

Untitled #228

From the History Portraits series

Cindy Sherman

1990 C.E.

Photograph

Cindy Sherman is a contemporary photographer who is widely recognized as a key artist in the Women's Movement. She is best known for elaborate photographs featuring herself in various staged roles. Her work focuses special attention on exploring stereotypical images of women. Sherman's *History Portraits* is a series of 35 photographs reinterpreting the construction of stereotypes in Old Master paintings.

JUDITH AND HOLOFERNES

The *Book of Judith* tells the Old Testament story of Judith, a beautiful and pious Hebrew widow who lived in Bethulia, a strategic town guarding the route to Jerusalem. Ordered to conquer the Israelites, the Assyrian commander Holofernes besieged Bethulia and brought the town to the brink of surrender. The emergency prompted Judith to devise an audacious plan. She successfully entered the Assyrian camp by promising Holofernes valuable information about the Israelites. Enamored by the beautiful widow, Holofernes invited her to a banquet. His plan to seduce Judith failed when he drank too much liquor and passed out. Judith then seized Holofernes' sword and cut off his head. Emboldened by Judith, the Israelites drove the demoralized Assyrians from their land.

JUDITH AND BOTTICELLI

Judith's heroic story inspired many Renaissance and Baroque artists. Between 1497 and 1500, the famed Florentine artist Sandro Botticelli became one of the first artists to portray Judith. His work, *Judith Leaving the Tent of Holofernes*, depicts the biblical heroine moments after she has decapitated Holofernes. Botticelli follows the biblical account by adorning Judith in beautiful robes. She holds Holofernes' razor-sharp sword in her right hand while holding the Assyrian general's severed head in her left hand. Despite the violent act, no blood stains the sword or drips from Holofernes' head.

JUDITH AND CINDY SHERMAN

Botticelli's and Sherman's compositions are strikingly similar. Like Botticelli, Sherman presents Judith standing against a backdrop of brocade cloth suggesting Holofernes' tent. She holds Holofernes' masklike head in her right hand and a dagger in her left hand.

Although Sherman's *Untitled #228* looks like Botticelli's painting, the two works convey very different messages. Sherman includes a number of details that depart from Botticelli's idealized portrait. Both Judith's hand and dagger are stained with Holofernes' blood. This underscores Judith's image as a clever woman who has outsmarted a heretofore invincible Assyrian commander. While Botticelli portrays Holofernes as a handsome man, Sherman presents him as a grotesque old man. These empowering images reaffirm Judith as a powerful woman who has overcome the limitations of her male-dominated society.

MAKING CONNECTIONS

CINDY SHERMAN & MARIKO MORI

Both artists create images starring themselves in various larger-than-life roles. For example, in *Pure Land* (Image 241), Mori depicts herself as Kichijoten, the Buddhist goddess of good fortune. Both Sherman and Mori use their works to address larger truths about cultural perceptions of women.

IMAGE 232

Dancing at the Louvre

From the series *The French Collection*, Part I; #1

Faith Ringgold

1991 C.E.

Acrylic on canvas, tie-dyed, pieced fabric border

Faith Ringgold grew up in Harlem, New York during the Great Depression. Despite the hard economic times, Ringgold did not feel poor or oppressed. Harlem was still an exciting center of African American culture and Faith's family exposed her to poetry, music, and art. Ringgold studied art education at the City College of New York and taught courses in the New York City public schools for 18 years. She left the classroom in 1973 to focus on becoming an artist. Ringgold quickly proved to be an accomplished creator of drawings, children's books, and especially story quilts. *Dancing at the Louvre* demonstrates her ability to combine painted images, quilting techniques, and an imaginative handwritten narrative into a unique and compelling artistic synthesis.

"I'M REWRITING HISTORY"

Dancing at the Louvre is the first work in a 12-part series of story quilts known as *The French Collection*. The series both illustrates and narrates the fictional adventures of Willa Marie Simone, a 16-year-old black girl who left Georgia in 1920 to pursue an art and modeling career in Paris.

Ringgold acknowledges that she uses *The French Collection* as a vehicle to "rewrite history." Willa is an amalgam of Ringgold's mother, Willi Posey, a talented fashion designer and dressmaker, Josephine Baker, a celebrated black dancer who left the United States to live and work in Paris, and Faith Ringgold herself. As Willa's story unfolds she experiences an improbable but still believable mix of encounters with Picasso, Matisse, and other famous artistic luminaries living in Paris.

The quilt borders contain Willa's letters to her aunt Mellissa. Written with a black fine (felt) tip Sharpie marker, the letters describe Willa's emotions as she experiences her first exhilarating taste of freedom. Willa's letters also enable her alter ego Faith Ringgold to express observations about art history and the obstacles faced by aspiring young women of color.

"NEVER MIND LEONARDO DA VINCI"

Dancing at the Louvre takes viewers inside the Louvre,

a museum renowned for its collection of European masterpieces. Willa and her friend Marcia, and Marcia's three young daughters are positioned in front of the *Mona Lisa*, the most famous painting in the Western tradition. Two masterful da Vinci depictions of the Holy Family flank the *Mona Lisa*.

Willa and her friend do not maintain a respectful silence in front of these three iconic paintings. Instead, they ignore the da Vinci masterpieces and in a spontaneous, almost mischievous moment of youthful exuberance they dance, play, and laugh. In her marginal letter Willa enthusiastically reports, "Never mind Leonardo da Vinci and *Mona Lisa*, Marcia and her three girls were the show!"

This unexpected scene signals that *Dancing at the Louvre* will not serve as a prologue for a conventional work of art. It is instead Ringgold's symbolic and passionate statement that she will not accept the traditional view that elevates fine art such as da Vinci's paintings above crafts such as her narrative quilts. It is also not an accident that *Dancing at the Louvre* features five black females. This underscores Ringgold's longstanding complaint that the Western tradition has marginalized black artists.

"BRINGING BEAUTY INTO OUR LIVES"

Ringgold used acrylic paint on canvas to create the central image in each of the 12 scenes in *The French Collection*. She then surrounded these paintings with patchwork cloth made of pieced-together fabric. Ringgold added pounds of batting fabric and countless yards of thread to complete her stunning series of story quilts.

Quilts have deep roots in African American history and in Ringgold's family. Slaves like Ringgold's great-great-great grandmother used quilting as a collective activity to keep their sense of dignity after spending long tedious days working in the fields. In one scene Willa explains that quilting also served an aesthetic function by "bringing beauty into our [the slaves'] lives." The collective nature of making quilts provides a contrast with the Western tradition that lionized masterpieces painted and sculpted by solitary male geniuses.

MAKING CONNECTIONS

FAITH RINGGOLD AND KARA WALKER

Both Faith Ringgold and Kara Walker share a focus on issues of race and gender. In addition, both blur the line between fiction and factual historical narrative. For example, *Darkytown Rebellion* (Image 243) uses over a dozen realistic silhouettes to depict a fictitious event. However, like Ringgold's *The French Collection*, Walker's work forces viewers to consider the historic legacy of racism and discrimination.

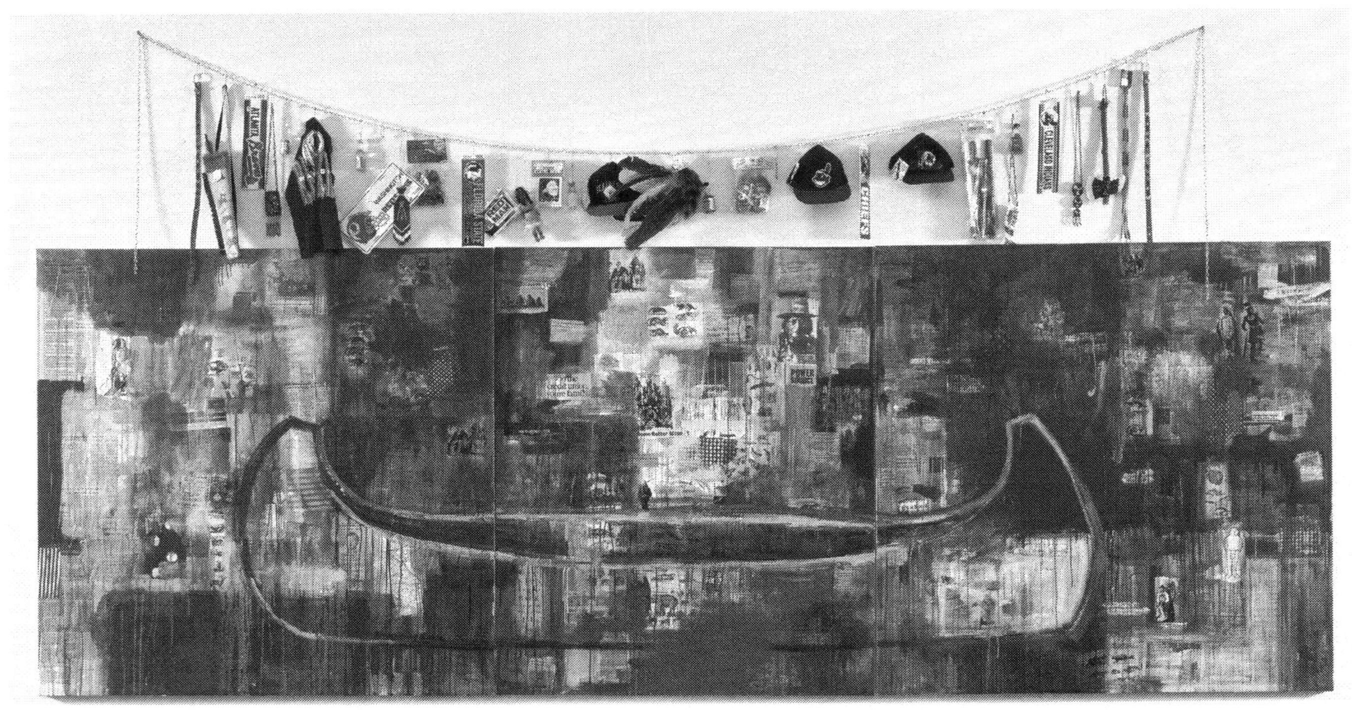

Chrysler Museum of Art, Norfolk, VA. Museum purchase in memory of Trinkett Clark, Curator of American and Contemporary Art, 1989-96.

IMAGE 233

Trade (Gifts for Trading Land with White People)

Jaune Quick-to-See Smith

1992 C.E.

Oil and mixed media on canvas

Jaune Quick-to-See Smith is a renowned Native American artist, curator, and political activist. She was born in a small town on the Flatland Reservation in northwestern Montana. Smith is an enrolled member of the Confederated Salish and Kootenai Tribes. Her grandmother gave Jaune the unique middle name "Quick-to-See" to describe her alert perceptiveness. Smith feels that her art, life experiences, and tribal identity are all "totally enmeshed." *Trade (Gifts for Trading Land with White People)* offers viewers a complex work of art that delivers Smith's strong personal commentary on Native American history.

THE QUINCENTENARY NON-CELEBRATION

Columbus Day 1992 marked the 500th anniversary of the explorer's arrival in what the Europeans would call the New World. For Native Americans, Columbus's "discovery" launched a catastrophic series of events that irrevocably changed their way of life. "The whole place was ours," Smith reminds Americans, "until the invasion came, the great invasion."

Smith did not view 1992 as an opportunity to celebrate the consequences of Columbus's historic voyage. Determined to challenge the traditional view of Columbus's achievements, Smith created a group of paintings known collectively as "The Quincentenary Non-Celebration." *Trade* is the best-known work in the series.

LAYERS OF ART AND MEANING

Trade invites viewers to inspect a multi-faceted work of art. The painted portion is a large-scale TRYPTICH that is five feet high and just over 14 feet wide. Smith first covered the surface of the three panels with a collage of images drawn from tribal newspapers, old photographs of Native Americans, and pictures of wildlife. The pages taken from the *Char-Koostah* News provide a diverse sample of stories about daily life on the Flathead Reservation where Smith grew up. This mix of memories provides an insight into Smith's personal and tribal identity.

Smith next covered the college with thin veils of red, green, and yellow paint. Her energetic brushstrokes are reminiscent of those in ABSTRACT EXPRESSIONIST paintings. Red is a particularly significant feature in many of Smith's paintings. In *Trade* she uses it as a metaphor for her identity as a Native American, her anger at how the American government exploited her people, and the bloody warfare that claimed so many innocent lives.

The outline of a canoe forms *Trade*'s central motif. During the colonial period, canoes symbolized and facilitated trade between Native Americans and European settlers. For example, in 1693 a fleet of 400 Native American canoes brought valuable beaver skins to Montreal. They exchanged their prized furs for European metal pots, iron tools, and colorful beads. In many transactions, Native Americans unwittingly traded their lands for trinkets and other inexpensive goods.

CHEAP TOYS AND SOUVENIRS

Smith completed her work by attaching an array of trinkets and souvenirs to a clothesline placed above her painting. The line of objects includes a toy tomahawk, an Indian princess doll, and a baseball cap worn by fans of the Atlanta Braves. These inexpensive mass-produced objects all reference stereotypical images of Native Americans. They remind viewers how objects unrelated to Native American culture have become substitutes for the heroic but often painful experiences endured by a proud people.

A PROVOCATIVE QUESTION AND A POINTED ANSWER

Smith's painting is more than a work of art; it is also a powerful political statement. According to Smith, if her painting could talk it would ask viewers these provocative questions: "Why won't you consider trading the land we hand over to you for these silly trinkets that so honor us? Sound like a bad deal?" Smith pointedly answers, "Well, that's the deal you gave us."

MAKING CONNECTIONS

JAUNE QUICK-TO-SEE SMITH AND MICHEL TUFFERY

Jaune Quick-to-See Smith and Michel Tuffery are both artists whose work displays great courage and conviction. Rather than acquiesce in the 1992 Columbus Day celebration, Smith used *Trade* to openly challenge the alleged benefits of the European colonization of North America. Rather than ignore the deleterious impact of imported canned goods, Tuffery created *Pisupo Lua Afe* (Image 237) to urge Polynesians to return to their traditional diet of fish and locally grown fruits and vegetables.

IMAGE 234

Earth's Creation

Emily Kame Kngwarreye

1994 C.E.

Synthetic polymer paint on canvas

Emily Kame Kngwarreye (1910–1996) was an indigenous Australian artist who began painting at the age of 79. She created over 3,000 works in a brief but productive career. These paintings established her as Australia's most prominent modern artist. *Earth's Creation* portrays Kngwarreye's exuberant response to the rhythms of the seasons in her native land.

FROM UTOPIA TO THE WORLD

Kngwarreye grew up in Utopia, a remote desert community located in Central Australia. An established elder of her community, she created decorative motifs on women's bodies for traditional ceremonies. She also demonstrated great talent applying wax and dyes to colorful fabrics called batiks.

The outside world discovered Kngwarreye when a prominent Sydney art gallery inaugurated a "Summer Project" seeking to discover, assist, and promote Aboriginal art. Within a short time artists in Utopia produced a stunning collection of original art. The Sydney sponsors selected Kngwarreye's first work, *Emu Woman*, for the cover of their exhibition catalogue. The exposure launched her artistic career.

"GREEN TIME"

Kngwarreye painted *Earth's Creation* to celebrate "Green Time," the annual arrival of life-giving spring rains. Her vibrant patches of yellows, blues, greens, and reds capture the explosive flowering of the previously barren desert landscape. She often worked with a brush in each hand as she used a "dump dot" technique to pound the acrylic paint onto the 9-foot by 11-foot canvas. In 2007, *Earth's Creation* became the first work by a female Australian artist to sell for over one million dollars at auction.

MAKING CONNECTIONS

EMILY KNGWARREYE AND ABSTRACT EXPRESSIONISM

Emily Kngwarreye's paintings reveal no outside artistic influence. Instead, they reveal how she saw her own world. Kngwarreye's works nonetheless share stylistic similarities with the works of ABSTRACT EXPRESSIONISTS.

For example, her forceful brush strokes convey a sense of movement across the canvas that resembles those of Willem de Kooning in *Woman, I.* (Image 145). In addition, both Kngwarreye's *Earth's Creation* and Helen Frankenthaler's *The Bay* (Image 149) use colors to present powerful abstract images of nature.

Copyright Shirin Neshat. Courtesy of the artist and the Gladstone Gallery, New York and Brussels

IMAGE 235

Rebellious Silence

From the *Women of Allah* series

Shirin Neshat (artist)

Photo by Cynthia Preston

1994 C.E.

Ink on photograph

Shirin Neshat is an Iranian-born visual artist. Her photographs, films, and videos explore the changed status of women in Iran's Islamic society. *Rebellious Silence* is part of a series of black-and-white photographs known collectively as *Women of Allah*. The photographs offer provocative glimpses into how Islamic fundamentalism and militancy have affected notions of femininity in modern Iran.

"BOTH FRIGHTENING AND EXCITING"

Neshat's family belonged to a prosperous class of educated, Western-leaning Iranians. In 1975, Neshat left Iran to study art at the University of California at Berkeley. However, she found herself stranded in America when the Iranian Revolution replaced the autocratic but pro-Western Shah with an Islamic fundamentalist government headed by Ayatollah Khomeini.

Neshat finally returned to Iran in 1990. The society she discovered bore little resemblance to the one she remembered. The Iranian Revolution led to the enactment of compulsory laws that restricted the lives of women. Cosmopolitan Iranian women who had worn colorful mini-skirts during Neshat's youth now appeared in public wearing formless black chadors. Neshat found the revolutionary changes "both frightening and exciting."

"INSPIRE, PROVOKE, AND MOBILIZE"

Convinced that she had a responsibility to create art that would "inspire, provoke, and mobilize," Neshat returned to the United States. Although she was not a photographer, Neshat conceptualized, directed, and posed for the *Women of Allah* photographs.

Rebellious Silence provides a striking example of Neshat's work. Clad in a chador, a determined Muslim woman stares defiantly at the camera. The long barrel of a rifle bisects her face. Inscribed across her face, modern verses in the Farsi language praise martyrdom as a courageous way to defend Islam.

"I AM ONLY ASKING QUESTIONS"

Rebellious Silence raises a variety of controversial questions as it offers viewers a complex image of a veiled Iranian woman. To Western eyes the gun symbolizes antagonism and violence while the chador represents Iran's repression of women. In contrast, critics argue that *Rebellious Silence* perpetuates derogatory stereotypes of Iranian women. They argue that the gun is a symbol of strength and resistance while the chador frees women from unwelcome male gazes. Neshat steadfastly refuses to either criticize or admire the woman portrayed in *Rebellious Silence*. She insists, "I'm an artist, not an activist...I am only asking questions."

MAKING CONNECTIONS

REBELLIOUS SILENCE AND *LA GRANDE ODALISQUE*

Neshat's *Rebellious Silence* and *Ingres' La Grande Odalisque* (Image 107) represent very different portrayals of Muslim women. Ingres' work invites male viewers to enjoy the fantasy of viewing an exotic and sensual nude female. In contrast, Neshat forces viewers to confront an armed woman prepared to reject the male gaze and accept martyrdom.

Courtesy Ronald Feldman Fine Arts, New York

IMAGE 236

En la Barberia no se Llora (No Crying Allowed in the Barbershop)

Pepon Osorio

1994 C.E.

Mixed-media installation

Pepon Osorio was born and raised in Puerto Rico. At the age of 20 he left the island to live and study in New York City. Osorio earned degrees in sociology and art history. Although he began his professional career as a social worker in the Bronx, he soon turned to art as a tool for making a difference within the Latino community. His richly detailed installations draw upon his Puerto Rican background and immigrant experiences. *En la Barberia no se Llora (No Crying Allowed in the Barbershop)* addresses the complexities of becoming a Latino man and father.

BIG BOYS DON'T CRY

En la Barberia no se Llora was inspired by Osorio's first experience at a barbershop. Although he was just five years old, Osorio vividly recalls the noise of the electric clippers as the barber trimmed his thick, curly hair. The unexpected sound frightened Osorio and he began to cry. The eagerly anticipated rite of passage quickly turned into an embarrassing disaster. As tears streamed down his face, the men around the young boy sternly admonished him that big boys don't cry.

A UNIQUE PROJECT

Osorio's traumatic childhood experience provided an important early lesson in growing up as a Latino male. He later recognized that the concept of masculinity plays a key role in issues such as domestic violence, homophobia, and teenage pregnancies.

In 1994, Real Art Ways in Hartford, Connecticut offered to sponsor a unique project that would help Osorio explore the world of Latino men and boys. The project called for Osorio to transform an abandoned store into a barbershop. The installation would be located on a busy street in the heart of Hartford's fast-growing Puerto Rican community. Known as Frog Hollow, the area had been the site of prolonged gang fighting that claimed 16 lives during the previous year.

Osorio built a strong base of community support by first touring the neighborhood and then collecting ideas from residents and merchants. Aided by local volunteers, he created a recognizable welcoming façade decorated with a painted scissors, a comb, and a traditional candy-striped red and white barbershop column. But the façade also included a distinctive red-lettered message warning visitors, "EN LA BARBERIA NO SE LLORA."

AN EXAGGERATED MASCULINE SPACE

The interior space featured a room packed with masculine symbols. Paintings of gang tattoos and scores of framed portraits of Latin American and Caribbean athletes, politicians, and entertainers covered the walls. Osorio positioned four bright red barbershop chairs on classic black and white tiles. He ornamented each chair with baseball caps, hair picks, off-track betting receipts, and other *churcherrios*, or trinkets.

Osorio's lavish attention to detail created an overwhelmingly masculine space. However, he also added one discordant feature. The head of each chair contained a small video monitor that played silent clips of males of all ages sobbing uncontrollably. Osorio hoped that the juxtaposition of strong male symbols with the unexpected and incongruous images of men crying would make visitors feel uncomfortable and encourage them to express their feelings about the meaning of masculinity in their own lives.

A MORE ACCESSIBLE APPROACH

The *En la Barberia no se Llora* installation marked a major step in Osorio's artistic development. His previous works had been shown in upscale galleries and prestigious museums. Although he was proud of this recognition, Osorio realized a disconnect existed between his work and the people he was trying to reach. *En La Barberia no se Llora* represents Osorio's attempt to place his art within the Latino community. He forcefully argues that this greater accessibility will enable his intended audience to visit his installations and leave thinking about "who they are in relationship to what they have just seen."

MAKING CONNECTIONS

EN LA BARBERIA NO SE LLORA AND *THE OATH OF THE HORATII*

En la Barberia no se Llora and *The Oath of the Horatii* (Image 103) both address ways in which cultures mold and maintain masculinity. The two works demonstrate that masculinity is a learned behavior. In *The Oath of the Horatii*, David places the father at the center of his painting. True to the ideals of the Roman Republic, the father teaches his sons to choose duty, discipline, and self-sacrifice as their supreme moral values. In contrast, the distraught female figures on the right side of the painting display feminine emotions of apprehension and uncertainty.

© Michel Tuffery MNZM / Museum of New Zealand Te Papa Tongarewa # FE010516

IMAGE 237

Pisupo Lua Afe (Corned Beef 2000)

Michel Tuffery

1994 C.E.

Mixed media, flattened corned beef cans

Michel Tuffery is a New Zealand-based artist of Samoan, Rarotongan, and Ma'ohi Tahitian heritage. He was part of the first wave of artists with Pacific ancestry to work within the contemporary art world. He is now one of New Zealand's best-known artists. *Pisupo Lua Afe* is a particularly vivid example of how Tuffery uses his art to address significant cultural issues affecting the Pacific Islands.

A CORNED BEEF BULLOCK

Pisupo Lua Afe is one of the most recognized works of art in the Museum of New Zealand. The work is a life-size three-dimensional bull made out of flattened, riveted, and recycled corned beef cans. On first glance, the sculpture appears to be a playful artistic joke. Tuffery's work, however, is not intended to be humorous. Instead, *Pisupo Lua Afe* is intended to make a powerful visual statement about the impact of global trade on Pacific Island culture.

PISUPO

Pacific islanders traditionally enjoyed a healthy diet that included fresh fish, local fruits, and coconut milk. However, they now live in a global economy in which inexpensive processed food can be shipped anywhere.

The arrival of canned pea soup ended the Pacific Islands' dietary isolation. Since all Samoan words must end in a vowel, pea soup became "pisupo." As the Polynesians imported more and more canned foods, pisupo became a generic term for all types of canned foods.

IMPACT UPON PACIFIC ISLAND DIET AND HEALTH

Canned goods now dominate food shelves in stores across the Pacific Islands. Polynesians have a particular penchant for canned corned beef. They often use cans of corned beef as prized gifts at weddings, funerals, birthdays, and other celebrations. Tuffery also points out that tin cans are replacing traditional woven bags and carved containers as storage devices.

The consumption of imported canned foods has impacted more than just traditional Polynesian celebrations and crafts; it has also created a significant health crisis. Processed foods contain an unhealthy combination of saturated fats, salt, and cholesterol that contribute to widespread obesity. Some island populations have reported obesity rates as high as 75 percent, the highest level in the world!

IMPACT UPON PACIFIC ISLAND ECOLOGY

Tuffery's bull is carefully crafted to convey a sense of scale and dominance. It is a pointed commentary on the impact that dairy farming is having on Pacific Island ecology. Within the last quarter-century cattle, have become an integral part of the economy of many Pacific Islands. Proponents of cattle grazing argue that it provides island farmers with an additional source of income and an important protein supplement. In contrast, Tuffery's bull asks viewers to consider the deleterious impact cattle grazing is having on island plants, streams, and landscapes.

MAKING CONNECTIONS

PISUPO LUA AFE AND *LIPSTICK (ASCENDING) ON CATERPILLAR TRACKS*

Pisupo Lua Afe and *Lipstick (Ascending) on Caterpillar Tracks* (Image 150) are both unconventional sculptures intended to facilitate discussions about controversial issues. Tuffery created *Pisupo Lua Afe* to place what he calls a "fresh lens" on pressing health and ecology issues in the Pacific Islands. Claes Oldenburg and Yale architecture students designed *Lipstick* to serve as a provocative stage for anti-Vietnam War speeches and rallies. Tuffery and Oldenburg provide examples of artists using their creative voices to deliver powerful protest messages.

Photo Credit: Smithsonian American Art Museum, Washington, DC / Art Resource, NY

IMAGE 238

Electronic Superhighway

Nam June Paik

1995 C.E.

Mixed-media installation, 49-channel closed circuit video installation, neon, steel, and electronic components

Nam June Paik is a South Korean-born visual artist who is recognized as the "Father of Video Art." In 1974, he coined the term "electronic superhighway" to describe the speed and potential impact of the emerging global communication network. Created in 1995, *Electronic Superhighway* is an ambitious mixed-media installation using video images to portray Paik's fascination with the diversity of American life.

PRESENTING AN ELECTRONIC COLLAGE OF AMERICAN LIFE

Electronic Superhighway presents viewers with a 15-foot-high and 40-foot-wide electronic map of the United States. Paik used almost 600 feet of multi-colored neon tubing to outline America's boundaries and those of all 50 states. The neon lights reference the glowing motel and restaurant signs that tempt motorists traveling along the nation's interstate highway system.

Paik captured America's diverse cultural mosaic by placing television screens within the boundaries of each state. Each screen displays a video clip representing Paik's interpretation of the state's unique history. For example, Alabama features clips of Dr. King fighting for civil rights while Kentucky features clips of championship horse races. Paik's fascination with movies led him to associate *The Wizard of Oz* with Kansas, *Meet Me in Saint Louis* with Missouri, and *Oklahoma* with (what else!) Oklahoma. Taken together, these 336 flashing video screens offer a unique electronic collage of the sights and sounds of American life.

CREATING AN IMMERSIVE EXPERIENCE

Like many global contemporary artists, Paik enabled viewers to become active participants in his installation. He accomplished this by cleverly placing a closed-circuit camera in Washington, D.C. As a result, museum visitors can see themselves as part of Paik's collage of America's ever-changing cultural landscape.

USING NEW TECHNOLOGY WHILE MAINTAINING PAIK'S ARTISTIC VISION

Paik prided himself on using cutting-edge video technology. The monitors in *Electronic Superhighway* use cathode ray tubes, long the mainstay of display technology. However, rapid advances in LCD (liquid crystal display) technologies are now making cathode ray tubes obsolete. As a legendary innovator, Paik would understand the dilemma faced by curators at the Smithsonian American Art Museum where *Electronic Superhighway* is a popular display. Officials will soon be unable to replace worn-out cathode ray tubes in *Electronic Superhighway*. As a result, they will face the challenge of installing new flat panel screens while still maintaining the integrity of Paik's artistic vision.

MAKING CONNECTIONS

NAM JUNE PAIK AND EADWEARD MUYBRIDGE

Nam June Paik and Eadweard Muybridge were both pioneers whose innovative work anticipated new forms of visual communication. For example, Muybridge's *The Horse in Motion* (Image 117) uses stop-motion photographs of a galloping horse to prove that all four of a horse's legs are briefly off the ground. His innovation paved the way for the emergence of the motion picture industry. Similarly, Piak's video art foresaw the potential of an instantaneous system of global communications.

Performer: Phil Esposito. Photo: Kira Perov

IMAGE 239

The Crossing

Bill Viola

1996 C.E.

Video/sound installation

Bill Viola is a leading contemporary video artist. *The Crossing* incorporates Viola's signature use of large-scale projections, extreme slow-motion, precise sound editing, and looping. The work is more than a technological tour de force. It invites viewers to contemplate the meaning of the universal cycles of life, death, and rebirth.

FIRE AND WATER

The Crossing is displayed on a freestanding, 16-foot-tall, two-sided projection screen placed in the center of a dark room. On one side, a man wearing khaki pants and a blue shirt walks slowly out of the darkness to eventually face the viewer. As he stops, a small votive candle appears at his feet. The flame gradually spreads, eventually becoming a roaring fire engulfing his entire body. The man remains calm as his body disappears and only darkness remains.

A second sequence simultaneously occurs on the opposite side of the screen, but with water. At first, a few drops of water begin to fall on the man's head. The light shower gradually turns into a torrential downpour, entirely submerging the man. As on the fire side, the man remains calm as his body disappears and only darkness remains.

A PIVOTAL CHILDHOOD EXPERIENCE

When Viola was six years old, he fell out of a boat and into a lake. When he reached the bottom, Viola did not panic. Instead, he felt a compelling sense of mystery and peace. This experience has had a pivotal impact upon Viola's art. Like many of his works, *The Crossing* uses water and submerged figures to help him investigate universal messages about the meaning of life. Deeply influenced by Christian and Hindu devotional art and thought, Viola insists, "There's more than just the surface of life. The real things are under the surface."

"WHAT'S IN YOUR HEART AND SOUL"

The Crossing is an expression of Viola's search for life's underlying realities. The work does not offer viewers definite answers. Instead, it invites an open-ended experience that encourages meditation and introspection. Viola reminds his viewers, "It's all about what's in your heart and soul."

Viola's own search for universal meanings has led him to believe that life can provide "intense moments of infinite feeling and acute physical awareness." Fire and water are universal elements that enable the figure in *The Crossing* to experience a brief but revealing moment before he vanishes and returns to what Viola calls, "the emptiness from which he came."

MAKING CONNECTIONS

THE CROSSING AND SHIVA NATARAJA

The Crossing and the statue of Shiva Nataraja (Image 202) both use fire as an element to help viewers search for the meaning of existence. Shiva dances within an arch of flames representing the endless cycles of birth and death. Although he is unleashing great cosmic forces of creation and destruction, Shiva's expression remains calm. Shiva's dance thus expresses an eternal truth about the endless rhythms of nature. Viola's *The Crossing* also explores the cycles of life and death. Like Shiva, the figure in *The Crossing* remains calm. He confronts the elements of fire and water knowing that death is not an end, but a crossing or gateway to birth and the beginning of a new cycle.

PA

IMAGE 240

Guggenheim Museum Bilbao

Frank Gehry (architect)

1997 C.E.

Titanium, glass, and limestone

Frank Gehry is one of the world's most renowned architects. His use of cutting-edge computer-aided technology enabled him to design and build the Guggenheim Museum Bilbao. When it opened on October 18, 1997, critics promptly hailed the museum as one of the world's most innovative and influential works of contemporary architecture.

BILBAO, SPAIN

The story of the Guggenheim Bilbao began in 1991. At that time, Bilbao, Spain seemed an unlikely city to host a world-class art museum. The city's location along the Nervion River in northern Spain had enabled it to become an industrial and commercial hub. However, as global economic conditions shifted, Bilbao's factories and shipyards closed, leaving an industrial wasteland and a dispirited city.

Bilbao's civic leaders were determined to reimagine their city. They undertook a major urban renewal program that included a new airport and modern rapid transit system. They then approached Thomas Krens, director of the Solomon Guggenheim Foundation, located in New York City, about the possibility of opening a branch of the Guggenheim in Bilbao.

Krens enjoyed a well-deserved reputation as an executive willing to take risks. At that time, he hoped to take advantage of the growing global interest in modern and contemporary art. Open to the possibility of building a museum in Bilbao, Krens invited Frank Gehry to tour the city. After exploring Bilbao, Krens and Gehry selected a vacant industrial site located beside a major bridge at a bend along the Nervion River. Gehry then submitted a bold design that in his words, "took on the bridge, the river, and the road." The jury accepted Gehry's proposal allowing the project to begin.

"THE GREATEST BUILDING OF OUR TIME"

Construction of the Guggenheim Bilbao began in October 1993 and proceeded with unusual speed. As the project neared completion, word began to spread throughout the architectural community that Gehry had created something special. The respected architect Philip Johnson visited Bilbao and pronounced the museum "the greatest building of our time."

Johnson's high praise captured an essential truth - Gehry's revolutionary design had a visual impact that changed the way people thought about museums. Unlike classically inspired museums, the Guggenheim Bilbao had no symmetrical row of Doric columns supporting a triangular pediment. Instead, Gehry created a DECONSTRUCTIONIST masterpiece based upon a series of asymmetrical shapes resembling a vast work of abstract sculpture. Viewed from different angles, the museum resembled either a metallic flower or a ship, evoking Bilbao's historic role as a major seaport.

CATIA SOFTWARE AND TITANIUM SHEETS

The Guggenheim Bilbao is one of the world's most technologically advanced works of contemporary architecture. Gehry's curved forms would not have been possible without CATIA, a three-dimension design software. CATIA precisely calculated the shape, size, and placement of every piece of metal in Gehry's complex steel skeleton.

While CATIA played an indispensible role in the museum's sophisticated design, titanium gave the building its distinctive identity. Named for the Titans of Greek mythology, titanium is stronger than steel, resistant to corrosion, and surprisingly light. It is also normally very expensive. However, an unexpected drop in titanium prices enabled Gehry to cover his round forms with 33,000 extremely thin sheets of titanium. These sheets provided a shimmering gold or silver surface depending on the time of day and the weather conditions.

ATRIUM AND GALLERIES

The Bilbao Guggenheim is more than just a striking structure; it is also a functioning art museum. Visitors first enter a soaring light-filled atrium that provides views of the river, city, and surrounding hills. As the museum's organizing center, the atrium contains a system of curved bridges and glass elevators that enable visitors to reach 19 galleries spread over three floors. The galleries include a range of shapes and sizes making them suitable for all types of art.

THE "BILBAO EFFECT"

The opening of the Guggenheim Bilbao sparked a revival of the city's distressed economy. Previously just 25,000 tourists visited Bilbao each year. The museum served as a powerful magnet that attracted four million visitors in its first three years. The revenue from tourist spending more than recouped the cost of construction. The construction of a world-class cultural institution to serve as a catalyst for spurring economic growth and creating a vibrant cultural identity is known as the "Bilbao Effect."

MAKING CONNECTIONS

THE GUGGENHEIM BILBAO AND THE SEAGRAM BUILDING

The Guggenheim Bilbao and the Seagram Building (Image 146) embody two very different architectural styles. The Seagram Building is an International Style office building illustrating Sullivan's famous dictum that "form follows function." In contrast, the Guggenheim Bilbao is a Deconstructionist art museum illustrating Bernard Tschumi's dictum that "form follows fantasy." Both buildings began with steel frames. However, while Mies Van Der Rohe designed uniform floors, CATIA software enabled Gehry to design a variety of curving forms.

Digital Image © 2013 Museum Associates / LACMA / Licensed by Art Resource, NY

IMAGE 241

Pure Land

Mariko Mori

1998 C.E.

Color photograph on glass

Moriko Mori is one of Japan's most recognized female artists. She began her career as part of Japan's cosplay, or costume play, craze. Like other young adults, Mori designed elaborate costumes to transform herself into futuristic characters inspired by comic books and videogames. As her career evolved, Mori turned to creating works that used traditional Japanese culture and futuristic images to convey universal spiritual messages. *Pure Land* illustrates Mori's use of complex images to provide a timeless message - everyone can achieve enlightenment.

THE DEAD SEA AS AN IDEAL SPIRITUAL SETTING

Pure Land provides viewers with an eerie, almost surrealistic image of the Dead Sea at dawn. The Dead Sea is one of the world's saltiest bodies of water. Fish and aquatic plants cannot survive in waters that are almost 10 times as salty as the ocean. Mori did not choose the Dead Sea setting by accident. Traditional Japanese Shinto rituals use salt as an agent of purification. The Dead Sea thus provides an ideal spiritual setting that encourages devotion, prayer, and meditation.

THE SYMBOLIC IMPORTANCE OF THE LOTUS FLOWER

Although the Dead Sea cannot support plant life, Mori nonetheless places a lotus flower in the center of her image. The lotus flower has the unique ability to flourish in muddy, stagnant water. While rooted in the mud, its flowers bloom on long stalks. In Buddhism the lotus bloom serves as a vivid symbol that beauty and purity can overcome worldly distractions and desires. Mori thus uses the lotus bloom to reinforce her message of spiritual awakening or enlightenment.

KICHIJOTEN, OUR GUIDE TO THE PURE LAND OF PERFECT BLISS

Mori's *Pure Land* is not devoid of human life. Look closely at the serene figure floating above the lotus bloom. It is none other than Moriko Mori! Dressed in an elaborate silk kimono, she has assumed the persona of a futuristic version of the female Buddhist deity Kichijoten. Beloved as one of the Seven Gods of Fortune, Kichijoten is a goddess associated with abundant harvests, happiness, and beauty. Kichijoten's left hand holds a wish-granting jewel, symbolizing her power to grant her devotees' prayers for good fortune. Kichijoten (Moriko Mori) will thus guide viewers into the "Pure Land of Perfect Bliss."

SIX ALIEN MUSICIANS

Six pastel-colored alien figures surround Kichijoten. As they float on light blue clouds, each figure plays a different musical instrument. Mori uses the alien musicians to function as futuristic bodhisattivas. In Buddhism a boddhisattiva is an enlightened person who helps others attain enlightenment.

A FUTURISTIC TIBETAN STUPA

In Tibetan Buddhism, a stupa is the representative of the Buddha's holy mind. Mori completes her *Pure Land* image by placing a futuristic Tibetan stupa on the far right horizon. The stupa is a physical representation of how Buddha's ethical teachings provide a path for an ordinary person to become an enlightened mind, as symbolized by the pinnacle at the top of the structure.

"WE'RE PART OF THE UNIVERSE"

Mariko Mori is committed to her belief that we are all spiritually connected. In order to work towards a peaceful future we must realize that, "We're part of the universe - part of a whole. We often forget the connection." Mori created *Pure Land* to help us perceive the connection. The purpose of her work is not to help a lone viewer reach the Pure Land. It is instead to achieve a global connection by helping everyone reach the Pure Land.

MAKING CONNECTIONS

MARIKO MORI AND CINDY SHERMAN

Both Mariko Mori and Cindy Sherman cast themselves in the principal roles of their artwork. For example, in her *History Portraits* series, Sherman places herself in a variety of historic roles including European aristocrats, clergymen, and women of leisure. Like Mori, Sherman creates a complete persona that includes costumes and make-up. In Image 231 Sherman assumes the identity of Judith, the famed Biblical heroine who saved the Israelites by slaying Holofernes, an Assyrian general determined to force her people to submit to King Nebuchadnezzar II. Although Judith and Kichijoten are very different characters, their images underscore the power of visual representation.

IMAGE 242

Lying with the Wolf

Kiki Smith

2001 C.E.

Ink and pencil on paper

Kiki Smith grew up in an artistic household in South Orange, New Jersey. Her mother, Jane Lawrence Smith, was a well-known opera singer; her father, Tony Smith, was a famed MINIMALIST sculptor. Now a major figure in contemporary art, Kiki is best known for her often controversial sculptural representations of the human form. However, her broad range of subject matter also includes installations, prints, videos, and drawings. *Lying with the Wolf* is part of a series of works using a distinctive feminist approach to explore the symbolic relationship between humans and animals.

A NUDE WOMAN AND A TAME WOLF

Lying with the Wolf focuses the viewer's attention on an unexpected image. Drawn with ink and pencil on paper, the seven-foot-high by six-foot-wide work depicts a nude female calmly reclining alongside a wolf. Normally a dangerous beast of prey, the wolf seems to welcome the woman's embrace as she strokes its ears and the side of its stomach. Smith provides no background imagery or contextual clues. As a result, the work raises a number of questions: Who is the woman? Why is she portrayed with a potentially dangerous wolf? How does the work address feminist perspectives in the Western tradition of the reclining female nude?

ST. GENEVIEVE AND ATTILA THE HUN

In an interview with Art21, Kiki Smith explained that while touring the Louvre, she paused to inspect a picture of St. Genevieve. The artist portrayed the beloved patron saint of Paris sitting peacefully among a group of wolves and lambs. The image inspired Smith to combine Genevieve and a wolf into a single work. Smith emphasized the significance of this pairing by insisting, "It's really important to put them together."

St. Genevieve's legendary life offered Smith an intriguing story. In 451 C.E., Paris faced a terrible threat. Led by Attila, a seemingly invincible army of Huns threatened to plunder and burn Paris. One contemporary writer reported that the Huns were like "wolves...fiercer than ferocity itself."

Panic-stricken Parisians prepared to abandon their city. But a 28-year-old nun named Genevieve persuaded her fellow citizens to remain calm. Commanding no troops and possessing no weapons, the pious Genevieve placed her faith in the power of prayer. Her strategy worked. Perhaps influenced by Genevieve's "prayer marathon,"

Attila spared Paris. In the popular imagination, Genevieve became a heroine who saved Paris from a ravenous army of wolf-like Huns.

THE BIG BAD WOLF

Lying with the Wolf references St. Genevieve's symbolic ability to tame an army of predatory Hunish wolves. It also references the wolf as a symbolic creature with deep roots in popular culture. For example, in their story *Little Red Riding Hood*, the Brothers Grimm describe the wolf as a "wicked creature" determined to eat both Red and her grandmother. In Disney's animated story, the Big Bad Wolf is a cunning villain determined to devour each of the three little pigs.

The identification of wolves as a traditional symbol of evil and danger demonstrates Smith's ability to use *Lying with the Wolf* to forge a new level of meaning. The wolf and the human are no longer predator and prey. Instead, Smith reimagines these traditional roles by portraying the wolf and the woman as nurturing companions.

A FEMINIST PERSPECTIVE

Kiki Smith's career illustrates the increasingly influential presence of women in the world of contemporary global art. Smith affirmed her debt to the women's rights movement when she acknowledged, "I came of age in the sixties and seventies and that I exist is a result of feminism."

Lying with the Wolf challenges conventional notions of gender stereotyping. The female figure is not a submissive woman cowering in fear next to a dangerous predator. She is instead an independent and empowered woman who is completely unafraid. Smith thus uses *Lying with the Wolf* to deliver a powerful statement of female strength.

MAKING CONNECTIONS

THE RECLINING FEMALE NUDE

Both *Lying with the Wolf* and *Venus of Urbino* (Image 80) illustrate contrasting examples of an artistic genre known as "the female reclining nude." The genre is a Renaissance invention created by the Venetian artists Giorgione and Titian. Completed by Titian in about 1538, *Venus of Urbino* depicts a young woman who proudly invites male viewers to admire her voluptuous nude body. In contrast, the woman in *Lying with the Wolf* is not an idealized object for male desires. Smith's work is thus part of the feminist challenge to the "male gaze," a tradition in which male artists portrayed nude women for the enjoyment of their male patrons.

Artwork © Kara Walker, courtesy of Sikkema Jenkins & Co., New York.

IMAGE 243

Darkytown Rebellion

Kara Walker

2001 C.E.

Cut paper and projection on wall

Kara Walker's work burst onto the contemporary art world during the late 1990s. Her drawings, films, and signature life-size silhouettes provoked strong feelings by openly confronting America's painful history of slavery and racism. *Darkytown Rebellion* provides a representative example of Walker's ability to create visually arresting images that question the stereotypes of plantation life in the Old South.

FROM STOCKTON TO STONE MOUNTAIN

Walker's childhood had an important impact upon her artistic career. She was born and raised in a comfortable middle-class home in Stockton, California, an integrated community east of San Francisco. As the Chairman of the Department of Art at the University of the Pacific, her father had the opportunity to expose Kara to the joys and beauty of art. But Kara's contented childhood suddenly changed when her father accepted a position as Director of the School of Art and Design at Georgia State University in Atlanta. The Walker family settled in Stone Mountain, a suburb outside Atlanta.

The move from Stockton to Stone Mountain posed a dramatic change for the then 13-year-old Kara. The small Deep South town exposed her to the continuing legacy of Jim Crow customs. Stone Mountain is located near a monumental rock carving depicting Confederate President Jefferson Davis and his two greatest generals, Robert E. Lee and Thomas "Stonewall" Jackson. The area was also the birthplace of the modern Ku Klux Klan and the site of frequent Klan meetings.

Living in Stone Mountain played an important role in shaping Walker's future art. After growing up in a tolerant California town, she now experienced the pain and confusion of being a marginal teenager who was not fully accepted by either black or white students. The constant reminders that she didn't fit in led Walker to question racial attitudes and stereotypes.

NEW CONTENT IN AN OLD FORM

Walker's experience with present-day prejudice prompted her to investigate the realities of slavery in the antebellum South. While earning degrees at the Atlanta College of Art and at the Rhode Island School of Design, she studied slave narratives, researched minstrel shows, and closely examined historical novels such as Harriet Beecher Stowe's *Uncle Tom's Cabin* and Margaret Mitchell's *Gone With the Wind*. Walker's research convinced her that America had chosen to forget or, even worse, romanticize the terrible realities slavery inflicted on black slaves and their white masters.

During the mid-1990s, Walker searched for an artistic form that would enable her to visually express the cruel realities of slavery. She found an engaging and revealing answer in an unexpected time and place - 18th-century French cut-paper silhouettes. At that time, French artists used paper profiles to capture the extravagant fashions worn by aristocratic lords and ladies. The term *silhouette* commemorates the name of Etienne de Silhouette, a French finance minister who gained a well-deserved reputation for his penchant for making black profile cutouts.

Walker discovered that silhouettes enabled her to create haunting images of stately plantation homes, petticoated Southern belles, and shackled and maimed slaves. She also discovered that this cast of caricatures could be organized into a variety of evocative installations addressing highly charged issues of oppression, race, and gender.

FROM DARKYTOWN TO DARKYTOWN REBELLION

The title *Darkytown Rebellion* suggests that Walker based her installation upon an actual historical event. In fact, an obscure painting by an anonymous 19th-century American primitive artist served as her source of inspiration. Called "*Darkytown*," the work depicted stereotypical images of well-dressed blacks enjoying an idyllic day on a rural Carolina plantation. Intrigued by the painting, Walker decided to reinvent the image by removing the figures and placing them in a new and much harsher reality.

Walker's reimagined *Darkytown Rebellion* evokes an entirely new feeling. She replaced its innocent serenity with a new and ominous sense of the underlying turbulence that characterized plantation life. Walker's work includes over a dozen life-size black-paper silhouettes affixed to a 37-foot-wide museum display area. A careful inspection reveals a hoop-skirted plantation mistress, a black man standing upright despite a severed leg, a teenager holding what appears to be a colonial ship sail, and a black figure Walker identifies as "a kind of rebel." Walker's procession of sharply drawn figures recall the satirical caricatures in William Hogarth's *Marriage a la Mode* (Image 98).

"YOU START RELIVING THE STORY"

Walker created *Darkytown Rebellion* to do more than just display a mix of historic fact and fiction. She also designed her installation to provide an immersive experience for museum viewers. Walker accomplished this by using overhead projectors to beam an array of colorful lights onto the museum walls, ceiling, and floor. When viewers step in front of the light source, they discover that their own shadows have been projected into the *Darkytown Rebellion* narrative. This forces viewers to confront the connection between slavery's horrifying past and its continuing impact upon America's racial attitudes. Noting the impact of her work, Walker observes, "It's interesting that as soon as you start telling the story of racism, you start reliving the story."

MAKING CONNECTIONS

STEREOTYPES

Kara Walker's *Darkytown Rebellion*, Jaune Quick-to-See Smith's *Trade* (Image 233), and Wangechi Mutu's *Preying Mantra* (Image 247) all use stereotypes to address the enduring legacy of racial attitudes. Smith's string of toys and souvenirs forces viewers to confront the mistreatment endured by Native Americans. Mutu's collage of an African woman is a beautiful and yet disturbing exploration of the conflicting perceptions of African women.

IMAGE 244

The Swing (after Fragonard)

Yinka Shonibare

2001 C.E.

Mixed-media installation

Yinka Shonibare describes himself as "a postcolonial hybrid." His bicultural upbringing includes a childhood spent in both Nigeria and Great Britain. Born in London in 1962, Shonibare was the son of a successful Nigerian lawyer. Although the family moved to Lagos, Nigeria, Shonibare spent his summers in London and later earned art degrees in Great Britain. His artistic works reflect these mixed cultural influences. *The Swing (after Fragonard)* is a large-scale mixed-media installation that explores the connections between Africa and Europe as it raises questions about the formation of personal and national identities.

FRAGONARD AND THE SWING

In 1767, the French Rococo artist Jean-Honoré Fragonard received an unusual commission from the Baron de St. Julien. A notorious playboy, the Baron requested a portrait of his beautiful young mistress. But that was not all. The mischievous Baron also specifically instructed Fragonard to "place me in a position where I can observe the legs of that charming girl."

Fragonard enthusiastically fulfilled the Baron's request. He created a delightfully frivolous scene featuring the Baron's beautiful mistress dressed in a luxurious silk gown. Perched on a swing pushed by her much older husband, she glides above a lush green garden. Fragonard captures a moment of joyful spontaneity as the flirtatious mistress gaily kicks off one of her tiny pink shoes. Carefully positioned so that he can look up her billowing skirt, the playboy Baron hides in the foreground.

SHONIBARE AND THE SWING (AFTER FRAGONARD)

Shonibare's three-dimensional installation deliberately paraphrases Fragonard's famous Rococo masterpiece. He preserves the young mistress perched on a swing. Her shoe is still suspended in mid-air, now held by a transparent wire. Shonibare's work also includes branches to represent the foliage in Fragonard's painting.

Shonibare does more than simply appropriate a familiar artistic scene; he also creates a new visual statement by both omitting and adding unexpected details. Shonibare's young mistress is a headless mannequin. She still wears billowing robes, but a new costume made from Dutch wax cloth replaces her silk gown. And finally, Shonibare excludes both the leering Baron and the clueless husband. Why did Shonibare change these details, and what issues is he addressing?

MODERN VIEWERS AND A HEADLESS MANNEQUIN

Shonibare's decision to omit Fragonard's two male figures allows modern viewers to participate in his installation. Like the Baron, viewers can now look up the young woman's skirt. This creates an immersive experience resembling the technique used by Kara Walker to project her viewer's shadows among the silhouettes in *Darkytown Rebellion* (Image 243).

Like most of Shonibare's sculptural installations, *The Swing (after Fragonard)* features a headless mannequin. Fragonard's beautiful young mistress enjoyed a hedonistic lifestyle dedicated to pursuing love and enjoying material comforts. Rococo paintings such as *The Swing* capture the spirit of this frivolous era. Shonibare's headless mannequin is a visual reminder of the cruel fate awaiting French aristocrats, many of whom would be publicly beheaded during the Reign of Terror.

The headless fiberglass mannequin also serves another important purpose. Shonibare does not want his figures to be readily identifiable. Since his "coffee-colored" mannequin in *The Swing (after Fragonard)* is neither white nor black, it represents what Shonibare calls a "post-racial" identity.

A FABRIC'S COMPLEX HISTORY

The cloth worn by Shonibare's aristocratic mistress has a surprisingly complex history. As they explored Indonesia, Dutch traders discovered Javanese batik or wax-printed cloth. They also discovered that the beautiful cloth commanded high prices because it required long hours to produce. Determined to make the fashion affordable for a mass market, Dutch textile mills used modern equipment to industrialize production. English manufacturers in Manchester soon copied the Dutch production methods.

The Dutch and English produced fabrics that became very popular in West Africa. The cloth's bright colors and geometric designs became associated with the struggles of newly emerging African nations for political and cultural independence. The fabric soon became erroneously thought of as an authentic or indigenous West African product.

"WHY DON'T YOU MAKE AUTHENTIC AFRICAN ART?"

While Shonibare was searching for an artistic identity, a white tutor challenged him by asking, "You are African, aren't you? Why don't you make authentic African art?" The question led to Shonibare's discovery that Dutch wax print fabrics had a history paralleling his own bicultural biography. Headless mannequins dressed in Dutch wax fabric became signature features of Shonibare's installations. They represent symbols of Shonibare's own multicultural identity.

MAKING CONNECTIONS

YINKE SHONIBARE AND EL ANATSUI

The global flow of goods influenced the artistic work of both Yinka Shonibare and El Anatsui. Shonibare's aristocratic mistress wears cloth inspired by Indonesian batiks, manufactured in British and Dutch textile plants, and sold in West African markets where it assumed a distinctively African identity. The flattened liquor bottle caps in El Anatsui's *Old Man's Cloth* (Image 248) also offer a commentary on the commercial and cultural interaction between Europe and West Africa. Shonibare and El Anatsui use fabric and bottle caps as artistic mediums to convey a message that all cultures are intertwined

IMAGE 245

Old Man's Cloth

El Anatsui

2003 C.E.

Aluminum and copper wire

El Anatsui is Africa's most widely acclaimed contemporary artist. Born and educated in Ghana, Anatsui has spent most of his career teaching at the University of Nigeria where admiring students affectionately call him "Prof." As we have seen, Yinka Shonibare (Image 244), Julie Mehretu (Image 246), and Wangechi Mutu (Image 247) are all African artists who left their homelands to live and work in Great Britain and the United States. Unlike these artists, El Anatsui is a native African who has remained in Africa. *Old Man's Cloth* provides an excellent example of one of Anatsui's visually arresting series of large-scale sculptures called Gawu or "metal cloths."

A COMMUNAL CREATION

Old Man's Cloth is a compelling and contradictory work of art. From a distance viewers see a massive object, 16 feet high and 17 feet wide, that looks like a glittering gold and silver tapestry. However, when viewers move closer they are surprised to discover that *Old Man's Cloth* is actually comprised of thousands of recycled liquor bottle caps connected by copper wire.

El Anatsui did not create *Old Man's Cloth* by himself. The work was a communal activity requiring thousands of hours of labor. Supervised by Anatsui, over a dozen assistants cut, flattened, and connected the bottle tops into blocks containing about 200 tops. Assistants then placed the squares on the floor where Anatsui directed their placement into overlapping patterns resembling the bright colors and geometric designs of West African kente cloth.

HISTORIC REMINDERS

Anatsui deliberately designed *Old Man's Cloth* to provide visual reminders of West African history. The gold color is a historic reference to Ghana's role as a major mining center. During the 14th century, West African miners produced about two-thirds of the world's supply of gold.

The tops from bottles of whiskey, rum, and gin also serve as reminders of the tragic role alcoholic beverages have played in West African history. During the 17th and 18th centuries, triangular trade routes crisscrossed the

Atlantic Ocean connecting the West Indies, British North American colonies, Great Britain, and West Africa in a web of commerce. *Old Man's Cloth* contains bottle cap labels such as Dark Sailor and Liquor Headmaster that reference the role rum played in the Atlantic slave trade. Anatsui also uses the labels as a reminder that West Africans now consume liquor as a way to escape the crushing burden of poverty created by economic disparities unleashed by globalization.

MAKING CONNECTIONS

OLD MAN'S CLOTH AND *SUNFLOWER SEEDS*

El Anatsui's *Old Man's Cloth* and Ai Weiwei's *Sunflower Seeds* (Image 250) share a number of characteristics. Both works consist of small, discrete items that take on new shapes each time they are installed. In addition, El Anatsui and Ai Weiwei both supervised teams of assistants who created the actual works. And finally, both works contain deliberate historic references. For example, *Old Man's Cloth* references the Atlantic slave trade and *Sun Flower Seeds* references Mao's Great Proletarian Cultural Revolution.

© Julie Mehretu, American, b. 1970. Carnegie Museum of Art, Pittsburgh: Gift of Jeanne Greenberg Rohatyn and Nicolas Rohatyn and A.W. Mellon Acquisition Endowment Fund, 2004.50. Photograph © 2017 Carnegie Museum of Art Pittsburgh

IMAGE 246

Stadia II

Julie Mehretu

2004 C.E.
Ink and acrylic on canvas

Julie Mehretu is the youngest child of an Ethiopian college professor and a white American Montessori teacher. Her family fled Ethiopia in 1977 when Julie was almost seven. While her father taught economic geography at Michigan State University, Julie earned a BA from Kalamazoo College and a Masters in Fine Arts from the Rhode Island School of Design. She is recognized as an innovative artist who has forged her own visual language of abstract marks. *Stadia II* is part of a triptych that uses abstraction to explore contemporary social and political issues.

LARGE AND COMPLEX

Stadia II is both large and complex. Hundreds of meticulously drawn abstract elements, including an array of geometric shapes, straight and curving lines, and clusters of small markings populate a nine-foot-high by 12-foot-wide canvas. The vast network of abstract forms and intersecting colors gives the work a sense of constant movement.

ORGANIZED CHAOS

The appearance of so many diverse elements creates a deceptive impression of structural chaos. In fact, Mehretu has carefully grounded *Stadia II* in the tradition of architectural drawing. As underscored by the work's title, a stylized rendering of a stadia or stadium dominates the painting.

Modern stadiums are closely associated with athletic contests. In a video Mehretu filmed for the Virginia Museum of Fine Arts, she explained that the build-up for the 2004 Summer Olympics played a role in how she conceptualized *Stadia II*. Olympic imagery can be seen in the many flags and pennants distributed across the work's upper register.

The 2004 Olympic Games were not Mehretu's only source of inspiration. The war in Iraq occurred at the same time as the games. The flags and pennants thus also serve as symbols of the nationalistic fervor that accompanied both the war and the athletic competition.

ART HISTORICAL PRECEDENTS

The narrative content of *Stadia II* is firmly anchored in the historic time in which it was created. However, Mehretu also made frequent references to art history. For example, the orange diamonds and circles and the red "X" at the top are clear references to Russian Constructivism and the work of Kasmir Malevich.

AN IMMERSIVE EXPERIENCE

Mehretu describes viewing *Stadia II* as "an immersive experience." The vast work contains many small paintings and images that require time to absorb. As a result, viewers experience what Mehretu calls "a perspectival shift" as their gaze moves back and forth from the whole work to its embedded parts. Viewers can thus experience a sense of standing outside the work, floating over it, standing within it, and even coming from underneath it.

A LAYERED WORK

Mehretu uses layered drawings to achieve the illusions of depth and movement. She begins by projecting architectural diagrams onto her work's blank space. When this layer is completed, Mehretu sprays it with a clear silica-and-acrylic solution. She then sands that to a smooth finish. Mehretu repeats this process until the work is completed.

MAKING CONNECTIONS

STADIA II AND THE ROMAN COLOSSEUM

Julie Mehretu painted *Stadia II* almost 2,000 years after Roman architects and engineers constructed the Flavian Amphitheater or Colosseum (Image 44). The two works are designed to provide spaces for spectacles. *Stadia II* focuses on the nationalist fervor generated by the 2004 Olympic Games and the Iraq War. The Roman Colosseum generated passionate emotions as over 50,000 spectators watched professional gladiators fight animals and one another. These bloody spectacles served an important political purpose by inspiring loyalty to the emperor, inculcating Roman values of courage and strength, and distracting the potentially volatile people who flooded into Rome. Mehretu argues that the modern media use war and athletic games for similar political and psychological purposes.

IMAGE 247 (IMAGE NOT AVAILABLE)

Preying Mantra

Wangechi Mutu

2006 C.E.

Mixed media on mylar

Wangechi Mutu is a global citizen who grew up in Nairobi, Kenya, attended college in the United Kingdom, earned a Masters in Fine Arts at Yale, and currently lives and works in Brooklyn, New York. She is one of the world's most exciting collage artists. Mutu specializes in creating portraits of women spliced together from disparate sources that include fashion magazines, medical journals, and issues of *National Geographic*. *Preying Mantra* illustrates her ability to engage in contemporary issues about the visual representation of the black female body.

POSE AND SETTING

Mutu places her female characters in the center of her works where they will never be marginalized. The figure of a reclining nude black woman dominates *Preying Mantra*. The figure's powerful legs are tightly crossed. Her right hand is positioned behind her crowned head while her left hand holds a green snake. The figure reclines on a geometrically patterned blanket situated in a grove of blue trees. The blanket resembles a traditional Kuba fabric created in the Democratic Republic of the Congo. Like many of Metu's works, *Preying Mantra* has a dreamlike quality that encourages reflection.

AN AMBIGUOUS TITLE

The title, *Preying Mantra*, is a considered reference to the praying mantis insect. Like the figure in Mutu's work, a praying mantis has long powerful legs. During mating season, the female praying mantis bites off her mate's head and then devours his corpse for nourishment. Mutu's title thus invites us to view her central figure as an aggressive and potentially dangerous woman. The presence of a serpent in her left hand reinforces this image while also serving as a reference to the Biblical story of Adam and Eve.

The central figure may be dangerous, but she could also be vulnerable. Mutu's title reminds us that African women were preyed upon by European imperialists. The Europeans justified exploiting their African colonies with an often-repeated mantra claiming they had a "white man's burden" to civilize illiterate and technologically backward Africans.

DESIRED OR DESPISED

Mutu often admits that she is "obsessed" with the perceptions and meanings attached to the black female body. "Anything that is desired or despised," she explained, "is always placed on the female body." *Preying Mantra* thus presents viewers with the image of a black woman who may be looking for her prey or who many be searching for the meaning of life.

MAKING CONNECTIONS

WANGECHI MUTU AND KIKI SMITH

Both Wangechi Mutu's *Preying Mantra* and Kiki Smith's *Lying with the Wolf* (Image 242) encourage viewers to explore nude images of recumbent female figures. The two works depict women who seem to be living at peace with nature. For example, Kiki Smith's heroine demonstrates spiritual power by taming a normally fierce predator. Mutu's female figure can also be viewed as a strong, confident women who is no longer afraid of foreign exploiters.

Gdobon

IMAGE 248

Shibboleth

Doris Salcedo.

2007–2008 C.E.

Installation

Doris Salcedo is one of Columbia's most renowned artists. *Shibboleth* took the form of a 548-foot-long crack in the floor in Turbine Hall, the main lobby of Tate Museum in London. Her installation is a powerful commentary on the experience of immigrants living in Europe.

ETHNOCENTRISM AND SHIBBOLETHS

Members of all societies use their own cultural perspectives to judge others. People accept what is familiar and reject what seems strange or foreign. Known as ethnocentrism, this process of cultural exclusion leads people to exaggerate and intensify their cultural and racial differences.

A SHIBBOLETH was originally a "test phrase" used to identify members of outgroups. Today the meaning of shibboleth has been broadened to include customs and beliefs that distinguish one group from another. Salcedo chose *Shibboleth* as the title of her work because it "refers to when you are recognized as somebody that is different."

A DISRUPTION

Salcedo's installation baffled many museum visitors. "There's some kind of message behind it, although I don't know what it is," admitted one confused tourist. *Shibboleth* uses a visible metaphor to convey an abstract message. Salcedo deliberately designed the long fissure in the Turbine Hall floor to disrupt the museum space. This physical disruption calls symbolic attention to the social fissures caused by the unwanted presence of marginalized immigrants in European society.

Shibboleth did not entirely disappear when its six-month exhibition ended in on April 6, 2008. After engineers sealed the fissure a scar remained on the museum floor. This permanent mark provides an enduring representation of the unresolved legacy of racial and ethnic discrimination.

MAKING CONNECTIONS

DISCRIMINATION

Both Doris Salcedo and Jacob Lawrence focus on how marginalized people experience discrimination. For example, Lawrence's *The Migration of the Negro, Panel 49* (Image 141) depicts a public dining room in a city located in the northern United States. A long yellow rope zigzags through the center of the painting separating the black and white diners. The rope functions as an example of the barriers symbolized by the scar in *Shibboleth*.

Nick Fielding / Alamy Stock Photo

IMAGE 249

MAXXI National Museum of XXI Century Arts

Rome, Italy

Zaha Hadid (architect)

2009 C.E.

Glass, steel, and cement

Zaha Hadid's career as a professional architect spanned almost four decades. Her unmistakable futuristic designs pushed the boundaries of what was architecturally possible. At the time of her death in 2016, Hadid was recognized as the most prominent female architect in the world. First opened in 2009, the MAXXI–a play on the words "museum of art" and the Roman numerals for the 21st century–is an important part of Hadid's unique vision of 21st-century architecture.

A FUTURISTIC ARCHITECT FOR TRADITIONAL ROME

Rome contains many enduring examples of ancient and Baroque architecture. However, the modern city has failed to embrace contemporary trends. But that changed when the Italian Ministry of Culture selected Zaha Hadid to design the new MAXXI museum dedicated to 21st-century arts. Hadid thus became the first woman to design a public building in a city traditionally dominated by male emperors and popes.

"I DON'T DO CONVENTIONAL WORK"

The MAXXI sent a clear message that Rome's special place in architectural history was not over. The glass, steel, and concrete structure presents an asymmetrical façade that lacks a distinct front or back. A cantilevered gallery jutting from the third floor underscores Hadid's defiant message, "I don't do conventional work."

The museum's vast interior spaces present visitors with a memorable experience. A large atrium leads to the museum's cafeteria, bookshop, auditorium, and galleries. A complex system of stairs invites visitors to explore a labyrinthine system of galleries. There are no predetermined focal points or rectilinear spaces. Instead, flowing tube-like galleries encourage visitors to discover works of art in unexpected places. Hadid's use of fluid spaces prompted Roman writers to label Hadid "the female Borromini" after the Baroque architect famous for his use of undulating convex and concave bays (see Image 88).

MAKING CONNECTIONS

MAXXI AND GUGGENHEIM BILBAO

MAXXI and Guggenheim Bilbao share three key characteristics. First, renowned DECONSTRUCTIONIST architects designed both museums. As a result, Hadid's and Frank Gehry's asymmetrical and curvilinear forms dominate both buildings. Second, new computer modeling software provided tools that made these groundbreaking designs possible. And finally, for many visitors the MAXXI and Guggenheim Bilbao have become must-see attractions, often overshadowing their artistic collections.

© Tate, London / Art Resource, NY

IMAGE 250

Sunflower Seeds

Ai Weiwei

2010–2011 C.E.

Sculpted and painted porcelain

Ai Weiwei is a Chinese contemporary artist and political activist who is an outspoken critic of the Chinese government's violations of human rights. In October 2010 Ai filled the Tate Modern's spacious Turbine Hall with over 100 million porcelain sunflower seeds. The installation invited viewers to contemplate a number of provocative economic, political, and social issues.

"MADE IN CHINA"

For centuries the phrase "Made in China" was synonymous with exquisite porcelain vases (see Image 204, *The David Vases*) that ranked among the world's most admired and prized luxury products. In contrast, the label "Made in China" is now synonymous with cheap mass-produced products. *Sunflower Seeds* forces viewers to reconsider the meaning of the "Made in China" label. Far from being industrially manufactured, each seed was sculpted and painted by specialists in small-scale workshops in Jingdezhen, a city famous as the historic center of Chinese porcelain production.

SUNFLOWERS AND CHAIRMAN MAO

Ai Weiwei grew up during the Great Proletarian Cultural Revolution (1966–1976). During that time, the Communist Party forced artists to create "Mao paintings" glorifying Mao Zedong. One of the most potent propaganda images depicted Mao as the sun and adoring Chinese people as sunflowers turning to gaze at the face of their benevolent leader. *Sunflower Seeds* references this famous image by asking viewers to consider how political propaganda can be used as a tool to suppress individual expression.

THE INDIVIDUAL AND MASS SOCIETY

Sunflower Seeds serves as a vivid metaphor for the relationship between individuals and an impersonal mass society. On first glance, the installation appears to consist of an enormous mass of identical pieces. But in reality, each life-sized seed is unique. Ai Weiwei does not tell viewers what to think. Instead, he uses his work to pose questions about the possibility of individualism within a collective society.

MAKING CONNECTIONS

SOCIAL INJUSTICE

Ai Weiwei and Doris Salcedo are both outspoken global activists committed to using their art to call attention to social injustice. Salcedo's *Shibboleth* (Image 248) created a crack in the Turbine Hall floor to allude to the discrimination faced by unwanted immigrants in Europe.

PRACTICE QUESTIONS

PRACTICE QUESTIONS

Your AP Art History exam will begin with 80 multiple-choice questions. You will have one hour to complete this section.

The 80 questions in this section will test your knowledge of the 250 images listed in the AP Art History Framework. The section will include about 45 questions grouped under specific images and about 35 discrete questions.

The 80 multiple-choice questions will count for half of your total score. As a general rule you should strive to correctly answer 75 percent of the questions to score a five, 60 percent to score a four, and 50 percent to score a three. Remember, there is no penalty for guessing.

The following 80 multiple-choice questions are designed to provide you with realistic practice. These questions focus on key information based upon Images 167–250. These are the images discussed in this volume. You will find an Answer Key following the questions.

Private Collection, © The Chambers Gallery, London / Bridgeman Images

Courtesy of Xu Bing Studio, Photo by Colin Doyle

Questions 1-5 refer to the above images.

1. Both works are most directly a response to which of the following historic events?

   A. The Open Door Policy
   B. The Boxer Rebellion
   C. The Great Leap Forward
   D. The Great Proletarian Revolution

2. The work on the left shows the influence of which of the following art historical movements?

   A. Neoclassicism
   B. Romanticism
   C. Impressionism
   D. Socialist Realism

3. The work on the left was intended to elicit which of the following emotional responses from viewers?

   A. Empathy for the suffering of a heroic leader
   B. Awe for the achievements of a heroic leader
   C. Disdain for the timidity of a previously admired leader
   D. Condemnation for the rash decisions of a previously admired leader

4. The work on the right is most similar to

   A. Dada works protesting the meaninglessness of World War I
   B. Cubist works fracturing form and providing multiple perspectives
   C. Surrealist works exploring the subconscious mind
   D. Post-Modern works incorporating a variety of different styles

5. The work on the right surprised its original Chinese audience because

   A. it offered spiritual enlightenment
   B. it rehabilitated Mao Zedong's reputation as a political visionary
   C. it presented imaginary words based upon invented characters
   D. it encouraged a revival of Daoist attitudes towards nature

6. **The Wall Plaque from the Oba's palace and *Jahangir Preferring a Sufi Shaikh to Kings* are similar in that both works**

   A. use famous mythological figures to convey important cultural values
   B. focus on issues of race and gender
   C. employ hierarchical scale to distinguish between figures of varying degrees of importance
   D. employ stylistic elements drawn from abstract expressionism

7. **The Guggenheim Museum Bilbao differs from the Seagram Building in New York City in that the museum**

   A. includes an architectural boundary between secular and sacred spaces
   B. uses a variety of curving forms
   C. employs an eclectic array of external decorations
   D. provides an efficient structure for conducting business

8. **The Qin Dynasty terracotta warriors' primary function was to**

   A. guard a ruler's tomb
   B. escort a soul to the celestial realm
   C. serve as symbols of individual achievement
   D. promote meditation

9. **The Great Mosque in Isfahan served as a model for the development of**

   A. four iwan mosques
   B. domed mosques
   C. hypostyle mosques
   D. pilgrimage mosques

10. ***Earth's Creation* by Emily Kame Kngwarreye shows the greatest stylistic similarity to**

    A. *Stadia II* by Julie Mehretu
    B. *Pure Land* by Mariko Mori
    C. *The Starry Night* by Vincent van Gogh
    D. *The Bay* by Helen Frankenthaler

11. ***Mana* is an importance concept of spiritual force associated with**

    A. West Africa art
    B. Islamic art
    C. Indian art
    D. Oceanic art

12. **A *lukasa* from the Mbudye Society of the Luba people served to**

    A. settle disputes
    B. honor women
    C. recall information
    D. promote trade

13. **Which of the following is NOT a characteristic feature of an Islamic mosque?**

    A. mihrab
    B. roofline sculpture
    C. minaret
    D. calligraphy

14. **Which of the following artists did NOT make works offering direct commentary on a social issue?**

    A. Pepon Osorio
    B. Michel Tuffery
    C. Jaune Quick-to-See Smith
    D. Jeff Koons

Gdobon

Questions 15–17 refer to the above image.

15. The installation was created by

    A. Yinke Shonibare
    B. Doris Salcedo
    C. Pepon Osorio
    D. Jaune Quick-to-See Smith

16. The installation was a response to which of the following historic events?

    A. The forced relocation of Native Americans during the Trail of Tears
    B. The plight of unwanted immigrants in contemporary Europe
    C. The immigration of New Immigrants to the United States in the late 19th and early 20th centuries
    D. The Great Migration of African Americans to urban centers in the North

17. The installation most directly addresses the issue of

    A. social exclusion
    B. iconoclasm
    C. exaggerated masculinity
    D. cultural exchange

18. The rich ornamentation of the Treasury at Petra was most directly influenced by the vocabulary of

    A. Mughal architecture
    B. Hellenistic architecture
    C. Egyptian architecture
    D. Sumerian architecture

19. Which of the following statements is true of the Golden Stool and the Jowo Rinpoche?

    A. They are both cultural icons believed to have celestial origins.
    B. They are both military trophies.
    C. They are both modeled after historic figures.
    D. They are both based upon aniconic imagery.

20. The walls of Great Zimbabwe's Conical Tower exemplify Shona architectural conventions because they utilize

    A. flying buttresses
    B. ceramic-tile roofing
    C. ashlar masonry
    D. *spolia* taken from ancient Roman ruins

21. In *Summer Trees*, Song Su-Nam sought to explore the ability of

    A. fractured forms to convey multiple viewpoints in a single scene
    B. ink to deliver nuanced gradations of shade
    C. atmospheric perspective to convey depth
    D. varied color schemes to deliver harmonious effects

22. When creating *Pure Land*, Mariko Mori was primarily influenced by

    A. Renaissance symmetry
    B. Islamic calligraphy
    C. Persian miniature paintings
    D. Buddhist symbols

PA

Nick Fielding / Alamy Stock Photo

Questions 23–27 refer to the above images.

23. Both structures were built as

    A. design schools
    B. art museums
    C. private residences
    D. office buildings

24. The building on the right was designed by

    A. Frank Gehry
    B. Zaha Hadid
    C. Julie Mehretu
    D. Maya Lin

25. Both structures are notable for their use of

    A. titanium surfaces
    B. classical allusions
    C. curvilinear forms
    D. cantilevered galleries

26. The style of architecture of the building on the left is best described as

    A. International Style
    B. Art Nouveau
    C. Post-Modern
    D. Deconstructionist

27. The construction of both structures was made possible by the use of

    A. computer-aided technology
    B. two-story colonnades
    C. marble facades
    D. repeating rectangular floor plans

28. Iconoclasts destroyed which of the following?

    A. Great Temple in Petra
    B. David Vases
    C. Ardibil Carpet
    D. Bamiyan Buddhas

29. All of the following are true about *Jahangir Preferring a Sufi Sharikh to Kings* EXCEPT

    A. it is a miniature painting
    B. it includes a blend of Mughal, Persian, and European styles
    C. it depicts an actual historical event
    D. it contains allegorical symbols

30. Which of the following is considered a site-specific installation?

    A. *The Gates* by Christo and Jean-Claude
    B. *The Crossing* by Bill Viola
    C. *Darkytown Rebellion* by Kara Walker
    D. *Pink Panther* by Jeff Koons

H.O. Havemeyer Collection, The Metropolitan Museum of Art, Bequest of Mrs. H. O. Havemeyer, 1929

Questions 31-34 refer to the above image.

31. The technique used in making the work is

    A. etching
    B. ink wash painting
    C. woodblock printing
    D. dump dot on canvas

32. Works such as this influenced

    A. Song Su-nam
    B. Fan Kuan
    C. Gottfried Lindauer
    D. Mary Cassatt

33. The work was created

    A. to inspire individual contemplation
    B. as part of a commercial endeavor
    C. for a public installation
    D. to reinvent and revitalize Korean art

34. The work includes all of the following EXCEPT

    A. a low horizon line
    B. a European chemical pigment
    C. a dramatic cliffhanger
    D. an allusion to a famous historical event

35. Nan Madol was built as a

    A. ceremonial and political capital for a ruling dynasty
    B. mausoleum for a beloved queen
    C. religious center for Buddhist monks
    D. commercial center for Silk Road merchants

36. Which of the following arts flourished during the reign of the Safavid rulers in Persia?

    A. miniature paintings
    B. stained glass windows
    C. Zen rock gardens
    D. monumental sculptures

37. The term tapa refers to

    A. navigation charts created in the Marshall Islands
    B. feathered capes created in Hawaii
    C. barkcloth created in Micronesia
    D. stone monoliths created in Rapa Nui

38. Jeff Koons' art focuses on

    A. the human form
    B. pop culture icons
    C. abstract forms
    D. symbols of civic pride

39. Gottfried Lindauer is well known for works in which genre?

    A. Still life
    B. Landscape
    C. Portraiture
    D. Photorealism

40. All of the following contain extensive narrative decoration EXCEPT

    A. the Bayeux Tapestry
    B. the David Vases
    C. *Night Attack on the Sanjo Palace*
    D. Trajan's Column

Gdobon

Questions 41–42 refer to the above image.

41. The work is an example of a (an)

    A. *lukasa*
    B. *mblo*
    C. *ndop*
    D. *ikenga*

42. The primary function of the work is to

    A. serve as a mnemonic device
    B. serve as an idealized portrait of a woman
    C. provide an idealized portrait of a ruler
    D. celebrate individual achievement

Werner Forman Archive / Bridgeman Images

Questions 43–46 refer to the above image.

43. Although the figure is now housed in a museum, it was originally placed

    A. inside a spirit house
    B. in a palace courtyard
    C. on the tomb of a clan chieftain
    D. beside a choir screen

44. The sculpture is made of

    A. wood
    B. marble
    C. terra-cotta
    D. painted limestone

45. Which of the following best describes the figure?

    A. It reflects religious unrest
    B. It communicates primarily through allegory
    C. It is more abstract than representational
    D. It is more ornamental than idealized

46. The figure's style most strongly influenced

    A. El Anatsui
    B. Michel Tuffery
    C. Alberto Giacometi
    D. Polykleitos

Geir Olav Lyngfjell / Shutterstock.com

Questions 47–49 refer to the above image.

47. The architect who designed this memorial is

A. Jean-Antoine Houdon
B. Auguste Rodin
C. Constantin Brancusi
D. Maya Lin

48. The memorial primarily shows the influence of

A. Neo-Traditionalism
B. Minimalism
C. Deconstructivism
D. Post-Modern pluralism

49. A key element in the memorial is its

A. close relationship to the site
B. reliance on sculpture to evoke patriotic themes
C. innovative use of a titanium surface
D. commanding but aloof presence

50. The Dome of the Rock is similar to the Great Mosque in Isfahan in that they both

A. use a four-iwan plan
B. contain two minarets
C. serve as mosques
D. contain decorative inscriptions from the Qur'an

51. The orientation of the moai on Rap Nui suggests that they originally functioned as

A. ancestors watching over their descendants
B. attractions for Polynesian tourists
C. guardians warning invaders to stay away from Rapa Nui
D. instruments designed to predict the summer solstice

52. The Longmen caves and Todai-ji both

A. contain huge statues of the Buddha Shakyamuni
B. contain statues of fierce guardian figures
C. served as capitals of ruling Buddhist dynasties
D. fell victim to attacks by iconoclasts

53. The Fang *byeri* and the female deity figure from Nukuoro are both

A. idealized images of the human figure
B. portraits of specific ancestors
C. statues made from carved wood
D. images of powerful war gods

54. The Marshall Island stick chart served as a

A. valuable trade item
B. guide to the lineage of an elite family
C. guide to help navigators reach a destination
D. didactic tool shared with the entire community

55. The concept of kitch is most closely associated with the work of

A. Ogata Korin
B. Bill Viola
C. Kiki Smith
D. Jeff Koons

Suraj rajiv

Questions 56-60 refer to the above image.

56. **The structure is a recognized symbol of**

    A. Persia
    B. China
    C. India
    D. Indonesia

57. **The structure functions as a**

    A. palace for a Persian emperor
    B. mausoleum for a Mughal queen
    C. mosque for devout Muslims
    D. temple for devout Hindus

58. **The structure's four identical facades all contain a central**

    A. iwan
    B. voussoir
    C. qibla wall
    D. relieving triangle

59. **The pool and garden represent a**

    A. Pure Land vision of nirvana
    B. Zoroastrian image of Ahura Mazda
    C. New Testament view of the heavenly city of Jerusalem
    D. Qur'anic description of Paradise

60. **The structure includes all of the following EXCEPT**

    A. carved floral designs known as *pietra dura*
    B. Indian pavilions known as *chhatris*
    C. balanced and harmonious facades
    D. an onion-shaped dome supported by pendentives

61. **Cindy Sherman and Mariko Mori are both known for creating**

    A. works featuring themselves
    B. mixed-media installations
    C. exuberant responses to the rhythms of nature
    D. incomplete forms to explore the effects of injustice

62. **Which of the following works uses mudras to convey symbolic meanings?**

    A. The David Vases
    B. The Ardabil Carpet
    C. Buk mask
    D. Shiva as the Lord of the Dance

63. **The Kei School of sculpture created the**

    A. *ndop* portrait figures
    B. Benin wall plaques
    C. fierce guardian figures at Todai-ji
    D. Buddhist statues at Borobudur

64. **Julie Mehretu's art most clearly reveals her strong interest in**

    A. Japanese prints
    B. classical mythology
    C. architectural drawings
    D. fresco techniques

Vera Tropynina / Shutterstock.com

Questions 65-67 refer to the above image.

65. The structure's *garbhagriha* is located

    A. adjacent to a central staircase
    B. in a centrally located inner sanctum
    C. at the end of a long line of horseshoe arches
    D. at the entrance to the temple

66. The main tower and the four subsidiary shrines are intended to evoke

    A. Buddhist concepts of nirvana
    B. Persian concepts of paradise
    C. Mount Meru, the mythical home of the Hindu gods
    D. Shiva and his four most important sons

67. The structure is noted for its

    A. ornate mihrab
    B. white marble façade
    C. freestanding statues of Hindu gods
    D. bas reliefs of sensuous nymphs

DR Travel Photo and Video / Shutterstock.com

Questions 68-71 refer to the above image.

68. The Great Stupa at Sanchi contains all of the following EXCEPT

    A. sacred relics
    B. sculptural programs
    C. an axis mundi
    D. an inner chapel for prayer

69. The *toranas* are primarily

    A. gateways
    B. portraits of ancestors
    C. guardian figures
    D. household deities

70. Indian stupa architecture served as a model for the plan of the

    A. White Temple
    B. Nan Madol mortuary area
    C. Borobudur Temple
    D. MAXXI National Museum

71. The *yakshi* statues represent

    A. fertility figures
    B. imperial wives
    C. revered ancestors
    D. sacred reliquaries

Photograph by Franko Khoury / National Museum of African Art / Smithsonian Institution

Jerry L. Thompson / Art Resource, NY

Questions 72–76 refer to the above images.

72. Both works were produced in

    A. Papua New Guinea
    B. the Torres Strait
    C. West Africa
    D. Rapa Nui

73. Both works were made principally of

    A. wood
    B. terra-cotta
    C. hollow-cast bronze
    D. painted marble

74. Both works emphasize

    A. the features of specific women
    B. the ideal of female beauty
    C. the importance of powerful goddesses
    D. the political power of women in matrilineal societies

75. Both works were made for

    A. tribal funerals
    B. religious festivals
    C. political coronations
    D. elaborate public masquerades

76. The image on the right is exceptional because

    A. the artist created a sense of impending action
    B. the projecting tubular pieces represent a royal crown
    C. the name of the artist and his subject are both known
    D. the artist employed classical proportions

77. Jean-Michel Basquiat's paintings best illustrate which of the following 20th-century artistic movements?

    A. Abstract Expressionism
    B. Photorealism
    C. Minimalism
    D. Neo-Expressionism

National Palace Museum

Questions 78-80 refer to the above image.

78. The artist who created this painting is

    A. Fan Kuan
    B. Mariko Mori
    C. Sultan Muhammad
    D. Bichitr

79. The work reflects the author's dedication to the principles of

    A. Daoism
    B. Legalism
    C. Hinduism
    D. Pure Land Buddhism

80. The artist created visual interest by using

    A. self-portraits
    B. bilateral symmetry
    C. chiaroscuro
    D. shifting perspective

ANSWERS

1. D
2. D
3. B
4. A
5. C
6. C
7. B
8. A
9. A
10. D
11. D
12. C
13. B
14. D
15. B
16. B
17. A
18. B
19. A
20. C
21. B
22. D
23. B
24. B
25. C
26. D
27. A
28. D
29. C
30. A
31. C
32. D
33. B
34. D
35. A
36. A
37. C
38. B
39. C
40. B
41. D
42. D
43. A
44. A
45. C
46. C
47. D
48. B
49. A
50. D
51. A
52. B
53. C
54. C
55. D
56. C
57. B
58. A
59. D
60. D
61. A
62. D
63. C
64. C
65. B
66. C
67. D
68. D
69. A
70. C
71. A
72. C
73. A
74. B
75. D
76. C
77. D
78. A
79. A
80. D

GLOSSARY

GLOSSARY

ABSTRACT EXPRESSIONISM

Images 227, 233, 234

An artistic style born in New York City in the 1940s. Artists used vigorous strokes to create what Jackson Pollock called "energy made visible." Emily Kngwarreye's *Earth's Creation* (Image 234) shares stylistic similarities with abstract expressionism.

ANICONIC

Image 185, 186, 188

Art that is symbolic or suggestive rather than literally representational. Islamic sacred art is aniconic because it forbids the use of human and animal representations. The Dome of the Rock (Image 185) and the Great Mosque in Isfahan (Image 186) provide excellent examples of the Islamic tradition of aniconic art in sacred structures.

ASHLAR MASONRY

Image 167, 213

Carefully cut and grooved stones that support a building without the use of concrete masonry. For example, architects used ashlar masonry to build the walls at Great Zimbabwe (Image 167) and Nan Madol (Image 213).

AXIS MUNDI

Images 192, 196, 199

A concept of an axis or pivot denoting a link between sacred sites and the celestial realm. For example, the top of the Great Stupa at Sanchi (Image 192) and the main tower of the temple at Angkor Wat (Image 199) both function as an *axis mundi* because they they connect earthly and heavenly realms.

BILATERAL SYMMETRY

Image 206, 209

Having the same form on either side of a central axis. The Taj Mahal (Image 209) and the Forbidden City (Image 206) both use bilateral symmetry.

CALLIGRAPHY

Image 187

Elegant writing as a decorative form of art. Calligraphy is held in high esteem in the Islamic world. For an excellent example see Folio from a Qur'an (Image 187).

CENTRAL PLAN

Image 186

An architectural design in which a dome covers a large open space. For examples, see San Vitale (Image 51), Hagia Sophia (Image 52), and the Mosque of Selim II (Image 84).

CIRCUMAMBULATE

Images 183, 192, 200

Pilgrims walk around the Kaaba (Image 183) in a counter-clockwise direction to emphasize that their action is not connected to a directional movement of the sun or planet. In contrast, Buddhist pilgrims circumambulate, or walk around, the Great Stupa at Sanchi (Image 192) or the Lakshmana Temple (Image 200) in a clockwise direction to emphasize that their action is in harmony with the cosmos.

CONCEPTUAL ART

Image 226

An American avant-garde art movement in the 1960s. Practitioners argued that the "artfulness" of a work lay in the artist's idea, rather than in a final concrete expression. Basquiat rejected the cold abstraction of conceptual art.

CONTINUOUS NARRATION

Image 203

A style in which multiple scenes are portrayed in the same space. As a result, the same figure will appear more than once. For example, both the *Bayeux Tapestry* (Image 59) and the *Night Attack on the Sanyo Palace* (Image 203) use continuous narration.

DADA

Image 229

Artists whose seemingly irrational images expressed revulsion against the horror and insanity of World War I. Some scholars link Xu Bing's *A Book from the Sky* to the Dada tradition of protesting the madness of political actions.

DAOISM

Image 201

An ancient Chinese philosophy based upon following a harmonious relationship with the natural world. For example, Fan Kuan (Image 201) retreated to a mountain wilderness in order to escape society and commune with nature.

DECONSTRUCTIONIST

Images 240, 249

Deconstructionist architects create an appearance of chaos with seemingly confused and random perspectives. For examples, see the Guggenheim Museum Bilbao (Image 240) and the MAXXI National Museum of XXI Century Arts (Image 249).

EMAKI

Image 203

In Japanese art, an EMAKI is an illustrated handscreen. For example, see the *Night Attack on the Sanjo Palace* (Image 203).

GANDHARAN

Image 182

Gandhara is the name given to a region in modern Pakistan and Afghanistan conquered by Alexander the Great in 330 B.C.E. The Gandharan style combined realistic Hellenistic elements with Buddhist subject matter. For example, the flowing robes in the Bamiyan Buddhas (Image 182) illustrated the Gandharan style.

HIERARCHICAL SCALE

Images 169, 199, 208

The use of differences of size to indicate a figure's relative importance. Hierarchal scale can be seen in the Benin wall plaques (Image 169), the Khmer bas-reliefs at Angkor Wat (Image 199), and in *Jahangir Preferring a Sufi Shaikh to Kings* (Image 208).

HYPOSTYLE HALL

Image 186

An architectural plan that uses rows of columns to support a roof. In an Islamic mosque, a Hypostyle Hall guides worshippers towards the QIBLA wall, thus orienting them towards Mecca. For an example, see the Great Mosque of Cordoba (Image 56).

ICONOCLASM

Image 182

Iconoclasm is destruction of religious and sacred images. For example, Taliban iconoclasts destroyed the Bamiyan Buddhas (Image 182).

INK WASH PAINTING

Image 227

A monochromatic style of painting, developed in China and revived by the Korean artist Song Su-Nam (Image 227). Ink wash artists use black ink in various concentrations to achieve subtle shades of black and gray.

IWAN

Images 186, 209

In Islamic architecture, a monumental barrel-vaulted hall with a wide-open arched entrance. The Great Mosque in Isfahan (Image 186) contains four facing iwans. This FOUR-IWAN PLAN became a prototype for mosques in Persia and across the Muslim world. For example, the Taj Mahal's four identical facades all contain a central iwan (Image 209).

JAPONISME

Image 211

A style in French and American late 19th-century art that was influenced by Japanese prints. For example, works like Hokusai's Great Wave (Image 211) fascinated Mary Cassatt (Image 121) and other Western artists.

KITCH

Image 230

Commercial art produced for mass audiences. For example, Jeff Koons uses cutting-edge techniques to create works like *Pink Panther* (Image 230) that are inspired by popular culture. Critics often dismiss works like this as kitch.

LINEAR PERSPECTIVE

Images 201, 211

A method of creating the illusion of depth on a flat, two-dimensional space. Linear perspective can be seen in the *Great Wave* (Image 211) and in *Hunters in the Snow* (Image 83). In contrast, Fan Kuan used SHIFTING PERSPECTIVE in *Travelers among Mountains and Streams* (Image 201).

LITERATI
Image 227
An educated class of Chinese and Korean intellectuals and scholars. Song Su-Nam is a modern Korean literati who attempted to revitalize traditional INK WASH PAINTING.

LOST WAX PROCESS
Images 169, 202, 221
A bronze casting method in which a figure is first modeled in clay and covered with wax. The whole is then recovered with clay. When fired in a kiln, the wax melts away, leaving a channel between the two layers of clay that can be used as a mold for liquid metal. Sculptors used this process to cast the Benin wall plaques (Image 169) and Shiva as Lord of the Dance (Image 221).

MALAGAN
Image 222
Refers to both the festivities and the sculptures created on New Ireland (Image 222). Malagan ceremonies reinforce a community's spiritual and social ties.

MANA
Images 214, 215, 216, 217, 220
In Oceania, a spiritual force that can be possessed by an object or a person. For example, the MOAI on Rapa Nui (Image 214), the 'ahu 'ula in Hawaii (Image 215) and the Maori chief Tamati Waka Nene (Image 220) all possessed *mana*.

MANDALA
Image 199
A sacred diagram of the cosmos. For example, the priest-architects intended Angkor Wat (Image 199) to be a mandala or model of the cosmos. Thus, the temple's five soaring towers represented the peaks of Mount Meru, the mythical home of the Hindu gods.

MANDATE OF HEAVEN
Image 212
Divine approval that legitimized Chinese rulers. *Chairman Mao en Route to Anyuan* (Image 212) is designed to convince viewers that Mao was destined to receive the mandate of heaven.

MASQUERADE
Images 173, 178
A type of performance art combining dancers, musicians, masks, and costumes. Both the *Pwo* mask (Image 173) and the Aka elephant mask (Image 178) were used in masquerades.

MATRILINEAL
Image 173
A society in which descent is traditionally through the female line. For example, the Chokwe are a matrilineal society. The *Pwo* mask (Image 173) underscores the prominent role of women among the Chokwe peoples.

MIHRAB
Image 183
A recess or niche set into the QIBLA wall of a mosque. It orients worshippers toward Mecca. Muhammad fixed the Kaaba (Image 183) as the QIBLA or direction for all five required daily prayers.

MINIATURES
Image 189
Small but detailed illustrations within albums or manuscripts. For example, both *Bahram Gur Fights the Karg* (Image 189) and *The Court of Gayumars* (Image 190) illustrate famous stories from the Shahnama.

MINIMALIST
Image 225
A design based upon unadorned geometric forms. The Vietnam Veterans Memorial (Image 225) utilizes a minimalist design created by Maya Lin.

MOAI
Image 214
Name given to large stone sculptures found on Rapa Nui. The Prehistoric people who lived on this isolated island carved and moved almost 900 of these monolithic statues.

MOKKOTSU
Image 210
A technique in which the artist paints a form without using an outline. For example, Ogata Korin used mokkotsu to paint the flowers in *White and Red Plum Blossoms* (Image 210).

MUDRA

Images 184, 202

A symbolic hand gesture used in Buddhist and Hindu art. For example, both the Jowo Rinpoche (Image 184) and Shiva as Lord of the Dance (Image 202) use distinctive mudras.

MUQARNAS

Image 186

In Islamic architecture, stucco decorations often stacked in tiers to decorate the vaults of a dome. Both the Great Mosque in Isfahan (Image 186) and the Alhambra (Image 65) contain striking muqarnas.

NEO-CONFUCIANISM

Images 201, 205

Philosophy stressing the importance of rulers who practice virtuous living and perform complex rituals. Neo-Confucianism also placed great emphasis upon filial piety, the honor and respect owed to one's elders and ancestors. The Joseon kings of Korea promoted Neo-Confucian principles. The *Portrait of Sin Sukju* (Image 205) reflects the high value placed upon Neo-Confucian principles.

NEO-EXPRESSIONISM

Image 226

An artistic movement popular during the 1970s that emphasized an artist's interest in the expressive capability of art. *Horn Players* (Image 226) by Jean-Michel Basquiat provides an example of an emotionally charged Neo-expressionist painting.

PIETRA DURA

Image 209

Technique derived from Italy, in which skilled artists carve floral designs into marble. The Taj Mahal's (Image 209) decorative program includes masterpieces of *pietra dura* craftsmanship.

PROPAGANDA

Image 212

The deliberate use of biased information to promote a particular individual, political cause, or ideology. *Chairman Mao en Route to Anyuan* (Image 212) and *The Results of the First Five-Year Plan* (Image 137) use propagandistic imagery to glorify totalitarian rulers.

RELIQUARY

Image 179

A container used as a repository for sacred or revered objects associated with a holy figure or revered ancestor. For example, in Image 179 a Fang *byeri* guards a wood bark reliquary.

RINPA

Image 210

A stylistic preference for vivid colors, bold abstract designs, motifs drawn from nature, and the extensive use of gold and silver. Pioneered by Ogata Korin (Image 210), the Rinpa style influenced several generations of Japanese artists.

SCARIFICATION

Images 173, 180

Decorative markings applied to the human body for cultural and/or aesthetic purposes. Both the Chokwe *Pwo* mask (Image 173) and the Yoruba veranda post (Image 180) use scarification patterns to signify great beauty and high social status.

SHIBBOLETH

Image 248

Originally a "test phrase" used to identify members of an outgroup. Doris Salcedo chose *Shibboleth* as the title of her work because it "refers to when you are recognized as somebody that is different."

SHIFTING PERSPECTIVE

Images 201, 207

An artistic technique designed to provide viewers with multiple vantage points. For example, Fan Kuan used shifting perspective in *Travelers among Mountains and Streams* (Image 201) to encourage a visual journey of his painting's many intricate details. Similarly, the designers of the Ryoan-ji rock garden used shifting perspective to encourage pilgrims to lose themselves in quiet contemplation.

SOCIALIST REALISM

Images 212, 228

An artistic style pioneered in the Soviet Union. Socialist realist artists focused upon painting positive portraits of youthful heroes overcoming obstacles to build a classless society. Liu Chunhua embraced socialist realism in *Chairman Mao en Route to Anyuan* (Image 212), while Magdalena Abakanowicz rejected it in *Androgyn III* (Image 228).

STRETCHERS AND HEADERS

Image 213

A construction technique used at Nan Madol (Image 213) in which builders employed a crisscrossing pattern of horizontal basalt logs called stretchers and perpendicular logs called headers.

STUPA

Images 192, 198

A dome-shaped Buddhist shrine containing sacred relics. The Great Stupa at Sanchi (Image 192) is one of the oldest surviving stone structures in India and an architectural prototype for other Buddhist stupas that followed it. For example, the concentric terraces at Borobudur (Image 198) rise to a giant central stupa.

TARASHIKOMI

Image 210

An artistic technique in which the artist dips paint onto an initial layer of wet paint. The pigments then merge and blur, giving the painting depth and a quality of unpredictability. Ogata Korin's skillful use of *tarashikomi* added great visual interest and variety to *White and Red Plum Blossoms* (Image 210).

TORANAS

Image 202

Gateways located at the four cardinal points surrounding a STUPA. The toranas at the Great Stupa at Sanchi (Image 202) include two upright posts and three elaborately carved horizontal lintels.

TORONS

Image 168

Distinctive projecting beams used in the Great Mosque in Djenné. The torons provide ready-made scaffolding, enabling volunteers to reach and repair all parts of the walls.

UKIYO-E

Image 211

Japanese pictures of a transient urban "floating world," populated by Kabuki actors and beautiful geishas. Katsushika Hokusai (Image 211) was an accomplished ukiyo-e artist.

YAMATO-E

Image 203

A distinctive style of Japanese painting developed in the 12th and 13th centuries. Yamato-e works like *Night Attack on the Sanjo Palace* (Image 203) distinguish Japanese art from traditional Chinese works.

Made in the USA
Middletown, DE
08 September 2018